HENRY SWINBURNE

THE COURTS OF EUROPE AT THE CLOSE OF THE LAST CENTURY

EDITED
BY CHARLES WHITE

Volume I

Elibron Classics
www.elibron.com

Elibron Classics series.

ISBN 0-543-97223-2 (paperback)
ISBN 0-543-97222-4 (hardcover)

This Elibron Classics Replica Edition is an unabridged facsimile of the edition published in 1841 by Henry Colburn, London.

V.

MR. BURKE'S
HISTORY OF THE LANDED GENTRY;

A COMPANION TO THE PEERAGE AND BARONETAGE,

COMPRISING ACCOUNTS OF

ALL THE EMINENT FAMILIES IN THE UNITED KINGDOM,

And of upwards of 100,000 Individuals connected with them.

Illustrated with the Armorial Bearings of each Family, Portraits, &c.

Complete in 4 vols., price 18s. each; or in 16 parts, price 4s. 6d. each.

This important work has been undertaken by Mr. Burke as a companion to his well-known and established "Dictionary of the Peerage and Baronetage of the United Kingdom," and upon a somewhat similar plan, in order that the two publications may embrace the whole body of the British Peerage, Baronetage, and Gentry, and may furnish such a mass of authentic information, in regard to all the principal Families in the Kingdom, as has never before been brought together.

*** Subscribers should give immediate orders to their respective Booksellers for the completion of their sets of this work, (a very small extra number of odd parts and volumes having been printed for this purpose) which will eventually become exceedingly scarce and valuable.

ALSO, BY THE SAME AUTHOR,

VI.

BURKE'S PEERAGE AND BARONETAGE

With important Additions, beautifully printed on a new plan, in one large volume, with an Emblazoned Title-page, and upwards of 1500 Engravings of Arms, &c., price 38s. bound.

Containing all the New Creations, and much other New Matter, the result of great research, and of Communications with the various Noble Families; forming the most complete, the most convenient, and the cheapest Work of the kind ever offered to the public.

VII.

BURKE'S EXTINCT, DORMANT, & SUSPENDED PEERAGES OF ENGLAND, IRELAND, AND SCOTLAND.

A COMPANION TO ALL OTHER PEERAGES.

New and Cheaper Edition, beautifully printed, in double columns, 1 vol. 8vo., with Emblazoned Title-page, &c., price 28s. bound.

This work, formed on a plan precisely similar to that of Mr. Burke's very popular Dictionary of the present Peerage and Baronetage, comprises those Peerages which have been suspended or extinguished since the Conquest, particularizing the members of each family in each generation, and bringing the lineage, in all possible cases, through either collaterals or females, down to existing houses. It connects, in many instances, the new with the old nobility, and it will in all cases shew the cause which has influenced the revival of an extinct dignity in a new creation. It should be particularly noticed, that this new work appertains nearly as much to extant as to extinct persons of distinction; for though dignities pass away, it rarely occurs that whole families do.

VIII.

QUEEN ELIZABETH AND HER TIMES.

A SERIES OF ORIGINAL LETTERS.

Selected from the Inedited Private Correspondence of the Lord Treasurer Burghley—the Great Earl of Leicester—the Secretaries Walsingham and Smith—Sir Christopher Hatton—and most of the distinguished Persons of the Period.

EDITED BY THOMAS WRIGHT, M.A., F.S.A. &c.

DEDICATED, BY PERMISSION, TO HER MAJESTY.

2 vols. 8vo, with PORTRAITS, price 32s.

"One of the most interesting historical works that have issued from the press for some time. The editor's object has been to do for English history what Bishop Percy did for English poetry; and by his judicious and instructive notes he has rendered his pages as interesting to the reader who may fly to them for amusement, as valuable to the inquirer who may resort to them for information."—*Literary Gazette.*

IX.

OLIVER CROMWELL AND HIS TIMES.

ILLUSTRATED IN A SERIES OF LETTERS BETWEEN THE DISTINGUISHED MEN OF THE PERIOD.

WITH AN INTRODUCTION AND NOTES, BY DR. VAUGHAN,

Author of "THE LIFE OF WICKLIFFE," &c.

2 vols. 8vo, with Portraits. Price 32s.

"These volumes are highly important; they give authentic information of one of the most complicated periods of English history, and exhibit the workings of some of the most powerful minds which ever guided or disturbed a state. They develop the general policy of the great leader of the Commonwealth with a clearness and an interest of the most explicit and satisfactory nature."—*New Monthly.*

X.

THE LIFE OF SIR EDWARD COKE,

LORD CHIEF JUSTICE IN THE REIGN OF JAMES I.

WITH MEMOIRS OF HIS CONTEMPORARIES.

BY C. W. JOHNSON, ESQ., Barrister-at-Law.

Second and Cheaper Edition, 2 vols. 8vo, with Portraits. Price 16s. bound.

"This is a very valuable work, illustrating one of the most important periods in our history, and written in a candid spirit, whose judgment is based on materials collected with great industry. Mr. Johnson has neglected nothing that could make his work complete; and it does equal honour to his intelligence and his industry."—*Literary Gazette.*

XI.

DIARY OF THE REV. J. WARD, A.M.,

VICAR OF STRATFORD-UPON-AVON,

Extending from 1648 to 1678, now just published, from the original MS. in the Library of the Medical Society of London.

EDITED BY CHARLES SEVERN, M.D.

1 vol. 8vo, price 12s. bound.

"This is one of the most curious and interesting works that for a long period has been presented to the public. The Rev. J. Ward was all but contemporary with Shakspeare; and part of the work before us relates to our poet, and throws much light upon disputed portions of his biography, and elucidates that relating to his death, of which hitherto we have been in ignorance. Dr. Severn has presented to the public, from these invaluable records, a selection of very singular interest."—*Dispatch.*

XII.

THE COURT AND TIMES OF QUEEN ANNE;

ILLUSTRATED IN THE

MEMOIRS OF SARAH, DUCHESS OF MARLBOROUGH.

BY MRS. A. T. THOMSON,

Author of "MEMOIRS OF HENRY VIII.," "LIFE OF SIR W. RALEIGH," &c.

2 vols. 8vo, price 28s. bound.

"The author of these volumes is so well known for her Memoirs of Henry VIII. and Life of Sir Walter Raleigh, that the readers of her new work will at once perceive in it the grace and vigour of style which so distinguish her former efforts. The political intrigues which so distracted the Court of Queen Anne are all very ably set forth. Circumstances have called public attention to these matters; so that we consider Mrs. Thomson's publication as peculiarly well timed. But even had there been no such introduction to our notice, the delightful manner in which she narrates the varied incidents of the Life of one of the most illustrious ladies who have become celebrated in our history, the anxiety to place the character of the Duchess of Marlborough in a right light before our readers, would recommend the work to general acceptance. It supplies a portion of history which was much wanted, and we are bound to say that Mrs. Thomson has executed her task with diligence, fidelity, and grace."—*Age.*

XIII.

THE DUCHESS OF MARLBOROUGH'S PRIVATE CORRESPONDENCE.

ILLUSTRATIVE OF THE COURT AND TIMES OF QUEEN ANNE.

(Now first published from the Originals.)

WITH HER SKETCHES AND OPINIONS OF HER CONTEMPORARIES

Second edition. 2 vols. 8vo, with PORTRAITS, price 28s.

"This is a very delightful work. We have closed the volumes with a confirmed impression that in many of the highest points of conduct, courage, and understanding, the Duchess of Marlborough was the most remarkable woman of her own or any other day."—*Examiner.*

XIV.

MEMOIRS OF THE BEAUTIES OF THE COURT OF CHARLES II.

WITH AN INTRODUCTORY VIEW OF THE STATE OF FEMALE SOCIETY, AND ITS INFLUENCE, DURING THAT REMARKABLE REIGN.

BY MRS. JAMESON.

COMPRISING

A SERIES OF TWENTY-ONE SPLENDID PORTRAITS,

Illustrating the Diaries of Pepys, Evelyn, Clarendon, and other contemporary writers of that gay and interesting period,—engraved by the most distinguished Artists.

NEW AND CHEAPER EDITION, WITH CONSIDERABLE ADDITIONS,

Now complete, in 2 vols. 8vo, bound, price 45s., or in Six Parts, price 7s. 6d. each.

"Nothing is wanting to make this publication perfect in its kind. We have the multum in parvo of the finest forms of female beauty in the world—the choicest excellence of England's school of portrait painting—the most masterly execution which modern engraving can bestow, and an interesting memoir of each of the celebrated characters thus brought before our eyes by the chaste and judicious pen of one of the most accomplished female writers of the day. The paper and typography are of the most superior description, and the price is moderate in the extreme."—*Dublin Evening Mail.*

XV.

DEDICATED TO THE RIGHT HON. GENERAL LORD HILL,

G.C.B., G.C.H., K.C., ETC.

LIFE OF FIELD MARSHAL, HIS GRACE THE DUKE OF WELLINGTON,

EMBRACING HIS MILITARY, CIVIL, AND POLITICAL CAREER, TO THE PRESENT TIME.

EDITED BY SIR J. E. ALEXANDER, K.L.S.

LIEUT.-COL. PORTUGUESE, AND CAPTAIN, BRITISH SERVICE.

In Two Large Volumes, 8vo, price 28s. bound; or in Eleven Parts, at 2s. 6d. each. Beautifully embellished with Portraits, Battle Scenes, &c., by Landseer, Heath, Warren, &c.

"Sir James Alexander's Life of Wellington has the treble advantage of being the cheapest—of inserting a large portion of the original correspondence—and of condensing within popular limits the dry military details."—*Globe.*

"Sir James Alexander possesses every requisite for this great undertaking. His work is peculiarly attractive. No doubt can be entertained that it will obtain a prominent place in the library of those to whose hearts their country's glory is dear, and be received as a standard work in all military circles."—*Dublin Evening Packet.*

"This work is likely to have a prodigious circulation. It contains the most complete, correct and authentic details of the eventful life of this exalted military hero, profound statesman, and patriotic politician."—*Bath Herald.*

XVI.

THE LIFE AND TIMES OF THE RT. HON. HENRY GRATTAN.

BY HIS SON, HENRY GRATTAN, ESQ., M.P.

In 2 vols. 8vo, with Portrait, &c., price 28s.

"This truly valuable work will unquestionably form one of the most important and interesting additions to our biographical and historical literature that our own day has produced. The large body of private correspondence which is here brought to bear upon the early and private life of Grattan will be read with an eager and intense interest. Moreover, there is a fund of personal anecdote scattered through the volumes, all of which is characteristic as well as new."—*Naval and Military Gazette.*

XVII.

THE LIFE OF WASHINGTON,

Commander-in-chief of the American Armies, and First President of the United States.

WITH HIS DIARIES AND SPEECHES, AND VARIOUS OTHER PAPERS.

BY JARED SPARKS. 2 vols. 8vo, with Portraits, price 28s.

"The Life of Washington is now first given to the world from original sources. Every information and document of value and undoubted authenticity that remain in the recollections and cabinets of America, France, and England, have been procured or examined, and here used at vast trouble and expense, and at the sacrifice of many years of labour. In short, the life of Washington is now complete; and every new addition to our knowledge of him only serves the more clearly to exhibit him as (in the resolution of Congress on his death) 'The man first in war, first in peace, and first in the hearts of his fellow-citizens.'"—*Sun.*

XVIII.

THE AUTOBIOGRAPHY OF JOSEPH HOLT,

GENERAL OF THE IRISH REBELS IN 1798.

Edited from his Original MS. BY T. CROFTON CROKER, ESQ.

2 vols. 8vo, with PORTRAIT, price 28s.

"We have read this work with great interest and satisfaction. It is a most remarkable piece of autobiography, teeming with romantic incidents."—*Chronicle.*

XIX.

WOMAN AND HER MASTER;

OR, THE HISTORY OF THE FEMALE SEX FROM THE EARLIEST PERIOD TO THE PRESENT DAY.

BY LADY MORGAN.

2 vols post 8vo. Price 21s.

"Lady Morgan has imparted to history the charm of romance. We have read her series of rapid but brilliant and vigorous sketches with an interest which many a novel fails to excite."—*Weekly Chronicle.*

"Lady Morgan has in these volumes undertaken to investigate the position which woman should occupy in society. She has sought in the records of the past, guidance and direction for the future: she has subjected the pages of history to a vigorous moral analysis, testing their facts with the skill of a critic, and deducing results with the wisdom of a philosopher."—*Athenæum.*

XX.

LIFE AND LETTERS OF BEETHOVEN.

BY HIS FRIEND, A. SCHINDLER.

Edited, with Notes, &c., by IGNACE MOSCHELLES.

2 vols. with Portrait, &c., 21s. bound.

XXI.

MEMOIRS AND LETTERS OF MADAME MALIBRAN,

WITH NOTICES OF THE PROGRESS OF THE MUSICAL DRAMA IN ENGLAND.

Second and Cheaper Edition, 2 vols. post 8vo, with Portrait, 16s. bound.

"These memoirs are full of interesting details, much of which is entirely new to the public, and of a nature to give new ideas and impressions of the extraordinary woman to whom they relate. We could fill several columns very pleasantly with those singular personal anecdotes and traits with which these volumes are filled; but extracts are unnecessary, as the book will be universally read. In addition to the chief memoir, there is a large body of miscellaneous anecdote, and a selection of Malibran's Letters, all singularly characteristic and amusing."—*Naval and Military Gazette.*

XXII.

THE DUCHESS OF ST. ALBANS' MEMOIRS.

Third and Cheaper Edition, in 2 vols. with Portraits, &c., price 16s. bound.

"A life of this very extraordinary woman, whose career was so plethoric of good fortune, and whose singular destiny placed her in so many and so varied situations, in which persons of every rank in life were involved, has at length been written with candour and fidelity. It would be next to impossible for us to give even an analysis of volumes so full of interest; every page teems with proofs of the late Duchess' kind-heartedness and good sense, while the numerous anecdotes, thickly interspersed, at once attract and instruct. The volumes are written with that taste and good feeling, which must command general approval, and will obtain the patronage, not only of those interested in theatrical matters, but of those who are watchers of the great stage of the world."—*Age.*

XXIII.

THE LIFE, CORRESPONDENCE, AND POSTHUMOUS WRITINGS OF M. G. LEWIS.

Author of "The Monk," "Castle Spectre," &c.

"Hail! wonder-working Lewis."—Byron.

2 vols. 8vo, with Portrait, &c., price 28s. bound.

"The Life of the great magician of horrors, whose genius partook of the very essence of German 'wonder-working' and mysterious creation—the Life of Monk Lewis, who knew, withal, every one of the choice spirits of his time, affords a most tempting subject. Crammed full of anecdote as these volumes are—theatrical, political, and literary—there is not a dull page throughout. The great body of the work has relation to theatrical matters, and gives us some capital stories about the most prominent members of the histrionic profession of both sexes; but the editor has introduced so much matter of a different kind—has presented us with so many varieties of wit and humour—that the work is as free from the fault of monotony as any we have read."—*Court Journal.*

XXIV.

NARRATIVE OF THE WAR IN AFFGHANISTAN.

BY CAPTAIN HENRY HAVELOCK,

In 2 vols. post 8vo, price 21s. bound, with a complete map of the seat of war.

XXV.

LIFE AND CORRESPONDENCE OF ADMIRAL EARL ST. VINCENT.

BY CAPTAIN BRENTON, R.N.

Author of "THE NAVAL HISTORY OF GREAT BRITAIN," &c. 2 vols. 8vo, 28s.

"To the several valuable records of the achievements and characteristics of our great heroes which late years have produced, these excellent volumes are now to be added. They will claim a permanent place in the splendid collection, as worthy to rank in design and execution with any work of the class."—*Court Journal.*

XXVI.

THE STANDARD NAVAL HISTORY OF GREAT BRITAIN,

BROUGHT DOWN TO THE PRESENT TIME.

BY CAPTAIN EDWARD PELHAM BRENTON, R.N.

2 thick vols. 8vo, price 31s. 6d. bd., comprising nearly 1400 closely-printed pages, with numerous PORTRAITS OF DISTINGUISHED OFFICERS, Plans, &c.

"This important work has long been an esteemed chronicle of the triumphant exploits of the British Navy, but its value is much further enhanced in this edition by the history being continued to the present time by the gallant author, who, in addition to his long experience of fifty years' service, has also been facilitated in the progress of his work by the assistance of most of the eminent men whose actions he narrates."—*Globe.*

XXVII.

THE MARINE OFFICER.

BY SIR ROBERT STEELE, KNT., K.C.S., ETC.

In 2 vols. post 8vo, with Portrait. Price 21s.

"Our 'Marine Officer' is a very pleasant, lively, and intelligent fellow; and we have accordingly great pleasure in directing the attention of our readers to his autobiography. In the commencement of the work the writer gives an account of his birth, parentage, education, and first entry into military life, which is admirably written, reminding us often of some of the best parts of 'Peter Simple;' but, Sir Robert Steele does not confine himself to his own adventures, he touches, from time to time, on most of the leading events of the late war—fighting many naval battles over again. For marine officers Sir Robert's book will have peculiar attractions, as it records many anecdotes of the heroism and fidelity of the corps which would not discredit the palmiest era of Roman valour."—*United Service Gazette.*

XXVIII.

CAPT. D. H. O'BRIEN'S ADVENTURES DURING THE LATE WAR.

COMPRISING A NARRATIVE OF SHIPWRECK, CAPTIVITY, ESCAPES FROM FRENCH PRISONS, &C., FROM 1804 TO 1827.

In 2 vols. 8vo, with Illustrations, 28s. bound.

"This is a work from the pen of a very distinguished officer, who has now added a literary fame to his professional reputation. Capt. O'Brien's adventures are numerous and extraordinary, and he narrates them in an unostentatious manly manner, and in a style, simple, natural, and effective. Every page bears the strongest features of truth and nature; so much so, that the reader makes the case his own, and vividly enters into all the scenes of danger and noble daring with which the work abounds."—*Dispatch.*

XXXV.

ITALY AND THE ITALIANS.

BY FREDERICK VON RAUMER,

Author of "England in 1835," "Illustrations of History," &c. 2 vols. price 21s. bd.

"The contents of this attractive book are multifarious, and put together in a familiar and agreeable spirit. It forms a most pleasant, varied, and interesting work upon Italy *as she is*."—*Atlas.*

XXXVI.

A SUMMER IN BRITTANY.

BY T. ADOLPHUS TROLLOPE, ESQ.

Edited by Mrs. TROLLOPE.

2 vols. 8vo, with Illustrations, 32s. bound.

"A work full of every species of interest and value which can attach to a book of travels. To the inquiring tourist who is tired of the beaten tracks of the Continent, the author opens an entire new field of travel, and smooths the paths through it. To the traveller whose journeys are confined to books, he offers one in which there is as much variety as novelty, as much entertainment as information. To the philosophic observer of human nature he presents a most interesting object of study—to the antiquarian a most fertile field of examination—to the lover of legendary lore, and the inquirer into popular superstitions, an ample fund of new and strange materials for thought and fancy. Finally, he puts on record a large body of singular and interesting facts, touching an actual condition of society to which the extraordinary social changes that are at hand throughout Europe, and especially in France, may, at no distant period, put an end for ever. Mixed with the graphic style of this book there is a liveliness and *bon-hommie*, which greatly add to its charm, and which make the work altogether one of unusual attraction. The volumes are embellished by many spirited and characteristic etchings."—*New Monthly.*

XXXVII.

TRAVELS TO THE CITY OF THE CALIPHS,

ALONG THE SHORES OF THE PERSIAN GULPH AND THE MEDITERRANEAN.

BY J. R. WELLSTED, ESQ., F.R.S., F.R.A.S., ETC.,

Author of "Travels in Arabia." 2 vols. 8vo, with Illustrations, 25s. bound.

"A publication of singular interest and entertainment."—*Naval and Military Gazette.*

"In these days of dull and flat common-place, it is quite refreshing to come upon a narrative of strange travel and wild adventure like this, which recals to mind the exploits of the old voyagers of Spain and England, when half of the world was undiscovered, and the other half unknown. Our traveller quits India by embarking on the Persian Gulf in a trading vessel bound to Muscat, and the first important features of his narrative relate to that remarkable city. Here he commences slave merchant, and embarks for Gambrun, visiting, in his way thither, some of the singular islands in the Persian Gulf, and particularly those where the pearl fisheries are established, of which he gives an interesting description. In due course he reaches Bagdad, the celebrated 'City of the Caliphs,' remains there a considerable time, and affords many details of it that are not to be found in the narrative of any other traveller. Among the most interesting of his adventures are those which take place among the Arabs of the Desert, particularly the Bedouins, with whom he passes a considerable period. Another point of great interest in these sketches is the celebrated city of Damascus, of which we have many graphic and characteristic descriptions. The first volume concludes with a visit to Tripoli, Lebanon, and Baalbec.—*Naval and Military Gazette.*

XXXVIII.

A WINTER IN ICELAND AND LAPLAND.

BY THE HON. ARTHUR DILLON.

2 vols. post 8vo, with Illustrations, price 21s. bound.

"The north of Europe presents much curious matter for investigation that has not yet been explored as it deserves. Iceland and Lapland are all but untrodden regions. Mr. Dillon, inured to the hardships of a northern winter, was induced by the interest he took in these nations to attempt the hazardous expedition of visiting them in their remote and unfrequented homesteads; and these volumes, full of information, historical and descriptive, are the result of a journey not less creditable to his literary character than his courage. Of Iceland he gives a very full account, tracing the progress of the country from the earliest records of the first piratical descent on the island in the ninth century to the present time. The history is a sort of sea romance, in which all the actors are marked by the strong features of a hardy clime and a daring spirit."—*Atlas.*

XXXIX.

A YEAR AMONG THE CIRCASSIANS.

BY J. A. LONGWORTH, ESQ.

2 vols post 8vo, with illustrations, 21s. bound,

"Incomparably the most valuable account of Circassia that has yet appeared."—*Court Journal.*

"This account of Mr. Longworth's residence in Circassia will deeply interest our readers. Whether perused merely with a view to amusement, or studied as to the duties which England has to discharge in the East,—in whatever aspect it is contemplated, Mr. Longworth's truly graphic sketch cannot fail to reward the reader's attention."—*Post.*

XL.

THE SPIRIT OF THE EAST;

BY D. URQUHART, ESQ.

Author of "Turkey and its Resources." Second Edition, 2 vols. 8vo. 28s.

"This is certainly one of the most interesting and valuable works of modern times. The information, the learning, the admirable pictures of mankind in the eastern countries which the author lays before us—the views of religion, legislation, social life, government and history—the errors he clears up, and the facts, hitherto almost unknown, which he establishes—the felicity of his illustrations, and the sprightliness of his narrative, make this one of the works of an age."—*Tyne Mercury.*

XLI.

LORD LINDSAY'S LETTERS ON THE HOLY LAND.

Third and Revised Edition, in 2 vols., with Illustrations. 24s. bound.

"Among the many travellers who have contributed to our knowledge of the interesting regions dignified by events recorded in Holy Writ, a prominent place must be assigned to Lord Lindsay. His abilities and accomplishments are of a high order; a spirit of inquiry and a glowing enthusiasm have been aided by various knowledge, and refined by a sincere piety. He exhibits a considerable store both of ancient and modern learning, but his draughts of Helicon have been abundantly tempered by—

'Siloa's brook, that flow'd
Fast by the Oracle of God.'

"Having gone out in the perseverance and devotion of a pilgrim, he has felt and recorded what he saw with the wisdom of a philosopher and the faith of an enlightened Christian."—*Quarterly Review.*

XLII.

A PILGRIMAGE TO PALESTINE.

BY THE REV. FATHER MARIE JOSEPH DE GERAMB,

Abbot and Procurator of La Trappe.

2 vols. post 8vo, with Illustrations, 21s. bound.

"These volumes are the most curious and interesting of their kind that we have lately met with. They may be looked upon as the first written record ever made public of the actual daily observations and feelings of a pilgrim to the Holy Sepulchre, and the other most famous scenes of Holy Writ. The strong and evidently sincere religious feeling which pervades the volumes throughout, will give them a strong interest with the religious portion of the community."—*Naval and Military Gazette.*

XLIII.

TRAVELS IN PALESTINE AND SYRIA.

BY GEORGE ROBINSON, ESQ.

2 vols. post 8vo, with Maps and Plans, price 21s. bound.

"Mr. Robinson has traversed the whole of Syria and Palestine, including the countries lying east of the Jordan and the Ante-Libanus, and also many interesting portions of Asia Minor. Of his travels he has here given a succinct, plain, and unornamented account. His journal is not merely the best, but perhaps the only, guide through these remote regions."—*Literary Gazette.*

XLIV.

NARRATIVE OF A TEN YEARS' VOYAGE OF DISCOVERY ROUND THE WORLD OF H.M.S. ADVENTURE AND BEAGLE, UNDER THE COMMAND OF CAPTAINS KING AND FITZROY.

In 2 large vols. 8vo, with Maps, Charts, and upwards of Sixty Illustrations, by Landseer, and other eminent Artists, price 2*l.* 18s. bound.

"One of the most interesting narratives of voyaging that it has fallen to our lot to notice, and which must always occupy a distinguished space in the history of scientific navigation."—*Quarterly Review.*

These volumes detail the various incidents which occurred during the examination of the Southern Shores of South America, and the Beagle's circumnavigation of the Globe, and add considerably to our knowledge of Hydrography, Geography, and Natural History, and of the Habits, &c. of the Aborigines. There will be found in them the materials of two distinct works, embracing everything worthy of notice in the expeditions during a period of nearly ten years. The first volume, by Captain P. P. King, F.R.S., relates to the expedition under his command, with an Appendix by Major Sabine, R.A., F.R.S., containing discussions on the magnetic observations made during the voyages. The second volume is by Captain Robert Fitzroy, and relates to the second voyage, with an Appendix, giving the determination of many positions and measurements of meridian distances, and other nautical information. The work is beautifully illustrated with etchings and engravings on steel, by Mr. Landseer and other eminent artists, from drawings by Mr. Martens and Mr. Earle; and with Charts and Plans by Mr. Gardner and Messrs. Walker: and an entirely new Map of South America, by Mr. J Arrowsmith, in which the position of places may be ascertained to within less than two miles. In the volumes notices will be found of the Cape Verd, Falkland, and other Islands in the Atlantic Ocean—of the coasts of South America, from Pernambuco to Guayaquil—of the Galapagos Islands—the dangerous Archipelago, or Low Islands—Otaheite—New Zealand—Australia—The Keeling Islands—Mauritius—the Cape of Good Hope.

XLV.

MR. BREMNER'S NORWAY, DENMARK, AND SWEDEN.

WITH NOTICES OF THE STATE OF PUBLIC OPINION IN THOSE COUNTRIES, AND ANECDOTES OF THEIR COURTS.

2 vols. 8vo, with Portraits, 28s. bound.

"There is not a single reader of Mr. Bremner's admirable book on Russia who will not be delighted again to encounter a traveller who unites in himself so many excellent qualities. With liveliness and *bon-hommie* to please the most idle of readers, with good sense and impartiality to satisfy the most critical, with activity, information, and judgment to turn all these good qualities to account, and a position in society that enables him to do so; these are the characteristics which Mr. Bremner brings to the concoction of this new work. On every subject which it touches—politics, statistics, public feeling, social habits and condition, agriculture, letters, science, personal character—all is treated with impartiality and strong good sense."—*New Monthly.*

XLVI.

MR. BREMNER'S EXCURSIONS IN THE INTERIOR OF RUSSIA;

INCLUDING SKETCHES OF THE EMPEROR NICHOLAS AND HIS COURT.

Second Edition, in two vols. post 8vo, with Illustrations, price 21s. bound.

"This ample and able work, the production of a man of sense and impartial observer, will soon be in the hands of the majority of readers throughout the empire, and not improbably throughout Europe also."—*Literary Gazette.*

XLVII.

AUSTRIA AND THE AUSTRIANS;

WITH SKETCHES OF THE DANUBE AND THE IMPERIAL STATES.

2 vols. post 8vo, with Portraits, price 21s.

"This is at once an instructive and amusing book. It contains a great deal of information, a vast number of anecdotes of distinguished persons, and a mass of general instruction, important and novel."—*Times.*

LIV.

HISTORY OF THE BRITISH TURF,

FROM THE EARLIEST PERIOD TO THE PRESENT DAY.

BY JAMES CHRISTIE WHYTE, ESQ.

In Two Large Volumes, 8vo, with Illustrations. Price 28s. bound.

COMPRISING :—

1. Memoirs and Anecdotes of remarkable Sporting Characters
2. The Performances and Pedigrees of celebrated Racehorses
3. Descriptions of the Racecourses in Great Britain
4. The Plates and Stakes annually run for over them
5. Accounts of the most approved Method of Breeding, Training, and Managing Racehorses
6. Notices of celebrated Jockeys
7. Description of the principal Races and Matches.

Also, every Particular, technical and otherwise, to which the Lover of Racing may desire to refer, either as a matter of business or amusement.

"This work must become a standard authority on the subject of horses and horseracing, and no one at all interested in such subjects will be without it, whilst the general reader will be delighted with it for the pleasant spirit in which it is written, and the singular traits of extraordinary character with which it is so profusely studded."—*Argus.*

LV.

THE SPORTSMAN IN IRELAND,

AND THE HIGHLANDS OF SCOTLAND.

BY R. ALLEN, ESQ., A.M., F.S.A., &c.

In 2 vols. post 8vo, with numerous illustrations, price 18s. bound.

" A most well-informed, humorous, and agreeable travelling companion. The leading features are all, more or less, of a sporting nature ; and in this point of view the work has uncommon interest. The details the author gives of his various ' experiences' in the beautiful lands which he passed over, cannot fail to send hosts of sportsmen thither who never before contemplated such a visit, and many more who would scarcely have ventured such an undertaking without the guide here placed at their disposal. The work is embellished with very many spirited and interesting sketches of remarkable localities, and is altogether one of the most readable and amusing books of its kind that we have had for many a day."—*New Monthly.*

LVI.

SCENES AND SPORTS IN FOREIGN LANDS.

BY MAJOR E. NAPIER, 46th Regt.

2 vols. small 8vo, with Nineteen Illustrations, 21s. bound.

" Through the medium of these pages the sportsman in England may enjoy his leisure by becoming acquainted with the proceedings of his brother sportsmen abroad, in climes where the game sought, instead of being confined to hare, pheasant, partridge, and similar timid denizens of our stubbles and coverts, comprises tigers, wolves, bears, jackals, buffaloes, elks, and other dangerous inhabitants of the tropical wilderness. But, whatever may be the risk attendant on their pursuit and death, our gallant adventurer will here be found seeking them in their desert and jungle retreats, eager to attack whatever might offer in the way of sport, from a snipe to an elephant ; the result of which is, that the wide 'preserves' of the far East are thrown open for the reader, and he is shewn the various methods pursued to bring down the game, while entertained with the amusing adventures of the daring hunter."—*Age.*

LVII.

SPORTING EXCURSIONS IN THE ROCKY MOUNTAINS.

BY J. K. TOWNSHEND, ESQ.

2 vols. post 8vo, with Illustrations, 18s. bound.

" Mr. Townshend supplies in these volumes a fund of very curious and entertaining matter. There is much variety and information of a practical kind in the book, and it will be especially acceptable to naturalists on account of the descriptions of the animals with which the regions traversed by the writer abound. On the whole, the work forms a most valuable addition to the library of American travels."—*Atlas.*

LVIII.

COMIC MISCELLANIES.

IN PROSE AND VERSE.

BY THE LATE JAMES SMITH, ESQ.

One of the authors of "Rejected Addresses."

With a Selection from his Correspondence, and Memoirs of his Life.

BY HIS BROTHER, HORACE SMITH, ESQ.

Second edition, with additions, 2 vols. post 8vo, with portrait, 21s. bound.

"One of the most amusing books that have seen the light, since the ever famous Rejected Addresses themselves."—*Globe.*

LIX.

COMMENTARIES ON THE HISTORICAL PLAYS OF SHAKSPEARE.

BY THE RIGHT HON. T. P. COURTENAY.

2 vols. post 8vo, 18s. bound.

"We have read this work with pleasure as the production of a scholar and a gentleman of refined taste and acute judgment. The many new points of view which he takes, and the many lights which he throws upon passages of the immortal bard, command our lively interest. It deserves the attention of the public as an almost inseparable companion to Shakspeare's Plays. Indeed, it is a work without which we do not look to see a respectable library, or collection of polite literature."—*Lit. Gazette.*

LX.

VISCOUNT DE CHATEAUBRIAND'S SKETCHES OF THE LITERATURE OF ENGLAND.

2nd Edition. 2 vols. 8vo, 24s.

"There has not appeared, for a long time, any work so calculated to pique the curiosity of the literary world as this new production of the celebrated Chateaubriand, in which he discusses the merits of Shakspeare, Milton, Byron, and the whole galaxy of ancient as well as modern English writers; drawing the most curious comparisons and analogies."—*Globe.*

LXI.

LORD BROUGHAM'S OPINIONS

ON POLITICS, THEOLOGY, LAW, SCIENCE, LITERATURE, ETC.

WITH A MEMOIR OF HIS LORDSHIP'S LIFE.

One very thick and closely-printed volume, price 12s. bound.

"The design of this volume is to afford a collective view of his Lordship's opinions and practical objects. It embodies not only the most brilliant passages from his celebrated speeches and writings, but also unfolds to the reader the gradual development of his mind on those great questions in politics, literature, and science, in which learned men of all countries and all ages must ever take a lively interest. To the selections is prefixed a prefatory memoir, which will be found more complete, accurate, and elaborate, than any that has hitherto appeared, containing particulars of his Lordship's early, and also of his more advanced, life, with a philosophical analysis of his mind and writings."

"This volume is calculated to be of infinite service, by teaching its readers to think, and think justly, on all the great political questions of the day."—*Sun.*

LXII.

THE AMERICAN IN PARIS;

OR, SKETCHES OF THE NEW INSTITUTIONS, THE EMBELLISHMENTS, THE SOCIETY, THE ECCENTRIC CHARACTERS, THE WOMEN, THE PRESS, THE LITERATURE, ETC., OF PARIS.

2 vols. post 8vo, price 18s.

"We cordially recommend this book to our readers as by very far the best, because incomparably the most amusing as well as informing, Guide to Paris that we are acquainted with in the English language, or indeed in any other."—*Naval and Military Gazette.*

LXIII.

SONGS AND BALLADS.

WRITTEN AND SET TO MUSIC BY

HIS ROYAL HIGHNESS PRINCE ALBERT, & PRINCE ERNEST.

Translated from the German, by G. F. Richardson, Esq.

DEDICATED, BY PERMISSION, TO H.R.H. THE DUCHESS OF KENT.

Imperial 4to, containing Fourteen Songs, and Forty-two Pages of Music, with a beautifully engraved Portrait of Prince Albert, price 12s.

LIST OF THE SONGS. THE WORDS IN ENGLISH AND GERMAN.

1. Farewell to Home.
2. To my Brother.
3. Italian Song.
4. The Bark dashes wildly.
5. The Wandering Harper.
6. Sleep, O Sleep.
7. Say, sleepest thou, Love?
8. To an absent Friend.
9. Yonder, thou shalt find the blessing.
10. All silent were the fountains.
11. Come, dearest, come.
12. How sweet this hour of pure devotion.
13. As the bark dashes wildly.
14. The star of splendour.

LXIV.

THE DREAM; AND OTHER POEMS.

BY THE HON. MRS. NORTON.

Second Edition, with Additions. In 1 vol., with Fine Portrait of the Authoress, after a Drawing by E. Landseer, R.A., price 10s. 6d. bound,

"A very beautiful poem. This lady is the Byron of our modern poetesses." — *Quarterly Review.*

LXV.

POPULAR SONGS OF IRELAND.

Collected and Edited, with Introductions and Notes, by

T. CROFTON CROKER, ESQ.

1 vol. with Illustrations, price 10s. 6d. bound.

"A volume of singular interest and curiosity. It is even more than this,—it is a publication of real value, as illustrative of the past and present condition, both mental and moral, of the most singular people in the world. At the same time, it is, as a collection of lyrical compositions, full of the graces and beauty of which that class of poetry is so eminently susceptible."—*Naval and Military Gazette.*

LXVI.

THE ROSE-FANCIER'S MANUAL.

BY MRS. CHARLES GORE.

New and cheaper edition, one elegant vol., price 6s. bound.

CONTENTS:

Geography of Roses—Culture of Roses—Glossology of Roses—Hybridity—Importance of Specific Characters—Comparison of Specific Characters—On Species—Distinction of Species and Variety—Bibliography of the Rose—Pharmacopœia of Roses—Monography of the Rose, comprising notices of 2500 Varieties—List of the Species admitted by Botanists, &c. &c.

"All the lovers of flowers, and especially the fairer portion of our readers, ought forthwith to have this elegant volume in their possession."—*Sun.*

LXVII.

THE ART OF NEEDLEWORK,

FROM THE EARLIEST AGES.

With Notices of the Ancient Historical Tapestries.

EDITED BY THE RIGHT HON. THE COUNTESS OF WILTON.

Second edition, revised, in 1 vol. post 8vo, 10s. 6d. bound.

"An admirable volume. It should be possessed by every lady."—*Times.*

"A charming volume. We congratulate our fair countrywomen on this valuable addition to their libraries."—*Herald.*

T. C. Savill, Printer, 107, St. Martin's Lane.

HENRY SWINBURNE ESQ^RE.

London, Published by Henry Colburn, 13 Marlborough St. 1841.

THE

COURTS OF EUROPE

AT THE CLOSE

OF THE

LAST CENTURY.

BY THE LATE

HENRY SWINBURNE, ESQ.

AUTHOR OF "TRAVELS IN SPAIN, ITALY," &c.

EDITED

BY CHARLES WHITE, ESQ.

AUTHOR OF "THE BELGIC REVOLUTION," &c.

IN TWO VOLUMES.

VOL. I.

LONDON:

HENRY COLBURN, PUBLISHER,

GREAT MARLBOROUGH STREET.

MDCCCXLI.

LONDON:
PRINTED BY IBOTSON AND PALMER, SAVOY STREET, STRAND.

INTRODUCTION.

Although Mr. Swinburne's career was not distinguished by any of those remarkable incidents, vicissitudes, or adventures, which give interest to the lives of mariners, soldiers, and explorers of distant regions, it is desirable that the reader should be made acquainted with the outline of his history, as well as with the circumstances that gave rise to the correspondence which I have undertaken to lay before the public.

I shall commence, therefore, by stating, that Henry Swinburne first saw the light in May, 1752, and that he was the third son of Sir John Swinburne, Bart., of Capheaton, in the county of Northumberland, and the youngest child of a numerous and very ancient Catholic family.

b 2

After receiving the first elements of an excellent education under the superintendence of his parents, Mr. Swinburne was sent to complete his studies at the monastic seminary of Lacelle in France. There he made rapid progress in ancient and modern languages, in history, philosophy, and the belles lettres, and moreover greatly improved his natural taste for painting and the fine arts. Thus he was subsequently enabled not only to enrich the literature of his country with two productions that rendered his name conspicuous amongst the travellers of the last century, but to execute an extensive series of drawings, as remarkable for their accuracy as for their beauty of design.*

By the death of his eldest brother, Mr. Swinburne came into possession of an annuity, as well as a small estate at Hamsterley, in the county of Durham; which, added to his own patrimony, placed him in independent, though not in very wealthy circumstances. He therefore determined to avail himself of an opportunity

* These drawings are in the possession of his daughter, Mrs. R. Walker, late of Mitchel Grove, Sussex.

which occurred at that period, for making what was called the "grand tour," and proceeded to visit Turin, Genoa, Florence, and other parts of Italy. After improving his classical knowledge and taste for antiquities by a careful examination of the pictures, statues, and splendid relics of architecture which he encountered during his travels, and having perfected himself in drawing, and in the language of the divine Alleghieri, he bade a temporary adieu to Italy, and retraced his steps, by way of Paris, towards his native land.

A circumstance occurred to him, however, ere he reached the end of his journey, which not only delayed his progress, but influenced the destinies of his future life; for it happened, during his passage through the French capital, that he met with and became tenderly attached to a Miss Baker, daughter of the then solicitor-general for the West Indies. This young lady, with whom he became acquainted at the house of Lady Webb, to whose superintendence she had been entrusted, was at that time placed for her education at the convent of Ursuline nuns; an establishment not only in great repute amongst the French nobility, but frequented by many young English and Irish ladies of the most distinguished Catholic families. To the advantages of considerable personal beauty, graceful manners, and a highly cultivated mind, Miss Baker added the attraction of a good fortune ; so that she no sooner made her appearance in Lady Webb's salons, than she became an object of general attention, and indeed received several flattering matrimonial offers. Amongst other persons of note who courted her smiles was Charles Howard, subsequently Duke of Norfolk.

Differing from the generality of the female sex in her views of the qualifications and ingredients necessary to ensure worldly and domestic happiness, Miss Baker was neither dazzled by the seductive allurements of rank, nor biassed by those of wealth. Having been as much struck by the pleasing exterior, interesting conversation, and superior endowments of young Swinburne, as he was fascinated by the beauty, grace, and intellectual powers of the fair West Indian, she soon gave him to understand that his attentions were not disagreeable, and at length rewarded his assiduities by conferring upon him her hand and fortune.

This marriage, which promised and ensured so much felicity to both, had not been solemnized many days ere Mr. Swinburne removed with his bride to England, and, after a short stay in the metropolis, proceeded to his estate in the county of Durham. There the young couple remained for some time, either occupying themselves with those studies that were so congenial to the tastes and talents of both, or devoting themselves to the embellishment of the house and grounds at Hamsterley. Indeed, the latter soon became remarkable for being the most picturesque and well laid out of any in that part of the country, as they combined the classic precision of the Italian style with the more wild and sylvan boldness of English park scenery.

Although few persons were more fully competent to comprehend and value the tranquil enjoyments of that retired and independent life so justly lauded by Horace, so beautifully described by Cowley, it appears that Mr. and Mrs. Swinburne had not long resided at Hamsterley ere they became desirous of a change. This arose partly from a mutual anxiety to increase their store of knowledge by travelling; partly from that restlessness and craving after locomotion, which is, perhaps, a distinctive characteristic of the English nation; and partly from their being disappointed in not finding the slightest sympathy or congeniality of taste and occupation amongst their country neighbours.

The contrast between Mr. and Mrs. Swinburne and the generality of their provincial acquaintance was, in fact, most antipodal; for, whilst the former almost exclusively devoted themselves to the cultivation of literature and the arts, the latter thought of little else than that of corn or turnips, unless indeed it were the pursuit of foxes. But the evil did not terminate there; for, as usual with provincial sportsmen, they were not content with hunting all day, but most unmercifully persisted in resuming, or rather recapitulating, all the incidents of the chase over the bottle, until the bottle eventually treated them as they had treated Reynard, and ran them to ground beneath the table; for it was considered in those days as discreditable for a true fox-hunter to retire to his couch sober, as it is now unseemly in a well-bred sportsman to over-indulge in his cups.

But though Mr. Swinburne bore no share in the roystering wind-up of the north country Nimrods' evenings, he was not reluctant to participate now and then in the manly pleasures of their mornings. He, therefore, had less reason to complain of a want of society than his wife, who found little enjoyment in that of her female acquaintance. These ladies, whose whole time and thoughts were absorbed in the performance of their maternal and domestic duties, and whose conversation rarely soared beyond the small gossip of the adjoining parishes, attached little merit to the possession of those accomplishments that distinguished Mrs. Swinburne. They were, in fact, as little able to comprehend or estimate her talents, as she was to appreciate the skill with which they executed those pickle and preserve accomplishments that constituted the glory of a north country housewife. It was, therefore, with no slight satisfaction that Mrs. Swinburne assented to her husband's proposal, that they should return to the continent, and proceed to Italy, after visiting the south of France.

When two persons are united, not only by the tenderest ties of affection, but by the utmost uniformity of taste, studies, and mental endowments —when no difference exists between them, save in the diversity of their acquirements—when no desire animates the one, save that of drawing forth and exhibiting in the most favourable light the talents and accomplishments of the other—and especially when fortune has placed them in a situation where they can gratify their inclinations—little time is required for preliminary discussion or preparation. Mr. and Mrs. Swinburne were not long, therefore, ere they concluded their domestic arrangements, and commenced those travels which furnished matter for his valuable descriptions of Spain and Italy, as well as for the following series of letters. These latter, as will be seen, were principally addressed to his brother, Sir Edward Swinburne, with whom he always lived upon terms of the most cordial and fraternal affection.

It is almost superfluous to dwell upon the merits of the two productions above mentioned, or to recapitulate the praises that were bestowed upon them by the critics of the day. I shall nevertheless observe that these publications raised his name to a high place as an antiquarian, philosopher and scholar, both at home and abroad, and that they were commended by men whose encomiums are of no ordinary weight.

Two of the authorities to whom I allude, are Mr. Eustace and the Baron de Grimm. The former thus speaks of Mr. Swinburne in his Classical Tour: "I quote this traveller with pleasure, because my observations enable me to bear testimony to his accuracy." The second, in his "Correspondence Littéraire," holds the following still more complimentary language: "Tous les voyages d'Italie connus," says Mons. de Grimm, "ne m'empêcheront point de lire encore celui-çi avec plaisir. Il a voyagé en philosophe et en littérateur. Ses observations éclaircissent très heureusement plusieurs passages des auteurs anciens, et son ouvrage mérite la réconnaissance de tous ceux qui s'appliquent à l'étude de l'antiquité."

Although this flattering eulogium was, of course, solely intended for Mr. Swinburne, it is but fair to observe that his wife was entitled to some participation in it; for it appears that her husband was accustomed not only to consult her opinions, previous to commencing his literary labours, but that he submitted his manuscripts to her inspection during the process of composition, and unhesitatingly followed her suggestions and corrections. In fact, no woman could have been better adapted for the companion of a scholar and man of science than Mrs. Swinburne. In addition to a competent knowledge of Greek and Latin, by which she was enabled to peruse the best classic authors in their original garb, she was mistress of several modern languages; she was an excellent musician, and, though no practical artist, she was endowed with no common tact and intuitive purity of taste, in all matters concerned with the schools of painting and sculpture. She was remarkable for her good sense, sound judgment, and quickness of perception, and possessed moreover that just and comprehensive *coup d'œil* which is so essential for the ready intelligence of the arts. But if Mrs. Swinburne was eminent for these endowments, she was not less distinguished for her diffident and unpresuming manners, and for a total absence of that pedantry and overweening vanity, which are too often observable amongst women who lay claim, or who are really entitled, to the reputation of superior intellect.

After quitting the north of England, Mr. and Mrs. Swinburne directed their steps to Paris, and thence to Bordeaux, where they passed the winter of 1776, with their relatives the Dillons, with whom they were nearly allied by the marriage of Mademoiselle de Dillon with Sir E. Swinburne. From Bordeaux they removed to the Pyrenees, where they were joined by their friend Sir Thomas Gascoigne, who urged Mr. Swinburne to accompany him on a tour through Spain. The only motive that prevented the latter from immediately accepting this proposition, was his reluctance to separate himself from his wife. Finding, however, that he should be able to establish Mrs. Swinburne and her infants in an agreeable and convenient house near Tarbes, and seeing also that she was extremely loath that he should let slip the favourable opportunity of visiting a country so little known to the public, and so badly described by previous travellers, he yielded to Sir Thomas's request, and in a short time the two friends traversed the eastern Pyrenees, and proceeded to Barcelona.

Following the shores of the Mediterranean from the ancient Saguntum (Murviedro) down to those of the no less celebrated Alhambra, Sir Thomas and his companion visited all the remarkable places that are scattered throughout those beautiful and once chivalrous countries. Then leaving behind them the Sierra Nevada, and the relics of the Abencerrages, they proceeded to Malaga, and thence to the shores of the Atlantic, where they passed a few days in examining the beauties of Cadiz and the warlike marvels of Gibraltar. Having satisfied their curiosity at these two places, they retraced their steps northward by Seville, Cordova, and Andujar to Madrid, whence they proceeded to Aranjuez, where they met with great attention from the Spanish court. After a sojourn of some days at this royal residence, the travellers once more turned their steps towards the Pyrenees, and having re-entered France by St. Jean de Luz, in due time reached Tarbes, where Mr. Swinburne immediately busied himself in arranging the materials which formed the groundwork of his first publication.

Having prepared his manuscripts for the press, and forwarded them to England, he removed with his family to Marseilles, where he took ship for Naples, intending, in the event of his first literary labours proving successful, to extend his travels, and eventually to give the result of his observations to the public in a second publication. Having been furnished with letters of introduction, from persons of the highest rank at Madrid, to those of the greatest eminence at the Court of Ferdinand IV., the Swinburnes received the most flattering marks of attention, not only from the Neapolitan nobility, but from the king and queen of the Two Sicilies. Indeed, the latter appears to have imbibed sentiments of great personal regard for Mrs. Swinburne, as was proved not only by numerous acts of kindness, but by autograph letter, expressive of her Majesty's friendly feelings.

Sicily being at that period little known to the English public, save through the inaccurate work of Brydone, Mr. Swinburne resolved to avail himself of its vicinity, and to pass a few weeks in exploring the relics of its ancient grandeur. Having procured letters of introduction to the most distinguished civil and ecclesiastical authorities, he embarked for Palermo, visited the most interesting portions of the island, and, after enriching his collection of notes and drawings, returned to Naples, where he had left his wife and children. From Naples Mr. Swinburne extended his excursions to Rome, Florence, and Pisa; and having completed the manuscript of his travels, he determined to proceed to England, for the purpose of superintending its passage through the press, as well as with the view of looking to his affairs in the north.

During Mr. Swinburne's visit to his native country, he was led to believe that if he were to return home with his family, government would not feel adverse to avail themselves of his talents, by conferring upon him some diplomatic or official situation. He therefore rejoined Mrs. Swinburne as soon as his new publication was ushered into the world, and, bidding adieu to Naples, directed his steps northwards. The kindness of her Sicilian Majesty was manifested on this occasion by furnishing them with letters of presentation to her mother, the Empress Maria Theresa, who, as well as the Emperor Joseph, exhibited every mark of kindness towards them during their short residence at Vienna. Indeed the former appears to have been so well pleased with Mrs. Swinburne, that she conferred upon her the order of the "*Croix étoilée*;" an honour the more remarkable, since her Imperial Majesty, in giving this decoration to a commoner, derogated from the statutes of the order, which limit the admission to women of noble birth, actually proving their sixteen quarters.*

From Vienna our travellers proceeded to Frankfort, Aix-la-Chapelle, and Brussels, and thence to England, where they had not long

* An account of the origin of this female order will be found in a subsequent note.

arrived ere they received accounts that the whole of their property in the West Indies had been devastated and utterly laid waste by the French and Caribs. By this misfortune Mr. Swinburne lost the whole of the fortune which he received with his wife. This occurred too at a time when a largely increasing family rendered the loss doubly painful; and there appeared little prospect of his obtaining indemnity, either from the French government or from his own.

Nevertheless, as the negotiations for the general peace, subsequently signed at Versailles in September 1783, were far advanced, he resolved to proceed to Paris, and to lay his case before the French government; trusting less, however, to the justice of the latter than to the generous protection of Marie Antoinette, for whom he was furnished with letters of introduction from her sister the queen of the Two Sicilies, from her mother the Empress Maria Therese, and from her brother the Emperor Joseph. Nor was he disappointed, for the ill-fated queen, who was then in the zenith of her power, not only promised him her mediation, but acted with so much energy and kindness, that she procured for him a grant of all the uncultivated crown lands in the island of St. Vincent, as an indemnification for the valuable property which had been devastated. This grant was recorded and acknowledged in the treaty of peace, and thence assumed the character of a sacred international act.

The value of the lands granted to Mr. Swinburne was estimated at £30,000; but Mr. Pitt, who was then premier, no sooner saw the island in which they were situated tranferred to Great Britain, than he offered Mr. Swinburne half that sum. This offer, being utterly inadequate, was rejected, and unfortunately, as the sequel will show; for, the government being then sore pressed for money, Mr. Pitt brought a bill into Parliament, the purport of which was to impose such heavy taxes upon all uncultivated lands in the West Indies, as would compel their possessors to abandon them to government at a comparatively insignificant price. The proportion of these lands being greater in St. Vincent's than in the other islands, the principal weight of this bill fell upon Mr. Swinburne. But remonstrances were vain ; the measure passed, and the government obtained for £6,500 property valued at nearly five times that sum.

The hardship of this case was considered so flagrant, that Mr. Swinburne was recommended to petition the House of Commons. But he wisely declined taking this step, well knowing that a private individual has no chance of success if he attempts to bring any measure before the legislature, the object of which is to prove that the ministry have been guilty of, or that the house has sanctioned, an act of spoliation. Mr. Swinburne submitted, therefore, to his fate with as much philosophy as possible, and retired to his small property in the north, where he devoted himself to the education of his eldest son and daughter.*

There is of course little in the ordinary routine of an English country gentleman's existence, no matter how intellectual or talented he may be, that can afford subject of interest to the biographer ; but it appears that Mr. Swinburne's domestic life presented so fair a picture of

* The latter married Mr. Paul Benfield.

tranquil ease and enlightened enjoyment, and the system of education pursued by him with his children combined so many moral and material advantages, that it made a deep impression upon the mind of the Marquis Ducrest, brother to Madame de Genlis, who paid a visit to Hamsterley during the course of the year 1787. Indeed, such was the captivating report made of it by M. Ducrest to his sister, that, according to her own acknowledgment, she founded her well-known work *Les Veillées du Chateau* upon his description. I must here observe that the Swinburnes had made the acquaintance of the Marquis Ducrest and of Madame de Sillery (Genlis), during their first visit to Paris in 1776, and afterwards continued upon terms of the most intimate friendship with that celebrated woman, with whom they maintained a most interesting correspondence during many years.

In the mean time the Queen of France was not backward in expressing profound regret that her kind intentions should have proved so little beneficial to the Swinburnes. In order to give them a further proof of the gracious sympathy she felt upon the occasion, she desired them to be informed that, if they felt disposed to proceed to Paris, in order to make personal application for further indemnification, she should be ready to support their claims with all her influence. Upon receiving this information, the Swinburnes again removed with their family to the French capital, where they remained until the eve of that direful convulsion which inundated France with innocent blood, and soon carried war and desolation throughout the rest of Europe.

Whatever might have been the good intentions of Marie Antoinette, they were unfortunately frustrated by the rapid developement and predominance of those subversive and sanguinary principles which soon dragged her down from the pinnacle of royal grandeur, happiness, and popularity, to the utmost abyss of human misery and degradation;—a contrast the more hideous, from the rank and sex of the innocent victim, and a consummation the more monstrous from the devilish and brutal insults heaped upon the royal victim.

However, although the power once possessed

by Marie Antoinette had so decreased as to render it impossible for her to obtain any pecuniary grant or indemnification for Mr. and Mrs. Swinburne, she evinced her kindness towards them, before their return to England, by directing their eldest son to be enrolled amongst the royal pages, and placed under the especial care of the Prince de Lambesc. This was a favour that had never before been conferred upon any Englishman, and was the more valuable, since the utmost care was bestowed upon the education of all these youths, who, as may be supposed, appertained to the noblest and most distinguished families, and who were subsequently provided for, either in the military or civil household.

Young Henry Swinburne was not destined to reap any of the ulterior advantages of this situation; for the aspect of affairs soon became so alarming, and the perils of all those persons attached to the royal household were so imminent, that it was considered advisable for him to return to England. Nor could he effect this entirely unscathed; for, having been involved in an affray, which took place at one of the theatres, between a party of royalists and demagogues, he received a severe wound in his head, and nearly paid the price of his attachment to the court by the sacrifice of his life.

Being aware of the advantage that he himself had derived from travelling, and an extensive intercourse with the world, Mr. Swinburne resolved that his son, who was a youth of remarkable promise, should participate in similar benefits. Consequently, as soon as the groundwork of his education was concluded, young Swinburne was despatched into Italy, under the care of the abbé Campbell, a highly respectable Catholic clergyman. In due time the worthy abbé and his charge reached Naples, where they were joined by Mr. Pelham, afterwards Lord Chichester, between whom and Mr. Swinburne's family the warmest friendship continued to exist down to the last moment of their lives.

Young Swinburne was of course most warmly recommended by his parents to the recollection and protection of their Sicilian Majesties; and it appears that the queen was so zealous in her desire to render him all the service in her power, that she sought out for, and offered him the hand of a ward of the crown, a young Maltese lady of ancient family, who, in addition to high blood, was said to possess an income of 50,000 ducats. But the young Englishman seemed to have been as disinterested, and as adverse to enriching himself through the medium of a matrimonial alliance, as had been Mrs. Swinburne when she rejected the brilliant offers that were made to her in her youth; for he respectfully rejected this advantageous offer, and, as the approach of the republican armies rendered it prudent for Englishmen to quit Italy, he lost no time in proceeding back to his native land.

Having fixed upon the career of arms as his profession, a commission was soon procured for him, and ere long he was appointed deputy assistant adjutant-general, upon the staff of Lord Moira; an appointment for which he was principally indebted to his knowledge of languages, and his skill as a draughtsman.

The hopes that had been held out to Mr. Swinburne, of his being employed by government, were not realised before the year 1796 ; for although interest had been made in his favour with Mr. Pitt and other members of the administration, it was not until Lord Spencer came into office that he received an offer, through Sir Evan Nepean and Mr. Huskisson, to proceed to France, as British commissioner for the adjustment of the proposed cartel for the exchange of prisoners. This delicate mission, which Mr. Swinburne consented to undertake, was rendered still more difficult in consequence of the capture of Sir Sidney Smith, whom the revolutionary government held in close confinement in the Temple, and refused to treat according to the ordinary usages of war. It was also simultaneous with, but entirely distinct from, that of Lord Malmesbury, who was at the same time appointed minister plenipotentiary, for the purpose of negotiating peace with the Directory.

The difficulties that Mr. Swinburne had to encounter are set forth in his letters, and are easily understood, when one considers the intricate nature of the subject, and the uncompromising tenacity of the men with whom he had to deal. But one is at a loss to comprehend why the British government should have recalled him from Paris, where he appears not only to have conducted himself with great prudence and discretion, but to have obtained the esteem of all persons with whom it was his duty to transact business. Such, however, was the case; for he was recalled at the very moment when there was every prospect of effecting his object, and was replaced by a Captain Coles, who was ere long compelled to return, after unsuccessfully attempting to establish himself upon the same level as his predecessor.

The abrupt termination of Mr. Swinburne's mission may perhaps be accounted for by the system too often pursued at the English Foreign Office in regard to its diplomatic agents; passive obedience, mechanical routine, and a mere adherence to system, being considered of much greater importance, and a much higher recommendation in the eyes of the minister at the head of that department, than the developement of extraordinary activity, brilliant talents, or zealous energy, unless indeed the latter be exhibited by some man who can boast of powerful patronage, or who can confide in his own parliamentary influence.

Mr. Swinburne's recal, which was in fact a species of diplomatic disgrace, was of course extremely galling to a man of his susceptible and honourable mind ; but all other sentiments save those of parental agony were merged in, and obliterated by, the terrible calamity which assailed him a short time subsequent to his return from France. This calamity, the most painful that could befal a parent, was the loss of the young and talented son of whom I have already spoken.

In consequence of some change that took place in Lord Moira's staff, young Swinburne was appointed aide-de-camp and military secretary to General Knox, then about to proceed as commander-in-chief to Jamaica. Little anticipating the melancholy doom that awaited them, General Knox and his suite joyously embarked on board a vessel called the Babet, and after a boisterous passage, during which they ran great risk, safely reached the island of Martinique. Here they put in to refit, and renew their stock of provisions, and eventually set sail for their ultimate destination. From that period no tidings of the ship or her ill-fated crew were ever received; she was therefore supposed to have foundered in the gale of wind which blew with fearful violence a few hours after they weighed anchor from Fort Royal. This supposition was the more natural, since it appears that the same neglect was shown in the selection of the Babet, formerly a French prize, as was too often evinced, during the late war, in the choice of unsound vessels for the transport of troops; a barbarous neglect, from which even the present epoch is not altogether free, but which was then the repeated cause of destroying many valiant men.

The regret evinced by the public at the melancholy fate of General Knox and his companions was universal; but the blow to the unhappy parents, who had centred all their hopes in this son, was irreparable. Mr. Swinburne more than once alludes to this calamity in his letters; but, with a generous desire not to afflict his wife, he glosses over his own anguish, and, in order to support her courage and soften her affliction, he endeavours to conceal the fearful agony that is undermining his own health, and filling his soul with the bitterness of death.

The difficulties in which Mr. Swinburne was involved by the sudden loss of his West India property, and the demands of a numerous family, of whom eleven were still living, induced him to apply to government for some official situation that might augment his limited resources. The application was met by an offer of the lucrative appointment of vendue master to the island of Trinidad, of which the valiant and much calumniated Picton was then governor. To this permanent office was added the temporary mission of restoring the islands of Santa Cruz and St. Thomas to the Danes. Mr. Swinburne would gladly have accepted any other employment than one which compelled him to separate himself from his family; but the proposition was too advantageous to be rejected, and he therefore bade adieu to his wife and children, and embarked on board the Danish vessel of war which was appointed to carry out General Waltershoff and the troops of his nation, destined to take repossession of the above-mentioned islands.

After executing the latter part of his mission, Mr. Swinburne proceeded to the island of Trinidad, where he sought to assuage the grief that was corroding his heart, by assiduously devoting his time to the duties of his office, and by occupying his leisure hours in the interesting study of botany, and the collection of an herbarium. He was destined, however, to terminate his earthly career at a moment when, to judge by his own letters, he least anticipated any evil effects from the unhealthy climate where he was doomed to reside. His overweening confidence in his own strength, and his contempt for the dangers that menace Europeans in Trinidad, soon proved fatal. Ere many months he was struck by a *coup de soleil*, as he was riding from his country residence to his office in the town, and died almost suddenly.

His obsequies took place at St. Juan's, where, at a subsequent period, his friend Sir Ralph

Woodford raised a monument to his memory. Of the eleven children who had to deplore the loss of this excellent parent and good man, some are still living. It is at the particular request of one of them, Mrs. R. Walker, late of Mitchel Grove, Sussex, that I have undertaken, with most imperfect materials, to write the foregoing brief introductory memoir. I have likewise added a few notes to the letters, some of which may be found useful in elucidating certain passages that might otherwise appear obscure.

CHARLES WHITE.

April 20th, 1840.

LETTERS,

&c.

LETTERS

FROM THE

COURTS OF PARIS, NAPLES, VIENNA, &c.

TO SIR EDWARD SWINBURNE.

Paris, March, 1774.

Dear Brother,

You request me to give you detailed accounts of my journey. The proposition is too flattering not to be complied with.

We left London on the 26th of February, embarked next day at ten in the morning, and landed at Calais at three in the afternoon.

The country near Calais is flat and poor, without enclosures. At the distance of some miles it grows hilly, with farmhouses and tufts of trees in the valleys. Near Boulogne it is hilly and open. Little wheat is sown, though all is arable. We slept at Montreuil. About Nampont are extensive woodlands, with heaths, junipers, and fine oaks. Near Bernayere are the ruins of a church, with very elegant arches. The farmers drive four horses in two-wheeled ploughs, attended only by one man. There are vast plains of corn. The roads are most wretchedly bad.

The part of the town of Abbeville by which we entered, was almost destroyed and depopulated. The churches and houses were in ruins, and the fortifications demolished. This desolation was occasioned lately by the wickedness of a keeper of the powder magazine. He had for some time supplied the deficiencies of his purse by the sale of the king's powder: at length, however, the time of a strict inspection approached, and the punishment he had reason to expect struck him with terror. Seeing that there was no way of preventing a discovery of his theft, he resolved to blow up the magazine, and thus to confound all accounts at once. It cannot now be known whether he meant to sacrifice or to save himself. Be this as it may, he set fire to the train, and blew up the magazine himself, and half the town of Abbeville into the bargain.

We there left the Paris road, and took that of Dieppe, which, during this season of the year, is scarcely passable; it runs through narrow lanes or hollow passes, in the middle of the boundless corn-fields, worn so deep that the top of the carriage did not appear. We were often obliged to cross ploughed lands and ditches, to escape dangerous holes, and I was sometimes compelled to call in a peasant to assist me in keeping the coach in its proper equilibrium. In spite of all our care, it was once overturned, but fortunately without occasioning any mischief. After many fatigues, we reached Eu in the evening. The next day we had to ascend a lofty hill, where there did not seem to be any trace of a high road. It was with difficulty the horses gained the summit, where we had an extensive view of the sea, and came within sight of Dieppe, situated in a deep hollow, upon an inlet of the sea, surrounded by high white cliffs. The roads after that were almost bottomless. A finer country then presents itself to the eye, with thick woods and great quantities of oak and birch, planted in regular rows. Lines of noble apple trees intersect the plains in every direction. The farmers take great care of the latter: they mat the stems round in winter, and, by cutting out all the exuberant wood, train them to one trunk, only leaving the small upper branches, which join together, and make a head like a mushroom.

Five miles from Rouen we descended through extensive woods and deep roads to a pavement, which brought us at last to the capital of Normandy, where we took up our quarters at "le cheval blanc" in the south suburb of St. Sever. Behind this suburb is a large gravelly heath, finely calculated for walking and riding: it abounds in butcher's broom.* Upon an eminence near it stands a large convent of Carthusian monks.

Rouen is built in the shape of a half circle, of which the Seine is the radius: it is a noble river. The quay, though little raised above the water, and poorly built, is much thronged with people. Several gates lead from it through the ancient walls into the city. A bridge of boats now supplies the place of a stone one, which was swept away by the impetuosity of the floods. Its piers still remain above water.

The streets of Rouen are dark, narrow, and have an antique and gloomy appearance. The churches are of a redundant gothic architecture. The cathedral of Notre Dame contains nothing curious, except the monument of Cardinal George d'Amboise, prime minister of Louis XII.

* *Ruscus aculeatus.*

He is represented kneeling on a tomb, overloaded with ornaments, figures, and escutcheons. The monument of Bréze, Maréchal de Normandie, is opposite.* John Duke of Bedford, Regent of France,† is commemorated only by a lozenge of marble fixed in the side-wall, with a modern inscription, behind the high altar. On each side of the choir is placed a heart, one of Richard Cœur de Lion, the other of his elder brother Henry.

St. Ouen, a rich Benedictine abbey, has a light gothic church. The Exchange is a grand edifice, situated in a dirty, narrow lane. Its hall, though dark, is spacious and noble. In the calf market Joan of Arc was burnt, and tradition points out the window where the Regent sat to see the execution. A bad statue of the maid was set up in the last century.‡ The en-

* Louis de Bréze, Count de Maulevrier, Grand Marshal of Normandy. His mother was a daughter of the celebrated Agnes Sorel and Charles VII. He married, in 1514, the no less celebrated Diane de Poictiers, whose charms had so great an influence over Henry II. Thus, as a French author observes, "the issue of this family could boast of being descended from the mistresses of two kings of France, a title not very honourable in our days; but for some people there is always a compensation."

† John Duke of Bedford, Regent of France, temp. Hen. VI.

‡ The best statue extant of the renowned Maid of Or-

virons of this city are beautiful, the hills well wooded, the meadows extensive, and the soil dry. Villas are dispersed on all sides. The Misses Ferguson, who are residing here, speak much in favour of the place and its society.

We left Rouen by the lower road; but the river Seine had so far exceeded its natural bounds, that we enjoyed little of the beauties of the prospect, or the agreeable windings in its course. We crossed it at the Pont de l'Arche. At Gaillon is a very large gothic palace of the Archbishop of Rouen, commanding a charming view of the river: woody hills rise on each side, ornamented with country seats; whilst the hollows are occupied by villages and rich arable lands, down to the flats near the water edge. The road to Mantes is very bad; there the pavement begins. The frequent appearance of the winding river, the thick vineyards clinging to the declivities, the diversified features of the vale, the distant broken banks impending over towns and villages, form together a group of objects that render this one of the pleasantest journeys a person can take.

leans is that in the gallery of Versailles, sculptured by the gifted and lamented Duchess of Wurtemberg, (Princess Marie of France,) whose premature death took place at Pisa, on the 2nd of January, 1839.

Mantes is well built, in a bold situation, and the most ancient part of its gothic church is very handsome. The surrounding country is clothed with vineyards and corn lands. At Meulan, in an island, is l'Isle Belle, a disagreeable low garden, with a ruinous house, once the much-admired seat of the Bignons.* We slept at St. Germain, and came next day to St. Denis, where we lodged with our friend Madame de Marcois, the mother of Madame d'Anglures. Forty-five kings of France lie within the abbey. I was shown in the treasury a very fine cameo of Nero, another of Augustus, and a third of Domitian, hung at the necks of saints, and a very beautiful agate vase. We then came to Paris, and have taken up our abode at Le Parc Royal, rue du Colombier.

I have been to Pigale, the statuary, to see his famous monument of the Maréchal de Saxe, destined for the church of Strasbourg. He is represented in armour, descending into the tomb, which death opens, pointing to an hour-glass: France, on her knees, tries to drive the spectre back: on his right hand lie the imperial eagle and the English leopard on their

* The De Bignons were of a very ancient family, which had furnished many illustrious members both to the bar and parliament.

backs, and the Dutch lion running away; and under them broken standards. A little boy, the genius of war or love, is weeping on the left, with an extinguished torch; behind is the French flag triumphant; whilst Hercules leans on his club, by the sarcophagus, in an attitude of grief.

The Marshal's portrait is said to be a strong resemblance: there is great puerility in the birds and beasts, and the Genius is highly absurd.

Pigale has also a naked statue of Voltaire, sitting crowned with laurel; a roll of parchment, which he holds in his hand, serves as a sort of covering. The periwig is not forgot, and altogether it is very ridiculous.*

Paris, April 30th, 1774.

On Tuesday I set out for Versailles early, pursuant to the directions I had previously received from Lord Stormont, our ambassador; and having nothing but mere curiosity to gratify, with no fear of disappointment, I made a tolerable day of it. The Duke of Dorset † was the only Englishman presented with me. We met in

* This statue of Voltaire is now in the vestibule of the Théâtre Français.

† John Frederick, third duke, who afterwards married Miss Cope.

the Salle des Ambassadeurs, and there made acquaintance. After a little waiting, the ambassador escorted us to the prime minister's levee, (the Duc d'Aiguillon.*) If he said anything to me, it was so little and so low, that I do not recollect a word of it.

In his antechamber the envoys of Europe were assembled, decorated with ribbons of all colours, and crosses and keys of all metals. Among the rest the famous Aranda,† late president of Castile; but now, to the astonishment of everybody, ambassador to the court of France, by his own request. He was the king of Spain's right hand when he planned the expulsion and destruction of the Jesuits, and his coming here seems to forebode some mischievous designs hatching in Spain against the peace of Europe, perhaps of England; yet some think Aranda only chose the journey, to take off the shock of an approaching disgrace.

About eleven, the introductors gave notice of the king's levee being ready, and so, in company of a German baron, we trudged up stairs,

* Minister to Louis XV., after the disgrace of the Duke de Choiseul.

† Le Comte d'Aranda succeeded Count Florida Blanca as minister to Charles IV. He was a man of eminent talents and enlightened views. He was overthrown by Godoy, Prince of Peace.

and surprised his most Christian Majesty in his waistcoat: for none but the family ambassadors may see him in buff.

After staring at us, talking about the opera with some few of the crowds of courtiers, and saying about one minute's prayer with his cardinal,* he drew towards us, who were ranged near the door in rank and file. All he said was, "*Est-il fils du vieux Duc de Dorset, que j'ai connu autrefois?*" and so marched off. However, as they talked much to others who stood near us, I can describe them better from this view than from the subsequent one.

The Dauphin is very awkwardly made, and uncouth in his motions. His face resembles his grandfather's, but he is not near so handsome, though he has by no means a bad countenance. His nose is very prominent, his eyes are gray, and his complexion is sallow. He seemed cheerful and chatty, and I think his aspect bespeaks a good-natured man. The second brother is a pretty figure, and so is the third, only his mouth is rather wide, and drawn up in the middle to the top of the gums.

They are not yet quite formed as to legs and strength, and have all a good deal of that restless

* The Cardinal de la Roche Aymon, grand almoner and confessor to Louis XV.

motion, first upon one leg and then upon another, which is also remarkable in some members of the English royal family.

The questions they ask seem very frivolous and puerile. I believe they find their time hang very heavy on their hands, for they ran with great glee to tickle one of the king's valets de chambre, as he was carryng out the king's dirty clothes.

Our next trot was to the Dauphin, who said nothing. The same silence reigned at the levee of his brothers, as to our share at least. The Comtesse de Provence is a little dumpy woman, and but a plain piece of goods; her sister, the Comtesse d'Artois, is rather prettier, having fine skin and tolerable eyes, but her nose is immense, and her toes are turned in. Poor thing! she seemed quite frightened, and could hardly speak.

I did intend to reserve Madame du Barré for the *bonne bouche,** but it must be the Dauphiness,

* This celebrated personage was born in 1746, of low parents, at Vaucouleurs near Orleans. Her father was one Gomart, a clerk in the municipal tax-office, (*octroi,*) and her mother was a girl called Becu, a sempstress. After sundry profligate adventures, she married William Count du Barré, with whose brother John she had lived during some time. Lebel, valet de chambre to Louis XV., being struck with her beauty, introduced her to his royal master. Ere long

who quite won my heart. I can give you no account of her particular features; but her air, eyes, shape, motion, her *tout ensemble*, were most charming. She spoke so cheerfully, and so easily, *comme si elle se sentait*, as the French say:

Elle avoit une grace,
Un je ne sais quoi qui surpasse
De l'amour les plus doux appas.

From her we passed to the three *not Graces*, but any other trio you may think would suit them. I mean the King's daughters: the Dauphin's sisters were not visible.

After all these perambulations up stairs and down stairs through the royal family, we climbed up a dark winding staircase, which I should have suspected would have led to an apartment of the Bastile, rather than to the temple of love and elegance. In a low entresol we found the favourite sultana in her morning gown, her ca-

she was established at Versailles, where she reigned despotically during many years. She and her family are said to have extracted thirty millions of francs from the public treasure. When Louis XV. formed his first intimacy with this fascinating woman, whose numerous adventures were known to all the world, he said to the Duke de Richelieu, "Well! at all events I succeed Du Barré."—"Yes!" replied the witty duke, bowing, "Just as your most gracious majesty succeeds to Pharamond, your illustrious predecessor."

puchin on, and her hair undressed; she was very gracious, and chatted a good deal, as every body else seemed to do at Versailles, about the opera. I could hardly refrain from laughing at an involuntary exclamation from my brother presentee, the Duke, whose mistress, Mrs. Parsons, has, you know, been long out of her teens. "Good heavens!" said his grace in a whisper to me, "why, her bloom is quite past."

She is of a middling age, just plump enough, her face rather upon the yellow leaf, her eyes good, and all her features regular; but I cannot think her a pleasing figure now, whatever she may have been, or may be still, when made up and decked out in her pride.

There ended our business, and then we proceeded to dine at the Duc d'Aiguillon's, where we found all the foreign ministers and some French. Among the women were the Duchess of Mazarin, once a famous beauty, and Madame de Forcalquier, a lady celebrated for her amours and her beauty, and cited as such by Helvetius in his posthumous book. It is she who, on some dispute with her second husband, (she is the widow of two,) received a slap in the face from him. Seemingly reconciled to the insult, she went out and staid so late, that Monsieur de Forcalquier, with a great deal of company, was seated at dinner when she returned. Upon his asking her why she came so late, she approached him, and said she had been all over Paris to find somebody who would take the *soufflet* off her hand, but as no one chose to receive it, she was under the necessity of returning it to him; and as she spoke, she discharged a most violent smack upon his cheek, and then flew off and took her seat composedly at the table.

Our dinner was very good, but our Amphytrion never spoke one word to us, and did not give us a very famous idea of *la politesse Française*. However, we ate our pudding, held our tongues, and then came away at our leisure.

The Baron, who was presented with us, is called Schwenckt, as I read his name given to the introductor; but his Hessian friend said there were a few consonants left out. He soon got acquainted with us, and let us into his history. This was his first *début* in the world, being quite *en droiture* from Westphalia. He stuck close to us for one, two, or three presentations; but the *introducteur* being called away, and none but ambassadors having the privilege of presenting, he was left in the lurch at the Dauphiness's. However, he got pretty well through this affair; but at Madame's he was unluckily placed behind the Swedish ambassador, whom he overtopped by head and shoulders; and whom should the princess address but this Swede, whilst our Baron, who was unpresented, felt *très mal à son aise*, grew as red as fire, and looked most pitiable.

This scrape was nothing to what he underwent at Madame du Barré's, where the whole company consisted of ten persons. Here he could not escape notice; and every time she stared at him, which she did very often, Monsieur le Baron ducked, and made a profound reverence. I thought I should have burst from the desire of laughing; but as we had patronised him so conspicuously all day, he could not do less than sit by us at dinner. To our no small amusement, but unfortunately for him, a large rabbit was placed by him, which it seems he had a great aversion to, and this was a new *désagrément* for him. If he publishes his tour, I dare say he will give it as his opinion, that being presented is an infinitely more trying ceremony than standing the fire of a regiment.

This morning news came of the King having the small-pox, that he had been bled for it, once in the foot, and had blisters clapped to his back *

* When some one told the Duke d'Ayen that Louis XV. had taken the small-pox, he shrugged up his shoulders, and

—the most extraordinary mode of treating this disorder I ever heard of: he must be in danger from his age and way of life. A few days will decide his fate. The royal family are all sent to Meudon, and his daughter, the nun, goes to-morrow to join her sisters, who are the only persons of his family left with him. The whole town is in motion between Paris and Versailles. What an epoch for ministers, both ins and outs!

Last night we were at the new opera of Orphée, by Gluck. I was vastly disappointed: the best of the music resembles in style and force the common burlettas; but, to do it justice, the performers sang it abominably, not quite in the French, yet not in the least in the Italian style. Some of the dancers are ridiculously grovelling and vulgar; but this he did in imitation of Boyes, I suppose, to make the rest of the opera show off better.* The dances are very bad, a thing uncommon on the French stage, where at least one sense should have repaid us for what the other underwent.

said, "*Je n'y crois pas—car il n'y a rien de petit chez le grands.*"

* This reminds me of the advice given by a wit to the composer of a French opera, interspersed with dances, which was not very successful upon its first representation. "What shall I do," said the composer, "to make it more popular?"—"Do!" replied the other; "why, lengthen the ballet, and shorten the dresses of the figurantes."

I have filled my paper with mere nonsense, but that is sometimes more agreeable in a correspondence than either solidity or business.

Paris, May 11.

Since my last, everything in this capital has worn the aspect of dulness and anxiety. No one could be totally indifferent whilst the life of the Grand Monarque was at stake; though it astonished me and all strangers to see how little the generality of the natives seemed to care about the event.

Louis XV. took to his bed on Monday, the 27th of April, the day after I was presented to him, and in a day or two the small-pox made its appearance. This was kept a profound secret from him, for fear of his being frightened into confession, and consequently into the banishment of Madame du Barré.

The physicians, whose constant practice is to kill in this disorder, bled him twice, and would have done it a third time, had they imagined he had blood sufficient for it. They also blistered him severely, and brought a deal of the humour out by that part of his body. Every day they issued bulletins, with an account of the progress of the malady, which, being posted up in the palaces for the inspection of the public, were intended to keep up their hopes. Could any credit have been given to these papers, the generality of people might have been lulled into confidence; but, from the known fallaciousness of these accounts, and the king's age and irregularities, nobody believed he would get over the disorder. Every body was therefore in motion, and endeavouring to prepare themselves for a great change of men and measures.

About six days ago, however, the king discovered the real nature of his case, which, it is believed, was made known to him by his daughter, Madame Louise, the Carmelite nun, who left her convent to attend him in his illness; and, though much against the inclinations of some people, he confessed himself, made a public avowal of his faults, and ordered the Cardinal de la Roche Aymon to repeat his words in the great gallery, and to have them printed and distributed. They expressed his sincere repentance for having so long scandalized his people, of whom and of God he asked pardon, and declared he only wished to recover his health, that he might devote the rest of his life to the service of religion and of his people.

The natives seemed in great spirits at this deathbed repentance; but whether they gave credit to such a thorough change, is what I cannot pretend to assume. The Viaticum was carried to him with all the pomp imaginable. The canopy was borne by the princes of the blood, and attended by all the principal personages of the court. It was observed that the Dauphin seemed the most affected of any, and wept profusely.

None of these spiritual aids availed, no more than the descent of the relics of St. Genevieve, nor the prayers of four hours in every church of the metropolis. On Friday, Sutton, the English inoculator, offered his services, but was refused, as he did not choose to let the French physicians into his secret. A mortification began to appear about the stomach, and upon Saturday the case was looked upon as desperate.

During the first days of his illness, Madame du Barré used to attend him at the hour of dinner, that is, as soon as Madame Adelaide retired from his chamber; but, just before the king's confession, she was sent to the Duke d'Aiguillon at Ruelle, whence she took her departure for Dauphiny.*

* She was proprietor of the splendid Chateau of Luciennes in Dauphiny, the furniture and decorations of which are said to have cost six millions of francs. After being released from the abbey of *Pont aux Dames,* near Meaux, where she was confined for some time by order of Louis

On Monday Sutton was admitted, as the doctors had given him over, the king being quite out of his senses, and almost in the agonies of death. Sutton administered emetics and cathartics, and brought him to himself so well as to enable him to speak and ask pardon of the Prince de Conti for all his usage of him. But all help was now in vain, and Louis XV. expired at half past three in the afternoon of yesterday, May 10th. He had caught the infection, I am told, from a girl who resided with some others in the Parc aux Cerfs, a kind of seraglio, near Versailles.* She was some time after taken into Madame du Barré's service, and being sent to Paris, where the small-pox appeared on her, she died last week.

XVI., Madame du Barré passed the remainder of her days at Luciennes, until she was arrested on the 22nd September, 1793, and guillotined by order of the Revolutionary Committee on the 9th of November following. Luciennes recently belonged to M. Lafitte.

* This establishment, which obtained such disgraceful notoriety, was originally a beautiful *campagne* called *l'Ermitage*, in the park of Versailles, and belonged to Madame de Pompadour. It was converted by that profligate woman to its scandalous purposes in the year 1753. It is affirmed that the expenses of the *Parc aux Cerfs*, and its contemptible inmates, many of whom belonged to the first families of France, was 150,000 francs per month. Lacratelle says that the total expenses of the *Parc aux Cerfs* absorbed one hundred millions of francs.

The royal family retired to Choisy yesterday. The king's daughters attended their father during all his sickness, but none of them have had the small-pox. The Duke of Orleans* waited on him like a servant. The Archbishop of Paris, though almost dead himself with a nephritic cholic, went to Versailles, but was not very graciously received.

On account of the infection, the body is not to lie in state at the Louvre, but will be carried to St. Denis, where it is to lie in state forty days; during which time no diversions of any kind are to be permitted. How black and dull then will be this land of foppery for six weeks! Mourning is risen high in price, cloth ten livres an ell. The mourning is to be for six months. After the forty days the new king will go to Rheims to be anointed. The processions for the king's recovery, which were marshalled out and regulated to last three days longer, are all at an end of course; and I suppose the canons of St. Genèviéve will seal up their relics again, and cover them, without any great parade.†

* The father of Louis Philip, better known as Egalité.

† The relics of St. Geneviève, the patroness of Paris, consisting of the bones of that saint, were preserved in the church of that name, afterwards the Pantheon, and were

It was my lot to be the last person presented to the king and Madame du Barré. We have been driven from our late hotel to one in the Fauxbourg St. Germains, Parc Royal, Rue du Colombier, for which we had several coercive reasons. One was, having a devil incarnate of a landlady to deal with, lazy housemaids, and moreover a very pestilential smell exhaling throughout, which is by no means an uncommon occurrence in this most brilliant of towns. Our present apartments are much better; the hotel is full. We have the Duke of Dorset, a Chevalier Douglas from l'Academie de Caen, Mr. Tuite, and Mr. Hall, son to Jamaica Hall, whom you know. He has been here six months, in which time he has made a shift to see the end of ten thousand pounds, what with play, a lady of the stage, and his tailor's bill. This last amounted (as my man heard from his) to no less than a thousand guineas! His French valet de chambre, after defrauding him by exorbitant bills, &c., of about the same sum, was detected at last by an English wine-merchant, and shown up to his

never brought forth, save in the event of the illness of the king, or of some other public calamity. An unbeliever in the miraculous agency of these relics having jeered the Abbé of St. Geneviève upon their inefficacy on this occasion, the satirical priest replied, "What more would you have them do—is he not dead?"

master, who discharged him. The other night Hall lost one thousand five hundred more, and would have been unable to discharge the bill of the house, if his principal winner had not lent him a sum sufficient for the purpose. He must be a thick-headed youth, and unless this his first expedition out of the British dominions should have refined his understanding as it has cleared his pocket, I think he will be fit for nothing but to be a mule-driver.

Mr. —— and Miss —— inhabit the back apartments of l'hôtel d'Espagne opposite our windows, and seem to live in great amity and cordiality. They have a young child with them. Madame d'Anglures goes on Friday to Orleans on her way to Blois, and we have some thought of joining her there, for a *séjour* in Paris will be a dull concern at this period, though the grief of the nation is by no means the cause of it. I never, indeed, saw joy more visible than it appears to be on the loss of this same Louis *le bien aimé*, whose illness was once the object of so much alarm and anxiety. Indeed, never did a king deserve more than he did to lose the affections of his people.

I have been to the gallery of the Luxembourg, where part of the royal collection is exhibited. There are but very few fine pictures. The *Jar-*

dins de la Boissière, in the Rue de Clichy, are in a fine commanding situation, but of wretched taste.

Orleans, June 1774.

We left Paris some days ago, and in compliance with your wish that I should send you a description of our tour, I will keep a sort of journal of all I see, and forward it to you *de tems en tems.* I intend giving way to my propensity to taking views, wherever I see anything worth admiring, and my letters to you may serve to illustrate them.

On leaving Paris, we traversed a rich arable country, full of quarries or pits of stone, worked by a wheel. There are fine valleys near Monthery, where the ruins of a castle rise boldly on the brow of a hill above the town, the approach to which is through avenues of trees. In the villages the peasants plant acacias before their doors, and the numbers increase as one advances nearer to Orleans. After passing the plain of Beauce, and the great forest of Orleans, which is all young wood as far as I could see, we came to a flat country full of villas and scattered cottages, and arrived at Orleans at nine in the evening.

The Rue Royale, regularly built, leads from the Place du Martery to the new bridge. This street is too narrow. In a recess on one side is placed the brass statue of the Pucelle, which was originally raised by Charles VII. on the old bridge. He is represented in armour, kneeling with her at the feet of the Virgin Mary, holding the dead Christ in her arms. There is no merit in any of these figures. The bridge is upon elliptical arches and almost without any ascent either way. It is remarkable for its simplicity and air of solidity; an iron gate between small turrets closes the south end, and opens upon a grand avenue. Near the north end, one arch of the old crooked bridge still remains; parts of the old walls are standing, thin and slightly built with pebbles buried in mortar. The church of St. Agnes is remarkable for having the upper part of its buttresses terminated with a filigree banister instead of the common pinnacle. Over the sacristy door are foliages like crisped cabbage.

The mall, or public walk, on the northern rampart, is one of the finest shady avenues I ever saw, but its being open to the north makes it unfit for winter use. The cathedral of St. Croix has been built at various periods. The west front is quite new; it is gothic in its ornaments, and upon the whole a grand piece of work, though it will not bear a comparison with the light elegant buildings of the thirteenth century. The choir part, which is ancient, is in a good style, but Grecian pillars and a heavy screen of the Corinthian order have been added to disfigure it, and to clash with the airy roof and the light cloisters of gothic columns.

The Benedictine convent is so white within, that no eye can bear to look upon it. Their library is open to the public. The pavement of the city is very strange, but clean. The inhabitants are a wealthy set of men, but unfortunately divided into jarring parties of nobles, financiers, merchants, burghers, Jansenists, and Molinists.* Their ton is vulgar, but they keep very good tables, and are extremely civil to strangers. Sugar refineries, traffic, and manufacture of Spanish wool, Levant trade for caps and coarse porcelain, are the great branches of commerce in

* The Jansenists were thus designated from their following the so-called heterodox but severe dogmas of Jansenius, Bishop of Ypres. The Molinists derived their name from their adhesion to the doctrines of the Spanish Jesuit Molina. The discussions and dissensions that arose between these two sects occupied France and Rome during fifty years, and might have continued to this hour, had not the revolution put an end to all theological disputes, and confounded all faith, all religion, in the same hideous proscription.

this town. There is a greàt deal of what is called devotion here.

In the time of the first French kings, Orleans was the capital of a kingdom. In 1429 it withstood the attack of the English, and the siege was raised by the famous Joan d'Arc. There is great abundance of fruit in the market here: the fashionable walk in winter is the cemetery of the cathedral of St. Croix, although there are heaps of human bones piled up in every corner. I could discover no traces of the fortifications mentioned in the history of the siege of 1488.

I have visited the banks of the Loiret—a sweet country. The river rises at La Sourée, a country-house belonging to Monsieur Boutin, two leagues south of Orleans. It was the residence of Lord Bolingbroke during his exile.* The present possessor, a financier, instead of following the dictates of nature, who pointed out such a scope for real beauty and embellishments, has lavished immense sums, and taken incredible pains, to distort every feature of her, and to degrade each part of the scenery. The spring, which bubbles up with great force and in a large volume of water in the plain at the foot of the

* Henry, first Viscount Bolingbroke, secretary of state to Queen Anne. He was attainted in 1714.

slope, is jammed up in a circular basin, and then let through a narrow gullet into a long canal, resembling in figure a child in swaddling-clothes. He has opened vistas where there is nothing to see, pruned up the trees till they look like broomsticks, and levelled the low ground till he has made a swamp of it.

There is one pretty retired walk of alders hanging over another stream, but its colour is muddy and inferior to that of the Loiret, which no sooner escapes from these shades of false taste, than it swells into a fine river, deep and full. The plain on the right hand is set thick with poplars and willows growing with pleasing luxuriancy. On the left is a cultivated ridge of hills, crowned with villas, gardens, and cottages, reflected in the crystal waters. Mills are at work, and boats ply upon the Loiret at a musket-shot from the spring, and shoals of fish are seen in every part of it.

The bridge of Olivet, near which Poltrot shot the Duke de Guise,* affords very beautiful prospects on both sides. About a mile below is a

* Francis, Duke de Guise, eldest son of Claude, first duke, one of the most eminent of this illustrious family, and one of the most bitter enemies of the Hugonots. He was shot by a Protestant gentleman, named Poltrot de Merey, on the 9th of February, 1563, during the siege of Orleans.

small country residence called La Motte Bouquin; the view from thence is delightful towards Orleans, which closes the northern horizon. The upper garden is laid out in flat terraces and parterres, and a small grove, all as pretty as the style allows; but the real beauties of the place lie on the edge of the river, which is here of a considerable breadth, with clumps of aquatic trees overshading its banks, and water-mills going in different points. A terrace by the water side leads to a covered walk between the Loiret and a canal, which receives a supply from innumerable springs, that gush out of the hills. The waters are extremely cold, and render the walk delicious in hot weather. A seat in an arbour commands a romantic scene down the water, and about a couple of miles lower down, the Loiret falls into the Loire.

La Boudon, a country house on the Loiret, is in a damp aguish situation. The river is dammed up by a mill into a pretty basin near it: there are many fine springs issuing out of the banks, and the walks are very rural by the water side, but it is by no means an eligible residence. I walked to the mouth of the Loiret, near the abbey of St. Marmin; an agreeable grove almost fills the angle at the junction of the rivers; but just at that spot are too many acres of barren sand, on which, however, grows a considerable quantity of asparagus from seeds washed down out of the extensive gardens that cover the plain above.

Monsieur Desfriches, a dilettante painter here, draws landscapes in a mellow style, and with fine lights; the foilage of his trees is remarkably light and well raised, and he enlivens his clear parts by drawing upon chalked paper and scraping, while he darkens the shadow of the crayon with touches of Indian ink.

Blois, July.

Having sent the baggage by water, we brought Madame d'Angloires and Madame de Marcois in our coach to Blois. As far as Mauny the country is a pretty vineyard, with an extensive view over the Loire into Sologne, which appears a forest from that distance. Near Beaugency is more arable ground. It is an ancient town on a declivity, with ruined towers and walls.

I dined with the Marquis de Marigni at Menars; he is the brother of the celebrated Madame de Pompadour.* The prospect from his house

* Jeanne Antoinette Poisson, daughter of a butcher to the Invalids, or, as others assert, of a M. de Tourneheim, a

is magnificent. The river forms a noble sweep in front, and there is a boundless view over the opposite plains, which are richly cultivated. The terraces between the house and the river are constructed in the best taste, and at an incredible expense. The furniture of the house is most superb: it consists of the finest Gobelin tapestry, real chintz beds, fine worked silks, paintings, china jars, mirrors, &c. The French may well say, "*Nous avons payé pour tout cela.*"

On the right of the chateau are an orangery and temple, adjoining a wood intended to represent an English shrubbery. It is cut into narrow winding paths, not deficient in taste: a small stream tumbles down little cascades by the side of it, and the walk is very judiciously extended to the machine which raises the water to the house, and occasionally keeps the rivulet running. The other part of the gardens is composed of a large extent of low, young wood, cut

rich fermier-general, who adopted her, gave her an admirable education, and married her to his nephew, M. d'Etioles. Louis XV. met her at a masked ball at the Opera—became forthwith enamoured of her, and it was not long ere she was publicly recognised and courted as his mistress. In 1772 she was created Marquise de Pompadour, an ancient and extinct title with which she had not the remotest connexion. Her brother, Poisson, was soon after created Marquis de Marigni. She died at the palace of Versailles in 1764.

into stars, and alleys with statues and temples. A group of zephyrs and Flora is a pleasing piece of sculpture. The park is divided, since Monsieur de Marigni had the great post-road brought on this side of the river, by order of government, for his convenience. It abounds with game, and contains about two hundred acres of wood.

Blois covers the steep slope of a rocky hill on the northern banks of the Loire. Its streets are precipitous, narrow, and crooked. The buildings of the upper town stand upon two knolls: the low town occupies a slip of level ground in the intermediate hollow, which appears to have been stolen from the river, that is said to have formerly run in several channels, and to have washed the foot of the hills. It has long been confined, however, to one straight bed, over which a noble stone bridge was thrown in 1717, to join the suburb of Vienne to the city. The walk and gates remain, and over each of the latter is an image of the Virgin. On the eastern point of the hill is the church of Solenne, which the Bishop of Chartres made an episcopal cathedral through the interest of Madame de Maintenon. Several livings attached to it form a revenue of sixty thousand livres for the bishop. The steeple is a barbarous tower of the Corinthian order, crowned with a kind of skull-cap, all which composes a heavy pile of building.

The bishop's palace and gardens command a very extensive view over town and country. Upon the western extremity of the hill is the ancient castle of the sovereigns of Blois. Twenty-three families have apartments in it. The size of the buildings, extent of the courts, and vestiges of terraces, gardens, and outworks, bespeak a royal though abandoned residence. The west front of the castle was built by Gaston d'Orleans, and Mansard was the architect. It cost three millions and a half of livres. The bad taste of the day led Gaston to destroy the noble gardens, planted far into the country by Catherine de Medicis, and to surround his palace with bulwarks like a state prison. The low building at the east end was built by Francis I., whose emblem (the Salamander) appears everywhere. Henri Duc de Guise was stabbed in the centre apartment, as he stood near the balcony.* His brother, the cardinal, was despatched in the

* Henry of Lorraine, Duke de Guise, commonly called the *Balafré* from a wound that he received in the face at the battle of Château Thierri. He was murdered by order of Henry III., by a certain Saint Malines, captain of the Cent Suisses, as he was about to enter the council chamber, December 23, 1558.

great tower near the west end, called La Tour du Château Reynault.*

Blois is not mentioned until the ninth century. It was afterwards governed by sovereign earls, of which Stephen, king of England, was one. It then devolved on the crown, and many kings of France resided there, and adorned it with noble edifices. The inhabitants, polished by the court, were long remarkable for the purity of their accent and language. Innocent XII. erected it into an episcopal see. The public walk here is over the bridge, a short and hot one, but pleasant.

The *conseil superieur* was fixed here† when the parliament was destroyed, and was composed of the members of the chambre des comptes, of needy Parisian lawyers, and people who were not bred to the law. The establishment has made house-rent dear, but has brought money to Blois. Society is here on a very easy footing;

* Louis, Cardinal de Guise, who was within the council chamber of the states general, and hearing the voice of his dying relation, sprang up and endeavoured to hasten to his assistance, but he was held back by the Cardinal de Retz and others, and conveyed to a distant chamber or cell, in which he was assassinated on the following day.

† These *conseils superieurs* were established when Louis XV. annulled the provincial parliaments.

all ranks intermix, and seem to be clear of parties and quarrels. Card-playing and evening walks constitute the chief amusements of the place, and certainly, "*toutes les femmes de Blois ne sont pas rousses et acariatres*," according to Voltaire's story, for we have met some very good-humoured apparently, with black eyes and black hair.

At St. Gervais, a small village south of the water, is prepared the famous *crême de Blois*, which is sold throughout the year in pots of one sous each. It is very savoury and rich, I suppose whipped into a lather and thickened by some art. The mills on the Loire are moored in the middle of the stream, and shifted as the currents vary. In summer, half the river disappears, and leaves large banks of sand.

At Blois they make liquorice cakes, but as it is extracted from the wild root, it has not the richness of the cultivated Pomfret plant.

Below the castle is the abbey of St. Jannes, not far from the bridge; south of it is a great extent of plain, bounded by the forest, and extremely fruitful in all sorts of corn except oats, of which I saw no fields anywhere in the neighbourhood. The gentle swellings that skirt the level are clothed with vines, plots of kidney beans, and hemp. Hay is abundant by the side

D 2

of the little river Gauchon, which comes from Chambord, and traversing the flat in a shallow black stream, overflows the meadows half the year. For this reason the hay is coarse and sour. The waters of the Loire are confined on both sides by high strong dikes, except where the land is of no value, and then the superfluous waters are allowed to spread in floods, to diminish the weight elsewhere.

The forest of Prussec covers the hills south of Blois. There are delightful rides in all parts of it, and great variety of thickets, open groves, and verdant lawns, but no valuable timber. The country people steal so much, and hack the trees in so clumsy a manner, that none can come to any size. The species most common in these woods are oak with the common broad leaf, a kind with narrow pale-coloured leaves, like those of the willow, beech, hornbeam, maple, ash, hawthorn, holly, juniper, laburnum, blackthorn, hazel, and tall heath.

Beauregard, the seat of the Comte de Gaucourt, stands on the verge of the forest in a fine situation.

I rode to Pont le Voye, a great Benedictine college, then across the plains to the *pont aux cailles*, where I had a charming view of the valleys at the edge of the forest, with a church rising under a hill. From thence we proceeded to Montels, a rambling village near the Beuvron, a deep and muddy rivulet. A large round ruinous tower, and a ditch or moat, still remain of the old hunting-seat of the Earls of Blois, on a bold pleasant site.

Pont le Voye stands on a small eminence in a valley surrounded with a vast plain and forests on all sides. The Comtes d'Amboise founded the convent, of which the church remains imperfect. The college is a separate establishment, and seems conducted on a liberal, comprehensive plan. All sorts of exercises and sciences are taught, as well as ancient and modern languages. Eight hours are allotted to study, play, and exercises. The annual charge is thirty pounds, everything included. The boys all sleep in separate beds. There is a servant for each dormitory; and three invalid soldiers parade all night to prevent fire, or alarm in case of accident. The monks have a large domain, and the students are indulged on holidays with refreshments at their different farm-houses. The English master is an Irish Abbé with a strong brogue.

The forest of Blois, north of the river, leads to the Abbey of La Guiche, founded by Jean de Chatillon, Earl of Blois, for nuns of St. Clare,

His monument, in black marble, is before the high altar. The convent stands close to the river Eisse, hemmed in by woody hills, and much exposed to inundations.

Chaumont is six leagues down the river. Through sandy plains behind the suburb of Vienne, and over the Cisson, up some pretty fields, I came to the village of Candé. The seigneur is a counsellor of the parliament of Paris, and has an elegant new house in an admirable position.

I crossed the Beuvron, and traversed a thick wood—was some time at a loss for the road, till I reached a cottage romantically situated in a small lawn under a steep woody bank. About half a mile further I got out of the woods, and rode through some fine meadows to the foot of the promontory on which the castle of Chaumont rises most majestically, overlooking the course of the Loire for many miles each way. The opposite hills are beautiful. Blois is seen plainly, and Orleans may be discovered on a clear day, as well as Amboise, distant to the west.

The castle in its present state was the work of Cardinal George d'Amboise, who was born in the old castle, the seat of his illustrious ancestors. Diane de Poitiers, Catherine of Medicis, Sardina of Lucca, &c., have possessed it in their turns. It consists of a great gateway flanked with towers, on which is carved a blazing mountain, meant for a quibble upon the name of the place.* The cardinal's hat and arms appear over many of the windows, and in some of the apartments are the devices and escutcheons of the Duchess of Valentinois,† viz. quivers, bugle-horns, and crescents. She ceded the castle to Catherine de Medicis, who took a fancy to it. This gateway leads into what was formerly a spacious court, but Le Roy pulled down all the north range, and made a terrace, which is a very beautiful walk in moderate weather. The situation is, however, so elevated, that there is almost always a great deal of wind, and frequently so much as to render the place extremely disagreeable.

* Chaumont, Chaud-mont.

† The famous Diane de Poitiers, created Duchess of Valentinois by Henry II. in 1548. The history of this renowned beauty is too well known to require observation; but the following epigram, alluding to the immense influence she had obtained over her royal lover, is perhaps less common.

> Sire! si vous laissez, comme Charles[1] désire,
> Comme Diane veut, par trop gouverner,
> Fondre, pétrir, mollir, refondre, retourner,
> *Sire!* vous n'êtes plus—vous n'êtes plus que *cire.*

[1] Cardinal Charles de Lorraine.

Another day I rode through the forests of Blois to the Vale of Chambord. There are delightful eminences on the skirts of the forest, covered with vines and coppice, through which innumerable country-houses and cottages rear their heads. The hedges abound in a variety of pretty shrubs. The waters of the Eisse, as clear as crystal, wind through large meadows divided by rows of poplars. The hills on each side are studded with houses. The ruins of the Château de Bury rise nobly upon an eminence. Its white towers make a fine contrast with the trees that grow amongst them.

Chambord is three leagues out of Blois.* Its park is above twenty miles in circumference, full of woods and corn-fields, but the walls are broken down in many places. The Cisson runs through it. The castle stands close to the river, in an ugly marshy bottom. It is a stupendous pile of building of stone, in a strange whimsical style of architecture, parts of which are neatly executed. The great staircase is exactly a double corkscrew; two persons may descend at

* Chambord was built by François I. It will be recollected that this chateau was purchased by the nation, and presented to the Duke de Bordeaux. The celebrated Paul Louis Courrier wrote a libel upon this subject, and was fined and imprisoned in consequence.

the same time, see each other on a level through windows that are opened in the niches, yet never join or overtake one another.

The apartments are royally spacious, but entirely stripped of furniture, except the bedchamber of the late Márechal de Saxe, and the theatre, which is completely fitted up. Nobody now resides in the main body of the house. It was a hunting-seat of the Earls of Blois. In the sixteenth century, Francis I. employed twelve hundred men in converting this place into a park. Stanislaus king of Poland resided here, and after him Maréchal Saxe. Its situation cannot fail to be unwholesome, as the palace is environed with immense woods and standing waters ; however, the inhabitants are thinning the forest very fast.

Bordeaux, August, 1774.

We left Blois after breakfasting with Lady Kenmure, who has resided there ever since her husband was attainted, and proceeded to Amboise, a rude heap of strange buildings. The castle is an uncouth compound of buildings of different ages, upon an irregular rock, and enjoys a noble view. On the hill west of the town is Chanteloup, the seat of the deposed minister the Duc de Choiseul.* The edifice is very extensive, of a flat form, with large office wings. An old wood runs behind it, and there is great variety of ground in front.

St. Levis, at a league's distance from Tours, runs close to a ridge of rocks that face a very long range of hills. They are excavated, with dwellings, and cellars with doors, windows, and galleries. Where there is sufficient room, villas and cottages are built before them, and hanging gardens are contrived in the bank. Some romantic ruins are placed on the point of the rocks, and, with the winding Loire, the city of Tours, and the abbey of Marmontier, compose one of

* Etienne François, Duke de Choiseul, prime minister to Louis XV., whose omnipotence continued intact until he and his party fell victims to the intrigues of Madame du Barré, who succeeded in getting him disgraced, and replaced by the Duke d'Aguillon and the Chancellor Maupeou. They mention the following anecdote of Madame du Barré, who was so intent upon the disgrace of Choiseul, and so inimical to him, that she discharged her head cook because he happened to bear a striking resemblance to her enemy. Having done this, she said to Louis XV. "I have discharged my Choiseul, when will you dismiss yours?" The disgrace of Choiseul took place in 1770, and was the forerunner of the exile of the parliaments, and thence of a great portion of the disasters that ensued.

the most beautiful landscapes in nature. The new bridge of Tours is of handsome white stone, with flattened arches. The interior part of the city is dirty, narrow, and ill built; but a street is now carrying round the town, a sort of Boulevard, which, although irregular, will be very grand. We had a broad excellent road here, in a vast open tract of arable country, bearing a resemblance to a disparked forest, studded with large tufted chesnut and walnut trees, thickening into woods and groves as the landscape retires up the hills ; there are many country-seats on the eminences, or at the verge of the wood.

The Creuse is a placid, muddy stream. Les Ormes, the chateau of M. de Paulmy, is a spacious new house, in a rich but false taste of decoration. The banks of the Vienne, on which the garden front looks, are fertile and pleasing ; it winds in a gentle picturesque manner between handsome eminences, clad with vineyards and woods. The higher plains are laid out in corn, and are full of fruit trees. Chatelherault affords a fine view, with its steeples and bridges, over the placid Vienne; but, on a nearer look, its charms vanish, and the town appears to the traveller in its true colours, the nastiest, worst built, and worst paved place in France. From hence a very beautiful road is cut in a direct line up a gentle acclivity through some large oak woods, with a chateau in perspective. The country grows barer on the approach to that city, and an enchanting view suddenly unfolds itself.

The river Clair, clear and silent, creeps through the willows in a narrow vale, which hems in the road on the left hand. Steep rocks close the right side, and in front rises a fine amphitheatre of villas, gardens, cottages, woods, and rocks. One beautiful cypress adds greatly to the general effect. At the extremity of this theatrical prospect, Poitiers appears on the point of a high brow, perched like an ancient fortress. There are some striking ruins in the bottom, some towers clad with ivy, and romantic vestiges of walls and cascades. It is a poor depopulated city, with some remains of Roman magnificence still extant. The public walks are very fine. It was at the distance of a stone's throw from the town that the battle was fought in 1356 ;* many of the slain lie in the church of the Cordeliers.

The country from thence is open, with a few straggling chesnut trees. La Costello is a pretty spot in a sequestered valley, shaded by oak woods, and watered by a clear rivulet. The views from the hills are almost boundless. Vi-

* The celebrated battle of Poictiers, won by the Black Prince.

vonne is a low dirty place, with a forest round it; its soil is gravelly and red. Pruffée, an ugly town on an eminence, belongs to the Comte de Broglie, a very tyrannical master.

Here begins a new mode of roofing: the roofs are almost flat, like those in the north of Italy, the chimneys rising out of them. The eye dwells with pleasure upon a rich landscape. Near Angoulême it is bare and rocky; it stands on a high, naked hill, with ugly walls and steeples. The Charente flows in the valley, clear and slow. Walnuts are the only trees. La Consonne, a large convent of Genovesan canons, is remarkable for the architecture of its cupola, and some elegant works in a screen before the principal entrance. We passed Barbezieux, an ancient fortified place. It is a marquisate belonging to the heiress of the house of Le Tellier.

At Montlieu we entered les Landes, or heaths, which are a deep black sand, overgrown with whins, furze, and heaths, with some oak and chesnut trees. In many places there are large clumps of pinasters of a small size. We were almost suffocated with dust and heat in these parts. At Carignan is a well-cultivated country, a great deal of Indian corn, and vines. At Cabrac we crossed the Dordogne in a boat, traversed the country called *Entre deux Mers*, which generally inclines to be wet and marshy. Many country-houses were dispersed about. After passing a ridge of woody hills, we crossed a broad plain to the Bastide, where we ferried over the Garonne to Bordeaux. We have taken a house on the *fossés du Tanneur*, and shall stay here some time.

Few towns in the world can boast of so fine a situation as this. The Garonne flows in a concave semicircle before it, and opposite rise the beautiful hills of *Entre deux Mers*. Its environs, for many miles every way, are covered with vines. The quay along the river is uniformly built for a great length. The square, with the statue of Louis XV., the exchange, the walks and ramparts, the Château Trompette, and beyond it the great regular suburb of the Chastroses, are such beauties as few cities can show. There is nowhere so great abundance of all kinds of provisions and delicacies. The trade is very considerable.

The elegant steeple of the Cordeliers was built while Guyenne belonged to the English, under the reign of Edward III., whose initials appear upon the tower. The Porte Basse, which is usually accounted a Roman work, is only built with the remains of some great ruin of that people. The English never settled in

Guyenne, except a very few families: one of the name of Knollys exists near Lisbourne. None but military men came hither, unless, perhaps, dealers in wool and wine, and none of these looked on Guyenne as their home. Borsis, a learned antiquary here, says he has never found in any contract, confrerie, or agreement, any English name whatsoever, and proves, by the memorandums of the chief mason, and the account of the expense, that the steeple of St. Michel's church was not built till the English had lost the country: he says he has discovered the ruins of a lion carved by the Saracens after they had demolished Bordeaux.

Bordeaux, March, 1775.

There has been a great piece of work and rejoicing here on the parliament being re-established by Louis XVI., *sous les auspices de son ministère:* the Comte de Noailles brought the intelligence. The exiled members returned to their station, and everybody seemed in an uproar of joy. M. de Noailles landed at the Château Rouge from the city barge, after rowing up and down the river through lines of ships with their colours flying, and saluting with their guns: he then walked up through the Fossé de l'Intendance to the government palace between a file of *bourgeoisie sous les armes,* and preceded by the town guards on horseback and on foot. The acclamations of the people and the crowded appearance of all the windows seemed to please him very much, and, like the Duc de Guise in the Henriade, he came along bowing and smiling to the spectators on either side.*

In the afternoon all the parliament men and women were assembled at la Chapelle de Barbet, a mile from the town, to receive the premier president at a grand banquet. A triumphal arch and the feast were prepared by the freemasons, who distributed invitations printed on satin, with various devices: he afterwards proceeded to Bordeaux, escorted by one hundred and sixty coaches full of all the town contains of people of fashion, besides many young men on horseback, and the Maréchaussée, each side of the road, every housetop, every window, being crammed as full as could be with spectators. It was an animated spectacle. He was received at his own house by

* The lines alluded to are these—

"On vit paraître Guise," &c. &c.

Henriade, chant troisiéme.

music, garlands and triumphant mottoes, and the mob filled the house so that it was midnight before he got rid of them.

We went next day to the palace, where M. de Noailles arrived with his guards *en habit de cérémonie.* The return of the exiles was applauded by a most numerous populace without, and a large assembly of gentlemen within, the hall. The *Manants*, or such as remained in 1771, were hissed and hooted at by the mob.* One of the *presidents à mortier*, M. d'Augeard, brought us by a side-door into the salle de conseil, where he placed us close to M. de Noailles.† There were not above twenty strangers admitted. The whole parliament was there, attired in red gowns. M. de Noailles opened the assembly with a short and proper speech, expressive of his joy in being the instrument the king had chosen to employ in restoring the parliament of Bordeaux to his people, recommending union, &c. The premier president then rose, and pronounced a good discourse, but very severe on the ministers of the late king, and replete with a

* The people of Bordeaux applied this term, which literally means a rustic, or boor, to all those members of parliament who did not follow their colleagues into exile.

† The *presidents à mortier* were so called from the peculiar shape of their black velvet official caps, which resembled a mortar.

greater spirit of resolution and freedom than the *Grand Monarque* might have liked to hear. The edict of re-establishment was then read, which is similar to that of Paris. The doors were then thrown open, and it was again read to the multitude. Your friend, M. de Salegourde, who had been exiled to Perregeux, having received a *lettre de cachet* like the rest, is come back and takes his seat.

The premier president desired to be remembered to you. It is a glorious epoch for him, and has repaid him for all the vexations of his exile.

We are all well here except Popsy,* who looks poorly. Her expectations of re-captivating the President de Verthamon are, I fear, vain; he seems to have no inclination to resume his chains. His apathy affects her much. Edward Dillon succeeds admirably at court. Monsieur has created a temporary charge of *gentilhomme d'honneur* for him, and the Comte d'Artois charges it upon his *caisse.* It gives him four thousand livres *d'appointemens,* and is a fine step towards the summit of Fortune's wheel.

* Mademoiselle Dillon, afterwards Marquise d'Osmond, sister-in-law to Sir E. Swinburne, who married her elder sister.

Bagnères, July 27th, 1775.

DEAR BROTHER,

I have delayed writing, that I might have time to collect materials enough to answer the purpose I propose in writing, viz. to amuse you in some of your long evenings. Before I proceed to give an account of my journey hither, or my discovery since I arrived, I shall pass in review what parts of yours may require an answer.

First with regard to Soreze, which I take to be the college you mention near Carcassonne, I have not been able to get much intelligence here. I passed very near it in going to see the reservoir at St. Ferrol, and believe it is situated close by Berrel, in a pleasant hilly country, and consequently cannot fail of being in good air. When I was at Pontlevry, they talked to me a good deal of their college in Languedoc; it is *bien monté*, and very numerous, especially in Spaniards, which perhaps may hurt the accent: they look upon it as rather on a higher footing and reputation than Pontlevry, but I can say no more of it. I shall let slip no opportunity of obtaining information, for in all probability I shall be in that neighbourhood in September, and perhaps may meet with somebody from thence before that time.

I knew of poor N. being ill some time before you mentioned it; but as ill news always travels quick enough, I was not eager to be the messenger. I hope, however, things are not so bad with the dear little fellow as you apprehend, and perhaps it may save him from future attacks by throwing out early the seeds of the disorder. I really expected a touch of the gout some time ago after drinking these waters, as I felt prickings and uneasinesses in my fingers, &c.; but they went off very soon, and upon comparing notes with other people, as I found these shootings to be the common effect of the waters in all constitutions, I became easy, and concluded my day was not come.

On the 16th of June I left Bordeaux with Sir Thomas Gascoigne and Mr. Harry Galway. From Austh to Rabastiens, the country is exceedingly hilly, but beautiful, rich, and well wooded; the roads the finest imaginable, carried down the hills in an easy manner at an amazing expense. From Rabastiens to Tarbes it is quite straight through the plain, and this last-mentioned city stands in the centre of one of the best cultivated extents of plain I ever passed through: though a bishop's see, it is but small, and contains no curiosities of any kind. Gentle eminences bound the plain on three sides, the Pyreneans on the south.

From hence to Bagnères, about twelve miles, is perhaps the prettiest drive in nature, gradually and imperceptibly rising as you advance into the valley of Bagnères: the road passes through or very near eighteen villages, besides cottages innumerable, fine open groves of oak and chesnut of great size, orchards without end, multitudes of clear streams running in all directions—small meadows, through which the water is conveyed so universally, and with so much skill, as to produce very fine second crops, large tracts of Turkey wheat, flax, corn, and millet. Hills gently rising from a point in the plain till they join the great chain of mountains, and the Pic du Midi, which is something like the large point of Cheviot, peeping up over the rest. These are the beautiful varieties that you are feasted with in this journey.

The valley grows narrower and narrower till the town of Bagnères, crossing the whole plain, seems to forbid any further passage, the mountains appearing almost to close behind it. Bagneres is very well built, every house being a lodging-house, and in general much better than any I remember to have seen at other water-drinking places; they are all white-washed, and covered with blue slate, the jambs of the doors and window-sills of a coarse bluish marble, got just above the town. Some have marble pilasters, in no great taste, on each side of their doors. The streets are crooked, and paved with small pebbles. Water runs continually in the middle of every street, and large canals, brought from the Adour for the use of mills, cross the town in four or five places. There are no considerable public buildings. The Coston, or public walk, is short, gloomy, and damp, therefore little frequented. Indeed, most people choose to walk out into the country, or upon the public roads, which are more pleasant than the town.

The country round Bagnères, north and south, consists of a circular plain without trees, crossed by the Adour, which is no more than a violent mountain torrent. On the east a very pleasant ridge of *collines* confine the vale, and on the west very high bare mountains come down upon the town, except that just above the houses are some very handsome large groves on the slope of the hills. All the smaller hills are beautiful, in great cultivation, and charmingly set off with cottages stuck irregularly on the summits and hollows, with each its clump of large trees and its orchard. Numberless fountains break out of these hillocks, and altogether form enchanting views, contrasted with the bare green tops of the mountains.

The mineral waters of Bagnères, notwithstanding the assertions of the physicians, are, I really think, all of one species, only varying in heat and accidental mixtures. The waters of "*Salut*" are a mile from the town, in a nook, under a bare rocky mountain ; a most delightful road winding up the valley leads to them, and they are the most in vogue of any of the baths. There are several in the meadows between the town and the "*Salut*," which is the weakest and coolest of all, scarce having any warmth, and not the least taste.

There are many baths in the town, with different properties assigned to them, really existing nowhere but in the idea or roguery of doctors. All come from the waters of *La Reine*, which issue out of a beautiful grove half way up the hill at the back of the town. They are boiling hot to the hand, but not at all so to the stomach, and I believe them to be far the most likely to be efficacious, if there is any virtue in these waters, which I believe to be small. I took those of the "*Salut*" regularly for a month, and found, with the help of very early rising, a good walk before breakfast, sober living and exercise, that they afforded me great lightness and greater ease in taking my long walks up the mountains. The baths are delicious.

I have not yet made any very long excursions, but intend in the first moon of August to go to Barèges and the Mature du Roy, which will be a long ramble through the mountains, of which you may expect a very minute detail. Meanwhile I will give you an abstract of what I have remarked in this neighbourhood, according as I find it in my journal.

Bigorre, being a *frais d'etat*, is much better off than its neighbours; the inhabitants more numerous, better dressed, and much more at their ease, scarcely any person being without some small landed property. The malady among the horned cattle has been kept out of this country by a timely exertion of their powers in indemnifying such as killed their suspected cattle.

The mountains hereabouts afford vast plenty of pasturage for innumerable herds of cattle and flocks of sheep, that travel up from the plains in summer, and constitute the riches of the province, which has no external commerce or manufacture at home. The plains produce immense quantities of hay, maize, rye, some bearded wheat and barley, and very bad wine from vines which are trained up to the cherry trees near Tarbes, but none near Bagnères, except against houses. The fruit here is not succulent or high flavoured.

The woods that cover some of the mountains

are of beech, more for fuel than for timber. Higher up are large tracts of silver fir, but not very large, being all hacked and hewed, as wood here belongs to the *communautés* of the neighbouring villages. I am told there are many sorts of firs and pines farther up. Oak does not abound in the mountains, but grows to a great size on the lower hills, where I was surprised to see whole woods of beech and oak, all planted about the thickness of a walking-stick with the head cut off, yet producing very noble sound trees, to judge by the fine old timber close by, which has evidently been planted.

This is very contrary to the received notions of gardening in England. It must be a very windy country, which in general hinders such plantations from thriving with us; yet upon the bleak ridges of their downlike hills I see every day rows of fine oak, beech, and birch, growing tall and healthy, and small single ones put in to supply the place of such as are felled for use, thriving very well without any prop or shelter, but a few briers to keep off the cattle.

The finest beechwood I ever beheld, which we rode in for hours, has all been planted out of nurseries or woods. The chesnut trees are very fine. It is surprising who can egg on the peasants to plant upon the heaths and hills, where it seems to be a kind of public undertaking. Large cherry trees abound in the cultivated parts. Great tracts of mountain have been by degrees cleared of wood, partly through neglect and partly by design, to procure more pasture for the cattle. The wood having been so long thick on the summits, has preserved them from the ravages of rain and torrents, and there is a fine verdure on most of them; but it is likely that now they are bare the snows and storms will get hold, and in time wash down all the soil, and leave the rocks bare and peaked like the Alps, which are infinitely less rounded and more irregular than the Pyrenees.

Of the shrub kind I have found great varieties of my acquaintance: some of the sides of the craggy mountains are clad with box. The lane hedges afford holly, dogwood, viburnum, privet, gooseberry-leaved currant, &c. Of the flower kind I have not discovered many that are out of the common beat.

Under the silver firs grow a great quantity of pale London pride and single yellow ranunculuses. This must suffice for the vegetable system. What I have to say of the mineral kingdom will be very short, as I hear of no mines near the place; the rocks are composed in general, near "*Salut*," of a large stony slate containing much pyrites of the cat-silver or pale false metal, kino, such as I have at Hamsterley. Other parts are marble, darkish blue and coarse.

In the vale of Campan, three leagues up the river, is a large quarry of very pretty green and white, and about the same distance south-east is a quarry of red and white, marble. Near Campan, half way up the crags, is a cave, about one hundred and four paces long, which I went to a few days ago. It is narrow and winding, not handsome or lofty, and though moist, contains no springs. They have broken and carried off all the fine pieces of crystal and stalactites, and there are only small pieces of either left, some of which I brought away for specimens.

Madame de Brionne has had the ridiculous vanity of having a marble plate put up in the bottom of the grotto, that the world may know that she and her company, among which even the lacqueys' names are engraven, penetrated so far in 1765.

Limestone abounds here, and very good cement is made with it. As for antiquities, all I can say on that head will go in a very small compass. The Romans knew of these baths, and probably Bagneres comes from Balnearia. There are three inscriptions in the town, one to the Numini

Augusti, another Marti, and a third "Nymphis pro salute suâ." There may be more, but I have not met with them, nor with any body like a cicerone. Henry de Transtamare, afterwards king of Castille, seized upon this place, and Marguerite de Valois exempted it from all *Lots et Ventes,* on condition of a certain sum of money received for apprentice fees, being appropriated to dancing, merrymaking, and bonfires, from St. John's to St. Peter's day. This privilege is well kept up. On those days every top of the neighbouring hills has its fire, and all the country girls assemble to dance in the town and neighbouring greens.

As to the people of the country, as far as I have any occasion for experience, they are fair and honest dealers, and not such dirty and pilfering scoundrels as the Bordelois. No Protestants among them. Their features harsh, and few pretty women, but a sound stout race of middling size. All go barefoot, except when they dance, an exercise of which they acquit themselves extremely well. The *paysannes* wear red cloth, short peaked veils, very unbecoming; on holidays, the better sort have them white, long, and transparent: they are an industrious set of people. Their patois varies in every village.

The only remnants of English conquest I have found out are, a ruined fortress without an entrance, on a very high hill, and the word *hay*, by which name they understand *foin*. But perhaps this may come from *heno*,* which is Spanish for hay.

To say anything of the way of life at Bagnères would be very unsatisfactory to you; let it suffice to say that the walks and surrounding country are charming. No public places but the wells early in the morning, and assemblies at private houses for cards, very dull and close. The Bishop of Tarbes, who is affability and politeness itself, has an open house, where he is always glad to receive strangers to dine and spend part of the evening.

There are here a large posse of Americans: "*vous savez ce qu'en vaut l'aune*," so need no further account of them.

We are threatened with a *troupe de comédiens*, and more gaiety; with how much foundation I know not. However, my time is so well filled with walking, riding, dining, sleeping, and that very, very essential part of life, sauntering away my time, that no part hangs heavy upon my

* The Spanish *heno*, like the Italian *fieno*, and French *foin*, is derived from the Latin *fenum*; the English word *hay* is from the German *heu*, but the root is the same.

hands, nor can I manage to find a sufficient quantity of it for reading, writing, &c.; so pray be grateful for that which I here bestow upon you.

Our present plan, *Deo volente*, is to remain here, where Mrs. Swinburne joined me on the 1st inst., till about the second week of September; then we intend going to Toulouse, and if Mrs. S. pleases she will spend the winter at Aix or Nice, whilst I and Sir Thomas turn off at Narbonne to pass a few months in Spain.

As Sir Thomas carries me, and it is an opportunity I never can expect again, I believe I shall be tempted to go. Don't mention it to anybody until I have taken my final resolution about the project.

If such nonsense can be allowed a place in a corner, I desire you will keep this letter till I see you, for fear my notes and journals should be lost in my frequent peregrinations. Adieu!

W. S.

August 20th, 1775.

DEAR BROTHER,

I wish you may not find this a much dearer letter than its contents are worth. But I judge you by my own sentiments. I am always reconciled to the postage of my friends' letters, provided they are but full, no matter whether of sense or trifles.

Our weather here is still very unsettled, rather rainy than fair. Mrs. Swinburne proposes passing the winter at a house in the plain near Tarbes, which is a pleasant situation but a dull town; but the acquaintance of the bishop, who resides there altogether, and is very civil to us, and the occupation her children give her, make her rather unfit for the enjoyment of a more dissipated winter residence. This has besides the additional merit of being extremely cheap, very near us, and consequently no expense or trouble in conveying bag and baggage thither; and is, moreover, in the way to any other place she many prefer to remove to. For my part, I shall go to Spain next month with my Pylades, by the way of Toulouse and Barcelona, and return by Bayonne.

How far we shall push our travels, or how long we shall be out, I cannot yet affirm, as it will depend upon circumstances; but our present intention is to go as far as Grenada, Gibraltar, Cadiz, perhaps from thence to Lisbon, and afterwards to Madrid. You may expect an account of my peregrinations, but will perhaps wait some time for it, as I have some thoughts of making up a pamphlet of it, if it answers my expectations. I also intend drawing everything worth notice on the route.

Direct to me "*poste restante, à Bagnères.*" Mrs. S. will take care to draw out the letters; and when you write, write a great deal, and pray remember, I know of nobody's marriage or death, or any one occurrence of the country, nor am I likely to know anything about it except from my friends. Jack Errington must be at home by this time, as he was lately at Bordeaux, on his return from Spain.

Mrs. S. made a prodigious progress in Madame d'Anglures' affairs, having, before she left Bordeaux, persuaded M. La Burte to see his daughter, and receive her in his house, to dine with her at ours, and carry her into the country with him. He has given her money, but how it will end I cannot yet foresee. This is after twenty-two years of complete abandonment of his child; and this is Mrs. Swinburne's doing, who is the most warm-hearted and indefatigable of friends.

Malaga, January 6th, 1776.

To Mrs. S.

I must write you a few lines from hence, because the consul's brother or cousin sets out this evening for Tarbes, so I could not resist the temptation of writing by him to wish you and the dear children many happy returns of the new year; but the heat in this place is so insufferable and oppressive, that I have hardly strength to hold my pen. What must it be in the summer-time?

We came here on horseback from Antequera, where we left our luggage. We ascended the Sierra by a most tremendous winding path over the rocks: this pass is called the Escaruela; there the Jesuits had a large estate. The hedges are full of beautiful flowers, almond trees in full blossom, marygold, myrtle, cystus, periwinkle, trumpet honeysuckle, and oleanders, in the beds of the torrents. We were glad to sit in the shade of a *venta** to eat our cold dinner, near a ruined village called Almoina, with a demolished castle in the very heart of the Sierra.

We descended a range of steep hills to the *Playa*, and soon arrived at the gates of Malaga. Our accommodations are horrid, but the consul,

* A small roadside tavern.

Mr. Marsh, is very civil. He has a sister in the seraglio of the emperor of Morocco. The cathedral here, which was built in the time of Philip and Mary, has the English arms over the altar. I saw beautiful double yellow roses in a farmer's garden in the *Playa.* The streets are narrow, the castle Moorish.

We staid a week at Grenada after I wrote to you. It took that time for me to make my drawings of that most curious of all palaces, the Alhambra, which is situated on a hill covered with wood, where fountains run through. There is a Moorish arched entrance of the castle with a horseshoe turn, mosaic ornaments, and a key in the keystone. There are fine views from the parapets of the inner court, beautiful basso-relievos added by Charles V. The doors are adorned with rings of bronze, a lion and eagle's mouth. The towers are lofty, built with cobble stones joined together in a smooth surface by mortar. We passed under the aqueduct which comes from the mountains, and supplies the castle with a fine stream.

We were assured that the last Moorish ambassador was as well acquainted with every part of this neighbourhood, as if he had spent his life in it. There are no remains of Morisco furniture.

We went to the play at Grenada—such a stupid thing—a friar and his ass the principal performers.

As late as twenty years ago, there were a great many Moorish families remaining at Grenada; but they were found out and driven away, after being pillaged of twelve millions of crowns. They made the trade flourish which now decays daily. There are still Moors at Rio Daro, with round faces, small bright eyes, little noses, and underlips advancing. They are humble and smooth-tongued, but it is hard to force money out of them.

Fruit and meat keep very well at the Alhambra, for the cellars are very cool. The air is extremely wholesome in the city, where in most houses a small stream of water runs through the rooms in which the family sleeps. We made acquaintance with an old parasitical officer of family, Don Diego Borroques. The Alhambra was opened on the 1st of January to the people, in commemoration of the surrender; everybody paid some acknowledgment to the governor, one Buccarelli, a drunkard, who lives like a toad in a hole, and has a little window over the door, where he sits and counts the people, calculating what the day will be worth to him.

I wrote my adieus on the wall behind the

door in one of the subterraneous rooms,* near the Moorish burial-place, in the two following concetti, and then took my leave of this most curious and well-watered edifice.

Hail prophet, most indulgent to mankind!
If thus on earth thy paradise we find,
What must on high thy promised raptures prove,
Where black-eyed houris breathe eternal love!
Thy faith and doctrine sure were quite divine,
Had so much water but a little wine.†

His regum heu! nimis infelicium deliciis die pro capta urbe triumphali mœstum, vale discernunt.—T. G. et H. S. Angli.

I walked up to see the *Generaliffe*, the Moorish monarch's spring palace. The great hall is well stuccoed—it is well watered, and has some

* These subterraneous chambers are similar to the *tahkhanehs*, or underground apartments of Persia and Afghanistan, which form a cool retreat during the extreme heat of day.

† Mr. Swinburne's *concetto* calls to mind the following old French drinking song.

Cet univers ah qu'il est beau!
Mais pourquoi dans ce bel ouvrage,
Le seigneur a-t'il mis tant d'eau?
Le vin me plairoit d'avantage.
S'il n'a pas fait un élément
De cette liqueur rubiconde,
Le seigneur s'est montré prudent—
Nous eussions bu le monde.

fine myrtle hedges. We were shown a large cypress, where the Abencerrage sat with the queen. The great drive of the town is on the Alameda, by the side of the Xenil; it would be a beautiful scene were not the river too shallow. The people still use the Moorish cry when they bathe or hear joyful tidings; for those who knew trades were suffered to remain when all the rest were expelled the kingdom.

We paid a visit near Grenada to the late minister, General Wall. At eighty-two he is very active, walks his five or six hours a day, my pace, which is a pretty brisk one, with his guns in his hand, talking all the way. He has a fund of the most entertaining anecdotes of courts and courtiers. His hunting seat belongs to the king, who has given him up the revenue of the territory. It is a most delicious habitation for winter. In the summer it is not tenable, for the vapours are obnoxious, and the heat insupportable. He then goes again to court for two months, and spends the autumn at his house in the suburbs of Grenada. He was extremely civil to us, and parted from us with great apparent regret, saying, "such birds of passage seldom alight in these parts." And indeed he sees very little company of any kind . . . . .

Cadiz, January 14, 1776.

DEAR BROTHER,

First, many happy new years to you all, and, secondly, thanks for your letter of the 29th October, which I found waiting for me here. You see I have surpassed even your most sanguine expectations, and have penetrated to the *ne plus ultra* of Hercules.

I have been more minute and inquisitive about every particular on the route, than a fellow of the Antiquarian Society in a heap of rubbish, and intend most bravely to get into print hereafter. The publication of a pompous book on Spain, by Mr. Twiss, damped my ardour when I heard of it; but upon the perusal of the work my colour came again, and the resolution has become doubly strong in me. It is scarcely possible to write a more shallow, pedantic, catch-penny book than that, and I think a plain, unaffected tour may go down after his bombast and trifles. I have besides drawn every antiquity, city, and remarkable view, in my way, with great attention and accuracy, which Mr. Twiss's prints are greatly deficient in. His Madonna is, no doubt, a fine print, but has as little to do there as a copy of any other picture in Spain.

I have employed several days in taking the

views inside and outside of the Moorish palace at Grenada,—the ornaments, capitals, dimensions, mosaics, &c., of its apartments,—by which means I have formed a collection that will give you a just idea of their architecture, &c. Though I ought not to anticipate, I cannot resist the temptation of running slightly over the journey with you, and faintly tracing the outlines of what I have seen in the course of this long peregrination; remember it is for your own private amusement.

On the 24th of October we entered Spain at Bellegarde, and arrived in four days at Barcelona. You know the route; therefore, as the roads are exactly as you left them, I shall pass over that much of Catalonia in silence. The hospitality of our countrymen, the politeness of the intendant, who was there in your time, and, by-the-bye, has a most charming daughter, combined with the general alacrity of the principal Spaniards to procure us a sight of everything curious about the place, made us pass our time very agreeably till the 19th of November, when we took our departure for Valencia and the coast. Before we quitted Barcelona we rode to Montserrat, and staid a day with the abbot. Here I made my first campaign in the Spanish language, having no other to convey our ideas by.

I am sorry to find, by what I can learn from St. Germain, that you neglected seeing this mountain in your way from Madrid. It is undoubtedly one of the greatest curiosities in the world. Its pyramidal rocks, the hermitages dispersed among its precipices, more like the nests of eagles than the dwellings of men, and the situation of the convent in a cleft of the mountain, are most singular and romantic. In this point, as in all others, you shall see my commonplace book, where I have entered into the most minute details, and in a rainy evening you will be able to bear the reading of them, as they will make the matter plainer to you, with the help of the drawings. The roads from Barcelona to the confines of Valencia are very rocky and disagreeable, the accommodation abominable, but the *paysage* most charming—one never loses sight of the sea, sometimes viewing it from a mountain, at others almost on a level with it, catching a light through the olive trees. We passed under an elegant Roman arch, and came near the tomb of the two Scipios, but were disappointed in our search for antiquities at Tarragona.

Tortosa and the Ebro afforded us no great entertainment, but we were highly delighted with our travels along the coast of Valencia. Nature and art have contributed to make a terrestrial paradise of it *to the eye*, for there is so general a want of taste in its productions, animal and vegetable, that any English stomach would be pursed up for want of matter to digest. Murviedro (the ancient Saguntum) has still a theatre, pretty entire, to show as its credentials.

From the Moorish castle that occupies the summit of the hill you command a matchless view of the plain of Valencia, perhaps twenty leagues along the coast, that city rising in a forest of olives, orange, palm, mulberry, and locust trees, that cover the whole level before you; the range of broken mountains on the right, and the boundless Mediterranean on the left.

Shut your eyes, and draw the picture in those of your mind. The sun was so hot that we could not stay long to enjoy the voluptuous feast. Perhaps you never saw any locust trees or *algarobas*, so it may be necessary to tell you that it is a large bushy tree, an evergreen.* The leaves are of a bright deep beech-green, set opposite each other on the branches. It produces a large pod, very sweet and palatable, and is the food of the mules in this kingdom of Valencia, where the country is covered with them. Here I ate, for the first time, the *belota*, or acorns of the ever-

* Robinia.

green oak, and do not at all pity the gentlemen of the golden age, for they are excellent eating.

Valencia is in so dead a flat, and so surrounded with trees, that one cannot get a full sight of it from any place; but it is a populous, large, dirty city, full of churches, like mosquitas, unpaved and unpleasant. From thence we proceeded to Alicant, a white town under a large rock that was partly blown up in Queen Anne's wars. Our countrymen received us, as everywhere else, with open arms and the greatest cordiality. Eletre, a large town not far from thence, is unique, being situated in the middle of an extensive wood, or rather forest, of palm trees, now loaded with their orange-coloured fruit; the branches are an object of commerce for Italy in Lent. The plain of Murcia deserves its reputation for richness and beauty; the mountains that run along each side of it prevent the eye from being disgusted with the sameness common to a view over so large a flat, but the city is nothing. Carthagena is a hole, but a most admirable port. The Spaniards seemed jealous of us, but the governor permitted us very politely to row all round it, and to see everything in the arsenal; this is very ill provided, and shipbuilding goes on slowly indeed, Fourteen hundred slaves, that work twelve or sixteen hours out of the four-and-twenty at a pump, to keep the docks clear of water, is a curious but an unpleasant spectacle for a man of the least humanity. Not half are Moors. The labour is so severe, the place so unwholesome, that they frequently drop down dead at the pump.

From Carthagena to Grenada, except in some hollows near rivers, the country is a perfect naked desert. On every pointed mountain along this coast are towers of alarm, or ruined Moorish fortresses, the only objects that induce the jaded traveller to stretch his head out of the chaise window. The inconveniences that we experienced in this long route, notwithstanding every possible precaution we could take to be well provided, are sufficient to deter all future travellers, if any such should ask my opinion ; but all difficulties vanish, all pains are forgotten, when once we arrive at Grenada—a heaven on earth.

The city is built partly on a high hill at the foot of the Sierra Nevada, so called from being almost always covered with snow ; partly on the slopes of this and two other eminences ; but the greatest extent of building runs along the plain at the bottom ; two small rivers, the Xenil and Daro, join and transverse its streets, where thousands of streams run down every alley, and through all its squares. The greatest quantity of water, and the best in quality, comes down from the Alhambra, an immense Moorish castle, built on the middle hill that overlooks Grenada, and this supply is brought in canals from the still higher hills behind, where the art and labour of the Moors are yet visible in spite of all the idleness and neglect of the Spaniards in keeping up and repairing their aqueducts and reservoirs.

Charles V. pulled down great part of the Moorish palace within the walls of the fortress, and built a very beautiful square palace with a doric circus in it, in an admirable, chaste style of architecture. Like many others of his projects, it was never finished, and now remains exposed to all the inclemency of the seasons. But they are so mild at Grenada, that if the mischievous hand of man does not accelerate its destruction it may still remain for ages. Adjoining to it are the palaces, destined by the Moorish kings for their baths, their concerts, and their women. The richness of the stucco work, the profusion of water, marbles, paintings and gildings, are truly wonderful, and utterly unlike anything I ever met with before. There is a light fairy kind of appearance in the pillars and ornaments not to be expressed, and the climate is so temperate that no moss or damp appears anywhere: the views from its windows are divine—over the city, and down the *vega* or plain, which is at least four leagues or more, before it is closed in by the mountains. But I could run on for hours on so favourite a topic—it is time to stop, that I may leave something for you to read hereafter.

We staid eight days, during which we have had the most delightful weather possible ever since we left France: except five days, whilst at Barcelona, there has not been a drop of rain, but rather too much sun. The Christmas holidays were delicious. Such crowds of pretty women, (for they are very pretty and clear skinned at Grenada,) sitting out on all the hills and public walks in the evening, and such serenity in the air, that it was always with the greatest reluctance we retired to our habitation.

We spent two days at the bottom of the vega with General Wall at his retirement, the *Soto di Roma.* He has fitted up a small royal shooting box very neatly, kills all his own meat, and employs himself in draining, and making beautiful drives through about four thousand acres of wood, which covers all that part of the plain. He is a charming, agreeable man of eighty-two; free and communicative, active and merry, walks five or six hours every day, and seems to enjoy life as well as other people can expect to do at fifty. From his house we came to Antequera, where we left our carriages and rode over diabolical mountains to Malaga, where we staid two days. Its church is very grand in the inside, the outside crowded. I am told it is almost as large as St. Paul's, but it did not appear of that size to me. From Antequera we had five days' deep road and much rain through the rich but naked plains of Andalusia ; and yesterday came hither from port St. Mary's in a bark.

The bay is superb, and gloriously crowded with vessels. It now rains very hard ; I hope it does not mean to last. As you will in all probability see Dr. Percy, tell him that I have been reading the romance of Don Alonzo de Aguilar, which he has translated in his reliques of ancient poetry, and being in the country, am able to inform him that he has been led into a slight error in the beginning, by the words *rio verde*, which he took to be only a poetical descriptive epithet, and accordingly has changed it to *gentle river*. Now *Rio Verde* (green river) is as much the name of that river, where the skirmish happened, as Blackwall is the name of the place to eat white bait in ; and it would be a little odd to make a copy of verses upon that, and change Black to *gentle Wall.* If you tell him this, mind I do not mean it as a criticism, only as a piece of information.

Rio Verde is a small torrent that falls into the

Mediterranean, near Ronda, at the foot of the Sierra Bermeja, between Malaga and Gibraltar.

TO MR. B.

Cadiz, Jan. 25, 1776.

Dear Sir,

You should have heard from me long before I got so far into this country, but for the following reasons—that I wished to send you an account of our journey properly digested, and free from all those errors that one naturally falls into at the first arrival in a strange place, before observation and experience have taught to distinguish solid and true information from vulgar and frivolous intelligence.

As my coming into Spain was quite an impromptu, I had not leisure to acquaint you with my motives, and left that office to Patty, which I conclude she has long ago acquitted herself of.

I hope I shall have no reason to repent having made this excursion, as I left her very well and commodiously settled at Tarbes, where, according to the letter she has written to me, she and the children enjoy perfect health, and she passes her time very agreeably. I have drawn accurate views of all the cities and antiquities, &c., on my route; and as no such things have yet appeared, I thought engravings of these might be acceptable to the public.

The publication of Twiss's book, I apprehended, would render my plan abortive; but on seeing it, I found his views few in number, and so wretchedly designed and executed, as to convey hardly any idea to me of the places he has meant to represent. I have taken notes of everything in the journey, and intend digesting them, to serve as an explanation to the drawing. I have enclosed the first sheet of it, and shall continue so to do till you let me know that the work is not worth the postage. I beg you will spend a leisure hour in perusing, altering, and correcting it.

My intention is to avoid all attempts at humour and witticisms, all trivial and puerile remarks, and accounts which can only interest myself,—such as dinners, and names of people that have been civil to us, trifling accidents, &c., which constitute the principal part of Twiss's book. The rest is made up of quotations, blunders, and nonsense. I never read so silly a book, Baretti's not excepted.

What I should wish to compass is to give a faithful, clear, gentlemanlike account of everything remarkable in this kingdom; and I have been fortunate enough to procure a great deal of authentic information from the principal Spaniards to whom we brought letters of recommendation in every tour, and who are much fonder of talking and acquainting one with every thing about their country than the French themselves. Besides, were Twiss's as excellent a book as it is a bad one, his tour and ours interfere but seldom, as he has not visited the northern parts of Spain.

I must now give you a short detail of our journey, first premising that we were everywhere received with the greatest kindness by the British families settled in the seaports, who loaded us with civilities during our stay among them, and with wine and provisions at our departure,—a very necessary help in this part of the world. After remaining in Barcelona long enough to make acquaintances, and branch out our letters of recommendation to all parts of Spain, we proceeded to Valencia; then through Alicant, Murcia, Carthagena, and Grenada to Cadiz; having had only two bad days, as to the weather, in our long journey from Barcelona to Andalusia.

About three days' journey from Cadiz, we got into the rainy country, and it has not ceased an hour since, which is near a fortnight. It had rained here for a fortnight before, and, if we believe the weatherwise, will continue a month longer. The roads will not be passable for some time, so that we are here kept prisoners, which is a great loss of time; but our quarters are good, for this town is reckoned the most agreeable in Spain. There is an excellent French comedy, a very indifferent Italian opera, and a Spanish theatre, open every night.

The factory is very numerous,* and glad to make travellers welcome; so that we are feasted and made much of, which keeps us in very good humour.

As soon as the weather permits, we propose going for a few days to Gibraltar, and return here and make the best of our way, by Seville, Cordova, and the Sierra Morena, to Madrid, where our stay will be very short. Our journey out of Spain will be by Segovia, Valladolid, Burgos, and Bayonne.

We have enjoyed the most delightful weather possible on the road. As we travelled almost always south, the sun was rather too powerful, but always so high as not to come into the windows and beam in our eyes. The pace we went was very slow, for the roads are wofully bad; but the fineness of the weather made amends for every

* The company of merchants. Each foreign nation had, and still has, its factory.

thing. I generally walked half the day's journey, or occasionally rode an ambling mule, which we purchased in Catalonia — the easiest *monture* in the world; you may sleep, or carry a glass of wine steady, though they go at such a rate as will keep a horse in a very long trot or canter. I have seen two that have gone from Rens, near Tarragona, to Barcelona, between sun and sun.

We made about two days and a half journey of it. As we carry beds and provision with us, we have been able to put up with the wretched hovels called inns. Without those precautions, one must be a muleteer to get a wink of sleep, and often run the risk of lying down on the floor supperless.

If these letters appear any way amusing to you, I shall continue them till I have completed this tour; if not, I shall drop the scheme, and keep my remarks to myself. The drawings, I think, stand a fair chance, as I am sure of their exactness and value.

TO MR. B.

Gibraltar, Feb. 29, 1776.

After long and weary expectation, the weather at last cleared up, and we were enabled to leave Cadiz last Saturday afternoon on horseback. We slept at Chiclana, a pleasant town, where most of the merchants resort, in spring and autumn, to spend a few weeks at their villas, which compose the greatest part of the town. The next day we were worse off, being obliged to pass the night at a small thatched house on the wastes. My bed was straw from the stable; the rest slept in the smoky crib on cork stools round the fire.

On Monday we reached San Roque, where the Spanish governor of the lines resides, and procured proper passes, with which we got into this extraordinary place next morning early. The whole country from Chiclana to San Roque is either forest or heath, with few signs of inhabitants, and the worst roads in the world even for mules.

General Boyd, and other persons to whom we brought letters, received us very politely. For a few days the bustle and military appearance of the place may be entertaining enough, but the style of life cannot please much longer. It was no small satisfaction to be once more on Britsh ground, to hear our own language spoken, and to see so many jolly roast-beef faces, after having so long been used to swarthy-peaked countenances and small-limbed people.

The soldiery here look like giants. The Hanoverians are tall, but not so well made below.

They agree very well with the English, being a quick, good-natured people, keeping much together, and disliked by none but the wine-houses, who have lost very good friends in the three regiments lately sent away.

While we were at Cadiz, there came in three American ships, consigned to a friend of ours. The cargoes and ships were sold. They had come from different parts of the coast, and all agree that the distress for every kind of necessary and convenience was very great among the provincials when they came away, and great murmurings among the sober part of the people. All the captains are North American born.

Our stay here will be short, and we intend to run over to Tangiers for a few days; for the Barbary coast looks so near that it is quite tempting, and the good oranges that come daily from thence are a further inducement to see the fine country which produces them.

This place is a tower of Babel: such a confusion of tongues and dresses! English, French, Spanish, Hebrew, Italian, Arabic! you may hear all in half the length of a street.

We have seven Dutch men-of-war here, with Admiral Hartsing; and one English frigate, the Experiment, Sir Thomas Rich. His lady is with him. Adieu.

Cadiz, March 20, 1776.

Dear Brother,

I think my last to you was from this place, about the middle of January; since which our peregrinations have not extended very far. Six weeks' incessant rain detained us here—half January, and almost all February. The carnival was not brilliant, as no public assemblies were allowed by the old fool of a governor. The theatres were the great resource. The French one, *monté sur le ton le plus magnifique*, with an excellent actress, La Vertueil, at the head, and every one much better than I ever saw together on a provincial stage in France.

The Italian opera is pretty well as to dancers, but infamous as to singers. The Spanish play is not so good as I have seen it in other places; but always full, as it begins directly after dinner; and a *bon ton* person may very easily make his appearance at the three houses in the course of the evening.

We had some private dances, but cards and conversation were the principal amusements. The number of English, Irish, French, and other foreign hotels, is very considerable. Most of the proprietors are women. There is a great deal of gambling; and take it all in all, Cadiz is not a very agreeable place even in fine weather; for it is so confined by the sea on every side, that one can hardly get a walk; and then such *mauvaises odeurs* in every street, that a foreign nose takes some time to get accustomed to them. It is moreover full of street robbers, who render it dangerous after the day is down; but I confess I have not met with anything of the kind. The place might be kept clear of all with a very moderate police; for it is a small town, shut up on every side, with a strong garrison.

All the streets are so constructed as to end in some square, or in the walk that goes round the city. The houses are very lofty, with flat roofs, and little kinds of towers or spires all along the parapets, to serve as supports to awnings in summer. The second story is the *etage d'honneur.* Every house has a vestibule, which is filth itself.

The bay surpasses all ideas I had of marine beauty. Its numberless creeks, islands, forts, windings, the great quantity of ships of war, and others constantly going in or out, or riding in the centre, altogether make an enchanting view.

On the 26th ult. we went by land (not at all the plan, for ten hours' sailing would have carried us into Gibraltar) to visit that celebrated rock.

Our journey thither, on muleback, was excessively tedious, being two days and a half tiresome riding, through very bad roads, over a desert country, mountainous and boggy. Some parts were pretty enough, such as fine woods full of uncommon plants, and large plains in pasture, well stocked with cattle: but the accommodations were bad even for Spain, and that is being superlatively so.

The great novelty we found in the situation of Gibraltar, the hurry and pomp of military music and parade, and the civility and hospitality of its officers, made us pass the first week with great pleasure. But when we had heard all the marches, and all the signals, &c., had dined round and seen everything to be seen, it began to tire us.

We made three attempts to get to Barbary; but the wind blew so regularly contrary, that we were forced to give up all thoughts of it—very much against the grain; for we had set our hearts upon it.

A Dutch fleet and one of our frigates enlivened the place, which has suffered much in its society by the departure of three regiments, and the arrival of the Hanoverians, who are a quick, sober, handsome set of men, speak neither English nor French, have no women with them, and live a very retired, parsimonious life. They do their duty well, are always exercising, but are not by any means so alert as our troops. They keep entirely together. Their dress is as near that of our soldiers as can be; but as they wear stiff black gaiters, with high tops, instead of the half-boots of the English, they march with bent knees, and look exceedingly pinched up.

We returned by the same road to this place last Sunday, intend staying a week longer here, and then proceed to Madrid, through Seville and Cordova.

We passed a day at St. Mary's with General O'Reilly, who was extremely polite to us, and, according to custom, very chatty. He is a fine, likely fellow, and we have promised to spend a few days with him when we leave Cadiz. I am curious to be well acquainted with a man who makes so much noise in the world. The Spaniards are certainly preparing for a second attack upon Algiers, unless they should choose to turn off, and try their strength against Gibraltar; which I apprehend we need not be very uneasy about.

Let me know a little how things go on with you, where you have spent your severe winter, and when you intend to bring your boys over to Liege; what new plans are carried into execution at Capheaton. All this, and a thousand such minutiæ, become of great importance when they have travelled some hundred of leagues.

Madrid, April 29, 1776.

DEAR BROTHER,

Upon my word I admire you for your assurance in saying you had written me a long letter —four short sides in your large hand, full of paragraphs and *puncta ad lineam.* You meant you thought it long enough for you to write, but I assure you it is full short when I come to read it.

Yours to Brigadier Vaughan goes off to-morrow to Coin, near Malaga, Costa di Grenada, which I believe will be his direction for some time, if you choose to write any more to him. We arrived here this morning, having left Cadiz on the 3rd. We stayed three days with General Count O'Reilly at Port Saint Mary, half a day at Xeres, three at Seville, four at Cordova, and one at Toledo. The remainder were employed in drawling through the rich plains and woody vales of Andalusia, and the bleak, bare, boundless plains of La Mancha.

You expect, no doubt, some light to be thrown

on the character of O'Reilly, a man who for some time past has made a noise in the world, and astonished by the rapidity of his rise and the greatness of the favour he is in at court. It must appear presumptuous in anybody to attempt to draw the character of another with whom he has lived only three days; but I sincerely think myself tolerably well qualified to sketch it, and perhaps hit it off with some degree of resemblance. He is so eager in all his conversation, and treated us with so much friendship and openness, that I am sure he acted and spoke without any intention to hide his real opinions from us. He speaks many languages, but expresses himself with most fluency in Spanish. His ideas are strong, and his conception of arguments and things above measure quick and forcible; his memory furnishing him with a knowledge of what has passed in different countries, that gives strength to his arguments on military and political subjects. His plans are upon a grand scale, and in discourse he is fond of expressing his admiration of Scipio, and those great heroes of antiquity who were above the opinions of the world, and who retired contented with the applause of their own conscience, and of the few virtuous men able to judge impartially of their actions.

In the inspectorship he is allowed to have great merit, and to despatch his business with celerity and regularity. He has seen, heard, and dived into all the arcana of war and politics, as well as what the French call ECONOMIE PUBLIQUE, and talks so much of honour and probity, that his hearers become alarmed lest he should be palming the appearance upon them for the reality.

I believe his ambition to be ardent and unbounded. He expatiated freely upon his Algiers expedition, said he saw all was lost and over as soon as he landed, as they had disobeyed his orders and deviated from his plans; at that moment he assured us he was twenty times in the mind *de risquer le tout pour le tout;* but, by what he he thinks the greatest effort of courage, he dared to retire baffled, and stand all that malice and envy would vomit out against him on his return.

He expressed great regret at losing us, probably *parceque j'ai de bonnes oreilles, et que je sais écouter.*

Seville is a most heavenly place in winter and in spring. We passed our evenings, whilst there, among the orange groves in the king's garden, watered by *jets d'eau,* in the style of those you have seen in Italy, squirting up along the walks. The cathedral did not answer my expectations, as it is encumbered with choirs and chapels ; nor is the gothic so light and airy as York minster. The Moorish tower adjoining is very handsome ; it is called La Giralda.

The Alcazar, or king's palace, has the arms of the two kingdoms represented in the Saracenic ornaments of the great entrance, which is quite oriental. Philip V., who died there, added a new part to this palace : the gardens are like fairy land, with galleries, waterworks, myrtle, and yellow jasmine hedges, and orange groves. Water runs through every part, and ends in a pond full of tench, where Philip used to fish by torch-light.

The orange trees about Seville are quite timber, loaded with fruit. We rode under them as in a forest, and crossed the plain to St. Ildefonso, a convent of Hieronymites, near which is Old Seville, or Italica, built by Scipio, and the birthplace of Trajan. Seven little hills form the situation of this ancient colony, of which very little remains except the rubbish and form of its amphitheatre.

There is a snuff manufactory at Seville, the only one in Spain. They make use of Brazil and Havannah tobacco. There are nearly five hundred people in one room making cigars.

Our acquaintance at Seville consisted only of the Marchioness de Malespina, and the Duke of Medina Cœli, who is a sort of king in effigy. He parades in great state along the Alameda with three coaches, each drawn by six mules, and lacqueys innumerable, in yellow liveries, every one stopping to bow to him as he passes.

My man, St. Germain, was clapped into prison for carrying my pistols through the streets to the saddlers, to have the holsters fitted to them. A strict police this!

We journeyed on to Cordova, having such bad accommodations on the road, as to be obliged to pass the night on a table. Cordova is an ugly-built city, with a fine country behind it. Its famous mosque, or mesquita, is one of the most ancient edifices in Europe since the fall of the Roman empire, having been erected in the eighth century. Although much spoilt, the chapels, and a vast choir in the gothic taste, built in Ferdinand V.'s. time, retain, in the greatest part of their extent, their ancient form and appearance. It is quite a wilderness of pillars and low-arched aisles, and is the most extraordinary sight you can imagine, especially as I first saw it by candle-light. It is the most ancient Moorish place of worship in Spain, but has none of that fairy character of ornament that sets off the Alhambra of Grenada. Indeed, its columns are all antique Roman, and many of its capitals Corinthian. The Moors capped such as had lost their capitals with rude massive imitations of what they admired in their ruins of ancient Cordova.

If my calculation come near the truth, and I believe it does, this square building stood originally upon near one thousand columns, all jasper and marble. But I pass over all this slightly, because hereafter you will be sufficiently tired of columns and arches, when you come to read my minute account of these places.

Don Pedro the Cruel built a part of the Alcazar at Seville, probably with Moorish architects, so like to the style of their buildings, that all the authors who have travelled this way have confounded them together, and called it the Moorish part; but a large gothic inscription in the principal front denotes the name of the builder, and the year of its erection;—besides, the arms of Castile and Leon are interwoven in the ornaments; and the Moors seldom put up the representation of any animal or living creature.* I own, had I not seen all those marks, the beauty

* The representation of any living animal or human figure is forbidden by the Koran.

of its court would have led me to call it Mussulman.

The women are very handsome at Cordova. Don Bart. Cesar took us in his coach to the bishop's country-house near the river. He (the bishop) has 220,000 ducats a year, but cannot bequeath it by will, and the king is his heir.

The Potro at Cordova, mentioned in Don Quixote, is a fountain in the street that leads to Madrid.

The most beautiful country I ever passed through, and most romantic, was after we left Cordova: hanging woods, dells, and purling streams—the Guadalquivir flowing to the right, one of the most charming drives in Spain.

There is more gilding in the church of Toledo than in all the French palaces put together; which is not saying a little. They have even gilt the lines of separation between the stones on the pillars.

I shall leave all these Christian and Mahomedan ecclesiastical topics, to give you an account of the colonies of Carlotta, Louisiana, and Carorina,* which, as an improver and an Agricola, will interest you fully as much. The two

* La Carolina is situated to the N. E. of Baylen on the high road from Cordova, by Andujar and Manzanares to Madrid. It is the chief town of the district called *Poblaciones de la Sierra Morena*, and is built on one of the spurs of those mountains.

first are a great way from, and much smaller than, the last of the three. As Carolina is the chief, a description of it will give every insight you can desire into the others.

The eastern extremity of the Sierra Morena, though a broken, hilly country, cannot be called a ridge of mountains when compared to the Alps and Pyrenees, but it is very high land. Eight years ago it was covered with forests, the receptacle of thieves and wolves; and before the colony arrived from Alsace and the neighbouring provinces of Germany, an hundred Catalans were despatched to clear it of the first of these vermin; the latter, cultivation was to eradicate. Of the first settlers the greatest part died from the immoderate use of liquor, the unwholesome herbs they culled in the mountains, and the heat of the climate; they, as well as all subsequent inhabitants, are bound to remain there for ten years, and care is taken to keep them to their engagement. The king fed them for three years, and gave to each family about thirty acres of land to clear, the implements of husbandry, ten cows, ten goats, a house, and one year's seed-corn. The unmarried had nothing. At the end of ten years the land is to become theirs in fee-simple, paying a small quit-rent to the king.

There is a great variety of all sorts of land,

but in general they have made it all arable. You may imagine, notwithstanding the king's good intentions, that many abuses crept into the management. The first director was a sad rascal, and used to remove the poor Germans from land they had tilled to others in waste, and for a valuable consideration put a Spanish family in their place.

I shall now proceed to sketch out a view of its present appearance. Carolina is built on an elevated plain not quite level, where eight years ago there was not a single house. From hence you command a most extensive prospect over almost all Andalusia and Grenada. The streets are broad and straight; the houses neat, though low and small; walks are planted and two or three squares built for public uses, as well as a governor's house, and a church; a large platform before the town is laid out in gardens. The roads are drawn in right lines all over the new country. The town is mostly inhabited by Spaniards, and Catalan manufacturers of cloth. The foreigners are settled at pretty equal distances over every part of the colony, in small houses proportioned to the size of their allotments; but in general they are run up in a slovenly manner. They have left the evergreen oaks standing in all the places where they were of any size; this, added to the prodigious extent of waving green corn, affords an enchanting prospect.

The new colony extends about three leagues breadthways and lengthways, but there are many straggling plantations in the nooks of the hills at a great distance from the rest. The great fault is a want of a proper quantity of water. The butter they make here is as fine as any I ever ate at home.

There cannot be a sight more pleasing to humanity than this new creation of industry and population; and we must not give way to the gloomy thought that the mismanagement and inconstancy of government, or the knavery of inferior men in office, will sooner or later injure, if not totally destroy, this rising colony. The number of the inhabitants of the Carolina department, I am told, amounts to eight thousand; but I could not learn how far that district extended, as there are several new villages erecting not far from it, such as Carboneros, and Agua-Romana, Vistaalegre, and Navas de Tolosa.

The latter is famous for a victory over the Moors. It is a strange mountainous place for armies to engage in. We had an adventure near it. Having sent our carriage on, we had walked through a woody dell by the side of a rivulet and found ourselves among a party of ladies and gentlemen dancing and eating sweetmeats, who politely pressed us to join their party and partake of an entertainment in the neighbourhood, which we were obliged to refuse. A capuchin seemed the GODELUREAU of the company, and was flirting with the prettiest of the ladies. The latter wore handkerchiefs and palatines. We had bad roads and an ugly country on entering Madrid: the corn-fields came up to the very houses.—Adieu.

TO MR. BAKER.

Madrid, June 1, 1776.

DEAR SIR,

A few days after my arrival here, which was on the 27th of April, we set off for Aranjuez, where the court is, through a hilly straight road and bare hills. The vale of the Tagus is fine, and the avenues noble. We visited Lord Grantham on our arrival, and attended a most execrable Italian opera. Next day we visited the Marquis de Grimaldi, who is the prime minister.

There are beautiful gardens in the island, where we met the Princess of Asturias walking.* If she encounters any presented person in her perambulations, he must necessarily attend her ; but we were not yet of the privileged number.

The prince was sailing in his golden galley on the Tagus. The king goes out shooting every day, and sometimes twice a day. He seldom speaks to young men, and likes old people best, especially monks.† We were a day or two afterwards presented to him, to the prince and princess of Asturias and Don Lewis, then to the infantas Donna Maria Josepha, Don Gabriel, and Don Antonio; and we dined out almost every day, at the Duke de Losadas, at the French ambassador's, the Marquis d'Ossuna, at the Duke d'Arcos, at Marco Zeno's, the Venetian ambassador's, and most frequently at Grimaldi's.

The Spanish grandees do not like to mix with other company. They *tutoyent* each other, and a grandee can only marry a grandee's daughter.

The ladies here wear no rouge, and have low heels. The life led by the young Spanish ladies of rank is very strange. In the evening they meet at the house of some relation, but never join in

* Marie Louise, afterwards celebrated as the wife of Charles IV.

† Charles III.

conversation, from whence they hasten home to dress their own suppers, and chat with their maids. In the morning they loiter and pray, dine on their *puchero*,* and the time passes till at last they attach themselves to a *cortejo*.† The married ladies whom I met seemed clever, but ill educated, pettish, and violent.

There is much talk here of the amours of the Count de Mora with the Duchess of Huescar, who has married his father Fuentes, and broke the son's heart.

We attended a bull feast, which is a shocking spectacle. An Indian of Buenos Ayres hampered and fastened the animal with a rope to a post; then got on him, cut the rope, sat upon him, and killed another bull.

On Good Friday the king absolves criminals by laying his hand on the sentences of those whom he chooses to pardon.

Don Lewis is so proud and ambitious, that the inquisitor general informed the king it was dan-

* A *puchero* is literally a glazed pipkin, in which the soup and bouilli is cooked. This soup forms the basis of the *olla*. It is the standing dish of all classes in Spain, and thence the name of the vessel is used figuratively for the contents. The Spaniards say, "*venga usted a comer el puchero*, as the French say, *venez manger la soupe*.

† The *cortejo* holds the same place as the Italian *cavaliere servente*.

gerous to take him out shooting. Five hundred thousand pounds sterling are spent on this place.

There are twelve thousand head of deer in the woods of Aranjuez. The king has one hundred and fifteen sets of mules, and ten thousand persons follow the court when it changes palaces.

We went to Villa Mayor to see the royal stud of asses, monstrous beasts with large heads and legs, fourteen hands high. On this occasion we met the princess, with a party, riding on some of these animals magnificently caparisoned.

Don Gabriel is a great mechanic and painter. There are paintings of his done with tufts of wool in the king's apartment. Don Antonio amuses himself in the gardens with filling and drawing an earth-cart.

Philip II. pulled up all the vines on these hills, and destroyed the villages, in order not to be overlooked. Charles V. was the first monarch who resided here.

The servants here are never discharged. The Duke of Infantado gives upwards of ten thousand pounds sterling in wages and pensions.

On our return from Aranjuez, where we remained about three weeks, I went to see the palace of Buonetiro, where are a fine portrait of Isabella of Castile, statues of Charles V., Philip

IV. and II., and Mary of Hungary. There is also a representation of an *auto da fè*. The new palace is richly decorated with marble busts, and some pieces of Titian. We have received our passports, and are on the eve of departure. I will conclude this letter on the road.

St. Jean de Luz, June 18, 1776.

Having now leisure to finish my letter, I will begin by our drive from Madrid, where we met a set of galley slaves, which reminded me of Don Quixote, and bevies of girls dancing round poles, holding ribbons in their hands. We passed through beautiful woods, and had a grand view of the Escurial. On arriving there, we sent in a letter from the Marquis Grimaldi to the prior, who appointed eight o'clock next morning for our seeing the convent.

I rose betimes to take a view of the Escurial, and at eight we were admitted. The staircase is grand. There is a magnificent organ in the church, and a lofty cupola. We descended into the sepulchre of the royal family, where some lines came into my head, which I shall send you herewith.

There are fine botanical paintings in the

library, and a gold book. But I will give no more description, as you will have it *au long*. On leaving the Escurial, we travelled along the foot of the mountains, through parkish grounds, full of deer and oak trees. Our muleteer amused us with singing romances. We had a view of the palace of Rio Frio, Segovia, and the immense plains of Old Castile.

When we arrived at St. Ildephonso, we waited on the *intendant* with Grimaldi's order, and were taken by him to the glass manufactory and bottle-houses. The glasses are cut with aquafortis. They make coloured glass there.

Mr. Dowling, the engineer, took us to see the gardens. The waterworks are most incomparable, and infinitely superior to those of Versailles, both as regards height and clearness of water. The fountain of the frogs and cascade are noble spouts.

The architecture of the palace is crowded and ugly. There is a vast collection of pictures. A St. Anne, by Morillo, teaching the Virgin to read, struck me most, as the girl is the very picture of my little Patty. There are also many antique busts and statues.

The king has already shot several persons in his shooting parties, from his badness of sight, which does not diminish his passion for the amusement. He pays annually thirty thousand francs sterling for damage done to the corn about Segovia.

We rode to the last-named city through an open corn country, so laid out for the convenience of the king's shooting. The aqueduct, a Roman work, begins at some distance from the city. The streets are straggling. The cathedral is a light, but solid gothic edifice. The alcazar, or palace, contains the mint; the view from it of the river and valley is suburb. The ceilings have the portraits of all the sovereigns of Spain from Pelasgus to Isabella.

We passed through a vineyard country, and saw numberless larkspurs in the waste, which are called, in Spanish, *espuelas de caballero*, (knights' spurs). At an inn we had a specimen of what Cervantes tells us served for the squire's beard; a cow's tail, which the hostess hung at her door, into which she stuck her comb. We regretted our Catalonian muleteers, for those of Madrid are very dull and slow.

On arriving at Valladolid we were joined by Mr. Geddes, the principal of the Scotch college. It is a vast city, seemingly run up in a hurry with bad materials. The streets have porticos on each side. Even the palace is old and ruinous. The river is considerable, and the walks very pretty.

Before we came to Villa Rodrigo we crossed the Puiserga, on a bridge of twenty-two arches. The women there wear hoods, the men *montero* caps faced with red and blue.

The position of Burgos, on a hill and its slope, is very picturesque. Its cathedral is a noble gothic building with statues on every part, even the pinnacles of the steeple. The gates of the city are adorned with those of the famous judges of Castile, by Diego Rodriguez.

We then travelled down a very handsome vale, bounded on the right hand by low woody hills, behind which appeared high blue snowy mountains. We met several Arragonian carts that were laden with chains and spears for bull feasts from Bilbao.

At Miranda we were ferried across the Ebro, for the bridge was swept away last year. The women seemed a sturdy race, working out in the fields, wearing lambskin caps, which they make themselves, for their wedding.

As soon as we entered Biscay, there seemed to be an air of wealth and liberty. It is a beautiful country, admirably cultivated. At Vittoria, the capital, we should have been delayed, had it not been for our passports.

The women of Vittoria are very pretty. The streets are dark, and are built on hilly ground, with steps of communication.

Our journey continued through a charming country ; fine corn plains, and every cottage having its garden. Here the females wear handkerchiefs and plaited hair for their head-dress ; the men woollen cloths or towels wrapped round their legs for stockings. Some women tie their hair in knots *à la Ramillies.* We met a grand wedding, so I could judge of the different fashions.

As Tolosa there appeared to be a numerous population. We saw two women riding in panniers balanced on the same horse.*

We had now arrived in sight of Fontarabia, Andayes, and the Bay of Biscay. We passed the Bidassoa in a boat ; the coaches forded it. We then left Spain, and entered France, where we went through a strict examination of our baggage.

In consequence of the dreadful state of the roads, we had the misfortune to have our axle-tree broken, which detains us here, and gives me time to complete my letter. Adieu.

* A remnant of the custom still in common use throughout the East, where the women are usually transported in *kejawehs*, camel panniers.

FRAGMENT OF AN ELEGY WRITTEN IN THE ROYAL VAULT OF THE ESCURIAL.

Through gilded halls, that daze our ravished eyes
With Raphael's magic and with Titian's glow,
Through sounding choirs where wreaths of incense rise,
The dark procession solemn moves, and slow.
Before it yawns the monarch's last abode—
Few are the steps the pageant has to tread,
Ere hasty priests consign their royal load
To dust, and silence on its marble bed.
The pomp retires—swift flies the courtly crowd,
With venal pace, to hail the rising morn;
And soon oblivion's soporific cloud
Will cling oppressive round the laurelled urn—
Save when some veteran, with an honest tear,
The sacred ashes of his chief bedews,—
Save when ambition, checked in her career,
The fatal change with bitter anguish rues.
Let us, my friend, awhile prolong our stay,
And take a lesson of th' impartial bier,
These vaults with philosophic eye survey,
And judge their tenants, without hope or fear.
What! even here must gold and marble glare,
Must architecture lend her art sublime?
Barely to second vanity's fond prayer
That dying pants to live beyond her time!
Shut out that light! the mansion of the dead
A salutary horror should diffuse;
No flow'ret gay should round the chaptrels spread,
But grave the forms and solemn be the hues.
In urns of porphyry, in rows of gold,

See where the mighty lords of Spain are laid—
In two short lines their history is told—
Upon the peasant's stone as much is said—
They lived, they died—high up and next to-day
Reposes Charles;* who late had learnt to rest,—
Charles, who so long had made mankind his prey,
Then sick, not satiate, left the bloody feast.
Ximenes † cleared the youthful monarch's way
Of every thorn which anarchy had nurst,
And happy Charles saw prostrate realms obey
Where that stern prelate's memory was curst.
What boots the hope that warmed Padilla's ‡ breast?
What boots the courage of his manly spouse?
Of what avail is liberty's behest,
That bids Toledo from her torpor rouse?
Dull falls her lance, defenceless is her shield,
And blunt her sword at Villalar is found.
The bird of Jove in triumph skims the field,
And bows her neck for ever to the ground.
Thus vapours, twinkling in the morning shade,
Hang o'er the fens, and dance with mimic glare;
The sun bursts out in fiery pomp arrayed,
And each vain meteor is dissolved in air.
A new-found world § by rapid conquest won,
At Charles's feet pours forth its precious hoard,
From temples watched by virgins of the sun,
And bloody shrines where Montezume adored.

* Charles, fifth emperor.

† Cardinal Ximenes, regent of Spain.

‡ Juan de Padilla headed the insurrection at Toledo against Charles's German ministers.

§ Conquest of Peru and Mexico.

On royal prey th' imperial eagle falls,
By Bourbon * lured to that luxuriant mead
Where rapid Tesin winds round Pavia's walls,
And Bruno's sons ten thousand heifers feed.
E'en now the Gauls with flattering accent tell
Their rueful story of that day of blood,†
When round their prince a line of heroes fell,
And Gallic corses choked the Lombard flood.
See gallant Francis, faint with many a wound,
At bay no longer keeps the pressing throng—
Bereft of friends, begirt with foes around,
He sinks and yields, in honour only strong.‡
Be noble, Charles, and soothe the pangs of grief,
To soften thraldom every succour lend;
The hour may come when some more favoured chief
Beneath his lance may make thy valour bend.
That hour is come; and fortune, fond of youth,
From Cæsar's temples takes the withered wreath—
Algiers and Metz enforce the sacred truth—
"Nought stamps man happy but the seal of Death."
Now foes with ancient enemies combine;
His veteran heroes sleep among the dead,
And spent in embryo is Potosi's mine;
Age and disease have cramped his active nerves;
No more he darts like lightning cross the world;
His hopes and fears in vast confusion hurl'd,
New to misfortunes, and untaught by woes,
Charles flies despairing to the monkish cell,

* Constable de Bourbon.

† Battle of Pavia in 1525.

‡ Francis I., king of France (*tout est perdu fors l'honneur.*)

But flies in vain, for hither also goes
The restless spirit death alone can quell.
Here it is quelled ;—in vain the march shall beat,
And martial sounds shall rattle round the dome ;
Victorious shouts, or shrieks of dire defeat,
Alike are lost, and cannot pierce the tomb.
From loathsome caves the bloated serpent sends
Infectious blasts to taint the vernal air ;
Its blighted head each sickening floweret bends,
The leaf is shrivelled, and the lawn is bare.
So Philip issues forth from his murky hall,
Tyrannic mandates traced with bloody hand;
Murder stalks forth at Superstition's call,
And streams of blood o'erflow the Flemish land.
Oh ! had he known, when with a jealous hand
He nipped the leading blossom of his crown,
That he had cast his offspring from the land,
To graft a bud of Bourbon on his throne !
Be to his mem'ry some indulgence given,
Whose daring genius bade this fabric rise—
Gaze on this mighty holocaust to heaven,
And view the founder with forgiving eyes—
The urns two Philips and one Charles contain,
Three kingly puppets, instruments of state,
Degenerate, weak, unable to sustain
A crumbling empire, sinking with its weight.
The sun of Austria, 'fore whose noontide ray
The dazzled world its head in terror bowed,
Now tumbled headlong down its evening way,
Pale, feeble, sick, involved in misty cloud.—
In scenes like these the moralising sage
Reads bitter lessons to ambitious man—
How weak his pride, how impotent his rage—
His schemes how empty, and how short his span!

Toulouse, September 3, 1776.

DEAR BROTHER,

We went to Aranjuez, where the court was on the 2nd or 3rd of May, and met with the most distinguished *accueil* possible from everybody; walking in the morning, eating a great deal, and sitting at cards, operas, or quietly at Lord Grantham's in the evening. All the ministers, especially Losada and Grimaldi, were remarkably kind and polite, the ambassadors very civil; as for Lord Grantham, he could not have behaved in a more cordial manner to his own brother, and I esteem myself peculiarly happy in having made his acquaintance, and obtained his friendship, as I have great reason to hope I have made that acquisition.

The king was anxious for us to see everything there and at Madrid, and we had every reason to be flattered with our reception. The fine woods on the banks of the Tagus, a great rarity in Spain, the luxuriant flower gardens, of which the island garden is as beautiful a spot as any I know, and the charming uniformity of the new streets, render Aranjuez a most agreeable residence in the spring months; but I do not believe it is wholesome, for I had a week's attack of the headache, which, however, passed over without any other bad consequences. We stayed about a fortnight at Madrid, where I got copies of many valuable translations from Arabic manuscripts, and the plans and measurements of the Moorish palaces, &c., with many other articles of great use and satisfaction to me.

I have since been labouring very hard in polishing and arranging my tour; I think it will be interesting from the great helps I have had, which few travellers can expect, and from the exactitude of the drawings. I hope to have the literary part ready this winter, but I am under great difficulties about engravings; however, I hope to get them over soon. As you are acquainted with the country from Madrid to Bayonne, I shall not enter into any detail on that head, except that the new road through the Biscayan mountains is very fine; rather too narrow, but perhaps the country is too rugged to allow of more breadth.

We arrived at Bayonne about the 19th or 20th of June, and rode post from thence to Tarbes, seventeen and a half posts, in ten hours, in one of the hottest days we have had this year; yet we were not in the least incommoded by it.

After a week's stay at Tarbes, where I found

all in perfect health, we went to Bagnères, where we passed six weeks most agreeably in a select society of people that were perfectly easy and *sans façon.*

Mrs. Dillon and Popsy were of the set, you may be sure. We usually dined at home, but spent the evening all together. The weather was very hot, but we were never without a breeze to refresh the air.

We came to Toulouse about the 16th of last month, and, after settling the nurse and children in lodgings, went to pass a week with the Bishop of Comminges, where Mrs. Dillon had already been some time. We there found a match already settled between the eldest Osmond, nephew to the bishop, captain in the regiment of Bourgogne cavalry, and Mademoiselle Popsy. It is a very sudden affair, having then only been *entamé* four days. I dare say they will be happy, for Popsy *semble prendre gout à la chose*, and they lived entirely for each other during our whole stay. *Les amans sont ennuyeux*, and therefore we did not repine at their making use of their privilege, and retiring into corners. Mrs. Dillon is in high spirits. The gentleman is not very brilliant in his person, but that is her affair. He seems very fond of her; and his good uncle, who is the best natured creature in the world, does everything to promote their happiness. The family is very good, from Normandy, and protected by the house of Orleans, so that he may hope to get promotion. The bishop was very polite to us.

We returned here, where the company of Madame de Saint Gery, a very lively, agreeable woman, and Mr. Macarthy's library, make us spend our time very agreeably.

We shall set out with Sir Thomas Gascoigne, on Monday next, for Montpellier and Lyons. After a short stay there to buy clothes, &c., we shall go to Marseilles, stay there a few weeks, and then take ship for Naples, where we shall spend the winter.

The Spanish ministers have been so obliging as to send us letters of recommendation to all the principal people at the Neapolitan court, and moreover have mentioned us in their private correspondence, which will ensure us a welcome reception. These are our schemes for next winter. As yet we have not thought where the ensuing spring and summer are to be passed, and when we shall be back in England.

I have been so great a rambler of late, that I can scarcely recollect having lived in a house of my own; and the inconveniences and wants of inns are becoming so habitual to me, that I am quite contented with them, and think of nothing better. I am afraid we cannot hope to meet you this year; the best thing you can do is to come and dance at the wedding. I have just heard that all the *noce* is coming here to-morrow.

I do not know if you were ever at St. Ildephonso; if not, it may perhaps be an object of curiosity to you. By particular orders, we had all the waterworks played off for us, and really they far exceeded my expectations. The statues and triumphant arches, from which the *jets d'eau* issue, are executed in a very good style, and, being all bronzed over, make a fine show. Their greatest beauty, however, is neither the height to which they sprout, nor the ornaments that hang round them; but the prodigious clearness and limpidity of the water, which is truly admirable. No rock crystal can reflect the rays of the sun with such brilliancy. We were fortunate enough to have a bright afternoon, without a breath of wind, so that the column of water went up perfectly steady and true. The gardens of this palace are pleasant and shady, but the trees do not thrive, from being planted too old, and in too shallow a soil. They have been at immense expense in digging and blasting round the roots, in order to put in fresh earth, and give them room to seek for nourishment.

Arts and sciences make great progress in Spain. They have arrived at a great pitch of perfection in printing, and, after having published Calderon, are now printing an edition of Lopez de la Vega. The academy has engraved several antiquities, but as yet offered none to public sale, except views of the Gothic cathedral of Burgos, which I have had sent me since I left Spain.

Casiri, Arabic librarian to the king, was prevailed upon to lend me the translation of all the Arabian manuscripts in the Escurial, or rather an analysis of them, and all the plans that the academy has taken at Cordova, Grenada, &c. I shut myself up for four days at Madrid to copy out what I thought useful for my project, and am sure nobody ever had the same opportunities. I am at present busy writing it out fair, and shall send it with all the Moorish architecture to England. The other views I shall get engraved where I can, or perhaps take a few lessons, and etch them myself.

I have not had a letter from England the Lord knows when; so can tell you no news of any kind, except that Lady Tyrconnel has made an elopement with Smith Lorraine, only to Marybone. She declined to see both her husband and father, who came to fetch her. Her lord has positively refused to sue for a divorce, as he would not give her the satisfaction of marrying her paramour.

Marseilles, Nov. 18, 1776.

Dear Brother,

Do you prefer a speedy answer, written by a sick body, with a cold and stuffed head upon him, to waiting till I am in better health, that I may furnish you with better entertainment? I can do either with a safe conscience, for I am very sure I run no risk of your having left Vienna easily in the winter. However, as I can get no answer at present to this *most sensible* question of mine, I must take it for granted you like me to go on with my letter.

We arrived here about ten days ago, and with great difficulty procured a lodging up three pair of stairs, at a most extravagant price. During a couple of days we exerted all our talents in ferretting out a better situation, and got into the best house I was ever in in France, just out of the town, in so fine a situation and air, so large, so well furnished and convenient, that I do not like the thoughts of leaving it.

The garden is very spacious, and the view over the harbour and court delightful. But however we have agreed to leave all this, and commit ourselves and all the fortunes of Ilium to the uncertainty of the waves, in the first week in December, having hired a large tight vessel for that time, to convey us direct to Naples. Sir Thomas, who is grown so well habituated to a quiet family life, that he cannot think of leaving us, goes also.

We left Toulouse on the 21st instant, and joined Lady Warwick and General Clarke at Montpellier, where we spent a month very agreeably, and I may say usefully, for I took lessons in botany of the king's gardener, to perfect myself in Linnæus's system. I drew and painted plants, wrote a great deal, and walked still more, having met with an intelligent cicerone, who procured me a sight of all that is curious in the cabinets of the town, among which the collection of birds of the Baron de Tongéres is the most remarkable.

General Clark has a house for the winter just out of Montpellier, and we had a great deal of their company. We then established our quarters for a week at Nismes, and I spent a great deal of my time, whilst there, in M. Seguier's cabinet. He has a valuable collection of antiques, medals, and natural history, with a noble library: he himself is a perfect assemblage of all kinds of knowledge.*

* Antoine Louis de Seguier, a descendant of the celebrated Chancellor, born at Nismes in 1703. He was renowned for

We made an excursion to Arles, where we found a great many Roman antiquities, but few in good preservation. It would be too tedious to enter into details; but that you may not have reason to think me very stupid, I will recapitulate what we saw in that city, which is out of the beaten track of travellers.

In the first place we were conducted to an unfinished amphitheatre, not equal in size and beauty to that of Nismes, probably built about the beginning of the empire of Christianity, and the last gasp of pagan worship and pagan shows; secondly, an Egyptian obelisk, without hieroglyphics, set up in the square; thirdly, two columns, twenty-five feet high, which supported the proscenium of the theatre, a work of Constantine's; fourthly, part of the pediment and two columns of a public hall or temple; fifthly, the model of the Venus found here, but ordered to Versailles by Louis XIV.; and lastly, the great burial-place out of the town, called the Elysian fields, full of enormous stone temples of various designs and dimensions.

his love for, and knowledge of, antiquities. He published the fruits of his travels and researches in various highly esteemed works. He died in 1784, and bequeathed his noble library and collection of medals and antiques to his native city.

From Nismes we went over the Pont de Gard, to which they have joined a bridge and made the great road, and thence to Avignon. I must commemorate the view of that city from the opposite rocks, as the finest I ever saw or expect to see. We visited Vaucluse which, being low in water, was little worth seeing,—Hareshaw Linn is worth fifty of it—and Orange, where we were well pleased with the circus or theatre, and the arch. From Avignon we went across the country (by a horrible road *par parenthèse*) to Berry, to see a Roman monument, which compensated us for our trouble.

About a mile from the town, on a small hill in a vineyard, stand together (but not directed towards each other, which puzzles me to find out whether they were meant to have any connexion, or whether they only form part of a great number of buildings,) the remains of a very much ornamented triumphal arch, and a perfectly entire mausoleum, the prettiest *bijou* I ever saw; it is square-built below, about eighteen feet every way. Upon the socle rises a square with small Ionic pilasters. At each corner and on the face are four different basso relievos, representing a combat between horse and foot, with triumphs, captives, &c. Upon this is raised a part with a Corinthian column at each angle, and pierced through with four ornamented arched doors. The entablement above is enriched with ornaments on the frieze, and on the architrave is an inscription which has been variously interpreted by antiquarians, but certainly denotes a sepulchral monument. Upon this entablement is placed an open circular temple, with its dome resting upon twelve very short Corinthian pillars.

Within this temple are two statues of unequal size, togatæ, without heads. I do not know how they got them in; for they are too large to pass between the pillars after the temple was finished. It is a charming edifice. The only thing that occurs as a fault, is the thickness of the columns, quite different from the regulated proportions of the Corinthian order; but they have not a bad effect, far from it; and who knows whether the architect, like Shakspeare, did not think himself at liberty to strike out new rules?

I do not think you ever passed that way; if you did, you will think all this description *de trop*. Aix was our next step, and then we came to this busy crowded town, which is brimful of English. You shall hear from me soon after we arrive at Naples, or, if we go to the bottom, my ghost shall come and pinch your toe at Vienna.

My Spanish tour is almost ready for the press;

I only wait for a proper hand to send them with, and to have answers from England about the publication, &c.

I know nothing new to add to the trash I have written above; so good night, for I have a symptom of a head-ache, which I have no mind to bring to a categorical answer. Yours, &c.

Naples, January 16, 1777.

We have got apartments on the Chiaia, which is the pleasantest situation here; the weather is fine, and Vesuvius is covered with snow. There are a great many English here at present, of which those I know are Lord John Clinton, Lord Tylney, Messrs. Osbaldeston, Dillon, Tierney, Molyneux, Lady Catherine and Miss Murray. No English minister is here at present, and Monsieur de Sa, the Portuguese envoy, does the business of presenting the English.

Sir Thomas and I went for that purpose to the king's palace at Caserta, through a wood of elms and a very fine road. I was not much charmed with the beauty and manners of either of their majesties. The king is thin but strong, of a fair complexion like his father. The queen is rather auy than otherwise. She did not say a word, and scarcely looked at us. We dined that day with the Prince de Jacci, who was extremely civil and attentive, and then went with him to the opera of Teseo. I know not by whom the music is composed, but it does not do credit to Italian fame, and as to the dancing, it was quite shocking. The house was finely illuminated, and very full of company. I have also been to the Teatro Nuovo, which is small, with a bad approach. The Buffo being ill, our amusement was not great.

This place is delightful, and more enjoyable than I can express. I have walked up the hills, and came down by the castle of St. Elmo, from whence the prospect is absolutely matchless. Nothing can be gayer than the town, nor kinder than we find its inhabitants. I know not whether it is in consequence of their natural good nature, nourished by the balminess of the climate, and cheerfulness of all nature around, *ou git dans son orgueil tout le néant de l'homme*, or whether the civility is caused by the letters I brought from the Duke Grimaldi and the Duke de Losardi. *Non importa!* The Princess Francavilla is all kindness: we have been with her to St. Carlos, and to a *rècevimento*, at a lying-in-lady's, the Duchess of Montecalos, and a ball at Madame Andres, wife of the Swedish Consul; also at Cavaliere Cecco Mauro's, an officer who, after making his fortune by play, is spending it all in giving balls.

We attended a profession, at St[a]. Chiara, of the sister of the Prince della Rocca, where there was much music, and a very fine gilt church. The nuns seem extremely rich, and enjoy great liberty. All the female convents are under the immediate jurisdiction of the sovereigns. The queen visits them in their turns in the summer, and takes a numerous suite with her to partake of the grand entertainment given by the nuns. The king is legate of the see of Rome by birth. All Neapolitan noblemen must ask leave of absence, which is generally granted for six months, and perhaps renewed twice, but never more: if they remained out of the country longer, they would have their estates seized.

The Sicilians are not under the same restraint. Where there is no heir within the fourth degree, the king is the heir to the noble fief, as the titles remain on the lands, which are plundered. Many of the princes are not gentlemen.

Lord Tilney has soirées every week, which are very agreeable.

We have had violent hail-storms, through

one of which I found myself taking a walk to Puzzuoli, which was very pleasant, notwithstanding the wind and occasional pelting of the storm. The sea was rough and grand ; the hills are nothing but a heap of cinders hardened. The weather is now grown more hot. I had a walk over the hills out of the Camaldola, by narrow hollow roads through the volcanic rocks, and returned through woods to the lake Agnano, which is full of wild fowl, not near so pretty as our lakes, as there is too much flat border to this.

I went in a caleche beyond the Torre del Greco and Monte St. Angelo, into the vineyards, to the spot where the lava stopped some days ago : it had just blocked up the road, overturned a cottage, and buried a vineyard before it ceased running. There is yet great heat in it, and at night it flames. During daylight there is only a trembling vapour which indicates the heat under it. The lava is very uneven and broken in the surface, dark and shagged like iron slag. It resembles the appearance of the first workings of a mine or slate quarry.

Mrs. Swinburne has been presented to the queen by Princess. Francavilla. She was very civil to her. Upon the following day there was a grand gala at the court on account of its being the king of Spain's birthday; we saw there the Prince of San Lorenzo, who last summer used to sit in the Calle Toledo without any clothes on, and orders were issued for him to be taken up and shut up in castle St. Elmo, if he did not wear them.

Lady Anne Severino is arrived, the eldest daughter of the second Lord Derwentwater, and heiress of the earldom of Newburgh, if her nephew have no children. She is married to a Venetian nobleman.

January 27.

There was a ball the other night in the Queen's apartments in dominos and masks. The king made one of them. Next evening the triumphal car of the four seasons of the Duke of Madelona paraded the streets, a festino of the Cavalièri on St^{a}. Lucia, which was stupid enough. There were few masks of character, and all seemed mute. We dined with Lady Orford, the daughter-in-law of Sir Robert Walpole, and now separated from her husband. She is very fond of whist, and is peculiar for always saying at the end, "*and two by honours*," by which declaration, if not always investigated, she often makes two more on her score than are her due, unless playing with those who are accustomed to her pranks. She is at the same time very severe with regard to others, and scolds famously both her partner and her antagonists.

We were amused the other night at Lord Tilney's card party by a *scena*. A Mrs. Sperme, who is a sort of toady of Lady Orford's, and generally makes up her whist party, happened to have thirteen trumps dealt to her. She was in great dismay, being frightened to death at Lady O., and feeling sure she would accuse her of cheating, at least by innuendos, if not openly. In her agitation she got up and asked leave to speak to Lord Tilney, to whom she told her distress, and asked him what she should do.

"Do, madam!" said he; "why play them out, to be sure."

The wind now is what is called *tramontana*, which is not very pleasant. I have been taking a walk through the grotto of Posilipo in a road to the left, where the peasants were very busy pruning their vines and poplars, and tying them together. Fellows at the top were singing as loud as they could bawl ditties like those of the Spaniards. I stopped opposite Nisida, to enjoy the pleasures of such a prospect, and ascended the neck of land on the left, where the violets were out, and the rock of tufo covered with purple stocks and gillyflower. Then I descended towards the sea of the bay, where I fell in with the Villa Maza. I there read a long inscription on marble, denoting that here were the fishponds of Pollio,* who fed his lampreys with human gore and flesh, and bequeathed these ponds, which are near Posilipo, to Augustus. I could not get admittance, as the farmer's people were at work, so I returned up the banks of ashes, washed into gullies by the rains, to the village, and came home by the stairs near Virgil's tomb.

There is a divine prospect from Capo di Monte. When the palace there was nearly finished, it was ascertained that there was no water. I saw a glorious collection of pictures and medals belonging to the house of Farnese.

February 8.

There have been magnificent balls at the court, but one of them the other night was stopped and put an end to *dans le beau milieu* by her majesty, who could not contain her jealousy of

* This monster was consul during the reign of Augustus, who having discovered the horrible practices of Pollio Videus, ordered the ponds to be filled up, and dismissed him from his favour.

the Duchess of Lucciana, and in her fury she ordered every one to depart. They say she is also very jealous of the dancer Rossi, whom the king admires, *é gelosia d'émpero, non gelosia d'amor.*

The French ambassador gives great balls, which are very agreeable; and a French theatre is set up, where we saw "*Les Dehors Trompeurs*" very well acted. We dined one day with Prince Francavilla, and went after dinner to see the procession of Don Marco Ottoboni through the Calle Toledo, consisting of sledges and hunters of various nations, richly dressed. The masks afterwards came to the court ball in their dresses.

There has been another profession at St. Mary's of Egypt. The devotee was daughter of the Duchess of Monterolendo. The duchess is very handsome still, as are most of her children, of whom she has had above twenty. She would much rather her daughter married, as it costs her more to make them nuns than to get husbands for such pretty girls. A thousand pounds scarcely defrays the musical and other expenses of these ceremonies, besides a pension to the nun, and something they reserve a power over in favour of the monastery, when they shall arrive at the great offices of the convent.

The Landgrave of Hesse Cassel is arrived, and made his *debut* at the French ambassador's ball. We went to the Fiorentini theatre, which had very pretty music, and good actors. "*Il Matrimonio per concorso,* or *in contracto,*" was performed.

The festinos are crowded, and there is no end to the balls.

February 12.

Yesterday we dined early to go to the house of the Marquis de Sambuca, the prime minister, where the king, queen, and chief nobility were present in the Calle Toledo. The street was lined with a double row of guards behind ropes, the coaches paraded in the middle, and the foot people crowded it as thick as can possibly be conceived. Every window was full of spectators, leaning upon tapestry and silk hangings. With difficulty could the postilions, by cracking their whips, make room for the five cars of the Madelona, and the sledges of the hunters with horsemen and hounds attending them.

This *parade* of Ottoboni was closed by the Bucentaur. The last that came was an English packet-boat, manned by the royal cadets. After these carriages had passed twice before their majesties, the street was cleared by the dragoons, and everybody driven behind the cords, and then, on the firing of a few *petards*, a dozen hack horses, with fellows on them riding bare backed, came galloping down the street. The prize was a piece of tissue. This was but poor work; but the next race of fine barbs without riders was very amusing, and its *coup d'œil* admirable.

Waiting until dark, the carriages returned in the same order, very well illuminated. Madelonas stopped opposite the king, and played off a pretty brisk firework out of the front of each car. The illuminations of the Bucentaur were beautiful beyond measure. I never saw finer sights than these.

From thence we went to the ball at court, where an excellent hot supper was served, each person eating on his knees, and in the best manner he could. In the ball-room the chairs were set so as to form a square in the middle of the room, and the company sat facing each other in a double row. The attentions of the Conte de l'Acerra to our table of English was beyond expression. We were served with pies, hams, wines, fruit in the greatest profusion. The king played at Macao, and at twelve went to the Festino d'Unione at the Casino. Soon after we broke up. Both the king and queen spoke much to us, and the king said, he had seen little Harry the day before pull off his hat to him, and look very pretty when he did so,

The king is very good-natured and well disposed, as many traits evince. He is boyish and romping, and very fond of amusement; excels in telling a story, and setting it off in the most ridiculous colours. He speaks Italian and French, but generally talks Neapolitan. His voice is harsh, and his gestures boisterous. He has no very strong passion for women, and what country girls and others he has taken a fancy to has been at the instigation of those about him, who put him up to it. He has no jealousy about him. His intrigues have lain in the sphere of Contadine, except a Madame Golard, wife to a French author on Economy, and an English woman. But he found out she had a cancer, and she and her husband were banished immediately. He has had some flirtations with ladies of rank, one of whom was exiled from the queen finding a note of her's to the king, with some extraordinary expressions. His present views are upon the Rossi, first dancer at the opera, and late mistress to the Duke of Arcos. She always comes to the balcony, when the king appears at his, to see the masks. They say he was in love with the Duchess of Lucciana, daughter of the Marquis de Gonzuala, secretary of state.

The queen has something very disagreeable in her manner of speaking, moving her whole face when she talks, and gesticulating violently. Her voice is very hoarse, and her eyes goggle. She has acquired a roundness in her shoulders, and is very fond of showing her hand, which is beautiful. If she sees or suspects the king to be taken with any woman, she plagues her life out, is in horrid humour, and leaves no stone unturned to break off all connexion between them; whether from real jealousy, or apprehension of losing the power she has over her husband, which is very great, since she has got quit of old Tanucci.* The king cries out in vain that his case is very hard, that he cannot go where he pleases, &c.

The disgrace of Tanucci had long been the main object of the queen, and the king was very glad to leave her free scope to follow that plan.

* Bernard Tanucci, minister to Ferdinand IV., a native of Pisa, where he was educated for the bar, and soon distinguished himself by his talents. He at length rose to the highest dignity, and died at Naples in 1783. He has not only left behind him several works on jurisprudence and philosophy, but the reputation of being an excellent statesman and liberal-minded minister

Wilseky, the imperial envoy, managed it by means of the interposition of the queen of France. The king of Spain reluctantly gave way, on condition that there should be no more masked balls at the theatre—a strange bargain!

Sambuca, who succeeded Tanucci, was a creature of Prince Jacci's, and looks very unlike a genius: his aspect is heavy and inanimate: his first manœuvre was very impolitic and blundering, in laying a tax upon oil, which he was obliged to take off the week after. The present system is to keep a strong garrison in Naples, and to take care that the inhabitants shall always be supplied with food at a moderate rate. These measures, it is said, will insure perpetual quiet in this, formerly, so turbulent a people.

A fund has long been established for purchasing corn, and selling it for less to the poor in case of a scarcity. Tanucci and his creatures are accused of having defrauded the king and embezzling most of the money, and one of the agents has absconded.

Ill-natured people say the queen's gallantries are numerous, and that her confidante was the duchess of San Severo, whose husband was at one time a great favourite with the king. For some unknown reasons, the queen has had a quarrel with the duchess, who, to revenge her self, persuaded her husband to inform his majesty of his wife's conduct, upon promise of his never divulging the name of his informer. The king, who was just then worried to death by the queen's real or affected jealousies, was quite enchanted with this discovery, and could not help telling her of it the first time she upbraided him with going astray. This attack made her furious, and she never rested till she learned from him the name of the person who had given him this information. The Duke of San Severo was banished from Naples, and his vexation brought on a fever, of which he died.

The king once carried his jokes so far as, at a grand supper at Posilipo, to take Guarini by the hand, and bring him up from the end of the table to the seat next the queen, saying that was his place: she boiled with anger, but was forced to swallow the affront, and, as soon as she could, had him removed to Turin, there furnished a house for him, and gave him a magnificent set of porcelain, which she had received as a present from the emperor, besides a very fine diamond star and cross. Her present favourite is an officer in the guards, son of the late prince of Marrico. They are much together at the masquerades, &c. She is only allowed 50,000 ducats a year for every expense, therefore cannot be very generous.

The streets of Naples are paved with square blocks of lava, which must be at least a hundred years old : each stone is laid in its place by contract, at a tarino, or two carlini. The Calle Toledo requires new paving once in seven or eight years. I cannot think this people so very wicked as they are represented to be by authors, who sometimes only copy one another ; for, during the vast crowding and *embarras* of the shows on Tuesday, not the least quarrel or tumult of any kind could be perceived, a thing I defy Paris or London to show the parallel of ; nay, in the great famine of 1764, the only violence a hungry populace (increased to double its numbers by the influx of people from the provinces, where every crop had failed) can be said to have committed, was storming one baker's house. It is written that winter and summer the streets are crowded with fellows that sleep on the ground and under bulks. I am sure all this winter the streets have been empty during night of all sleepers, nor do I think it possible for any creatures to have lain out in such weather.

We have had parties at the house of Gensano, at Princess Feralito's and Lord Tilney's, where I met the Polish Prince Solkonski and his wife. It is he who was taken prisoner, when he was fighting for the Russians, by the king of Prussia, who sent him prisoner to the fortress of Glogau, and compelled the troops he had levied to enter the Prussian service. We had a grand dinner at Lord Dalrymple's, after which a puppet-show and conversazione.

February 25.

Mrs. Swinburne and I went to Puzzuoli, where we took a boat to Agrippina's tomb, and landed below Baia, from whence we walked to the Piscina Mirabile and the Elysian fields, and dined at a cottage, where we drank some excellent wine, of the growth that is bought up, carried about at sea for a few months, and then sold at Naples for French wine. We had also some good buffalo cheese, called *Caccio di Cavallo.* We then visited the Monte Nuovo, which is covered with low shrubs, the remains of the Lucrine lake, passed up to Nero's baths, then took a boat in the bay of Baia, and rowed along the Via Appia, which appears very plainly. The Piscina Mirabile, built by Agrippa for watering the Roman fleet, supplied by an aqueduct carried along the hills for many miles, was a noble work. We picked up on the shore some mosaics, small medals and marbles.

We visited Pompeii with Sir Thomas, Mr. Stanley, and Mr. Pelham ; and words cannot express how much I was interested and delighted. I will not send you a description of it, as so many are in print.

Sir Thomas and I went to court at Santo Leuci, near Caserta, dined at San Nicolo di Strada with some Italian gentlemen, then to the prime minister's at Caserta, and accompanied the Prince of Sweden into the park, where the king and queen were under an arbour of leaves, facing the flight of steps, down which the waters of the aqueduct were let off at the signal of a gun which the king fired. Immediately after this the fire was repeated over the hills by a crowd of chasseurs and peasants, who hallooed, and popped away as they advanced down the hill to drive the game towards us. Some wild boars came down, and one plunged through the cascade. The king did not fire at them, but shot a hare. Upon the whole, though there was not much in it, the scene was rural and pleasing.

We then drove to the king's hunting box in the park upon a hill, where we played at cards with his majesty, till about nine, and then returned to Naples. The king was very courteous and good-humoured. Before he sat down, he begged there might be no ceremony, as this was only a *casino.* He told us a long story of an escape he had from a wild buffalo once, near Nola, by climbing up a tree. He is apt to give into the marvellous, a trick his father is very often caught at.

Lady Orford gives many dinners. We met there the other day some pleasant people, Cavalier Mozzi, Lord Dalrymple, Lord Graham, and Mr. Crosbie, with whom we made a party the next day to Portici, where Princess Francavilla informed us an excavation was about to be made of more rooms. It was a charming excursion. Traversing the beautiful fragrant plains, and crossing the winding river Sarno, which is as clear as crystal, we ascended through a vineyard over heaps of ashes to the excavation which has been made on the brow of a hill, from whence is a view of Ischia, Procida, Naples, Portici, Vesuvius, and the Appennines, which extend beyond Castela-mare, and all the vale of Nola. The principal place now opened here is a vapour-bath, with its flues. The superintendent treated us with a magnificent basket of fruit. The grapes were curiously dried with pine-apple kernels in each. The oxen here are singularly large and white.

On our return we had the pleasure of finding our friend Mr. Bankes arrived, and took him with us to spend the evening at the Duchess of Cotossiano's.

Naples, March 12.

We have made many excursions—one, of course, to the top of the mountain, on a mule from Portici, which I rode to the point where vegetation ceases; there I left it, and ascended the cone by the help of a man, who went before with a handkerchief round his waist for me to hold by. We met and followed several persons on the same errand. I confess I was disappointed at the summit.

We have visited Cumæ and the Lake Avernus. The ruins of the ancient city are numerous—broken pieces of marble and stucco lie about everywhere. The people go forth after the rain to see what has been washed down, and find many curious things.

The other day I took a boat and rowed round the Punta di Posilipo to the island of Nisida, which belongs to the Marchese di Petrono, and is farmed at seven hundred scudi. It produces honey and rabbits. The Porto Savono is a circular crater, very strongly characterised. I saw some very large black snakes in the grass and on the walls. The ships perform quarantine here. I found in the corner of a house in a vineyard north of the grotto the Colunna Milliaria of white marble, with this inscription—*Imp. Cæsar D.M. Nerva Nervæ Germanicus De Maximus Trib. Potestate vis.*"

The Pisciarelli are hot boiling streams that issue out of the side of the Solfaterra towards the Lake Agnano. You hear the great caldron boil with vast violence through a narrow canal. The waters smell disagreeably of sulphur, and the earth around is red and yellow.

Some days ago we dined at Caserta, at Prince Francavilla's, and walked in the boschetto, a charming grove of evergreen and common oaks. The king has cut down a large portion of it to build a foolish dirt pie of a fortress for his amusement. At the end of the wood is the Peschiera, a square pond, with a pretty thatched room, and an island in the middle. They have two tame pelicans there. We then went to the aqueduct, which conveys the Acqua Julia to Caserta, over the valley through which the king of Spain marched his army to Nantes.

The Recollets is a beautifully woody spot. Old Cascita rises on the crown of a lofty hill. We continued mounting and winding to a ruined chapel, from which we commanded the finest land view imaginable over all the *Campania Felici*.

Thence we drove to the palace, which is perhaps the most perfect, sumptuous, and extensive in the world—such profusion of marble, all the produce of the two kingdoms of the Two Sicilies.

The Prince Francavilla has his stud at *Difesa*, where we dined with him. It is a flat grass country, very unwholesome in summer. On our return we stopped at the king's haras, and saw all his horses and mares, sad cattle indeed, never crossed or improved.

The husbandmen hereabouts bury their beans and lupins before flower for manure, and hoe and dig all the plain under the vines, harrowing and smoothing with oxen.

The excursions we make are delightfully amusing and interesting; for, except in taking views, my wife has the same propensities as myself for antiquities, and our mode of life is so pleasant in this delicious climate, where no impediment of weather prevents our daily journeys of discovery, that it is impossible for me to express how agreeably the time passes. "*Vedi Napoli e poi mori,*" is the Neapolitan proverb; but I say, on the contrary, that after living at Naples it is impossible not to wish to *live* that one may return to it. However, at present we have no thoughts of quitting it, and that is still better. *Mais enfin ce mauvais tems viendra! L'on ne peut pas se domicilier hors de son pays.*

April 8.

The English have clubbed to give a puppet-show burletta. The other day the city magistrates walked in procession to seven churches; all were dressed in black velvet, embroidered, with scarlet tissue sleeves and waistcoats. The ladies here are carried about in rich sedan chairs, and their liveries are very magnificent.

The queen is very generous, but has not a large allowance. When she first took a fancy to Nasarino, she told the Princess of Stigliano, whose cecisbeo he then was, that she must give him up to her, and the Stigliano consented; but the gallant himself was restive, and would not be disposed of, and devoted his time and attendance to a third lady whom he really loved.

The Prince of Stigliano is extremely timorous. He refused the viceroyship of Sicily, until the king allowed him to take the Spanish regiment of Arragon cavalry with him. He sailed with it, and landed with it. It happened soon after his arrival that he assisted at a procession, at the end of which the whole crowd threw down their torches, and bawled out "*Viva Maria! muora l'Inferno!* The poor frightened viceroy, thinking the rebellious Sicilians were crying "*Muora il governo!*" was seized with violent convulsions, and forced to be carried into the sacristy.*

Another time one of his coach-horses fell down on the parade, and the mob ran to help his people. Stigliano, supposing it was a revolt breaking out, jumped out of the coach, and flew for refuge to a neighbouring church, calling out to the cavalry to follow him and save his life. Certainly Sancho Panza was fitter for a viceroy.

The king was educated by a friar of no good

* A similar but more amusing qui pro quo took place, in a humbler sphere, at Paris in 1829. A German company of comedians proceeded to that capital to give a few representations. The reputation for beauty of the prima donna, Fischer, had preceded her. The piece chosen for the début was the Freischutz, in which Agathe (Madame Fischer) appears in the first scene with a bandage over her forehead. Some wag in the pit being impatient to see her face, called out *à bas le fichu!* which Agathe, who understood little French, mistook

reputation, one Tanucci Samiandro, of the Sof frada family, which claims to be descended from the Lombards. His Majesty's manners are not very refined: when the emperor was here, and standing at a balcony with his brother-in-law, the latter made a very unwarrantable noise, and by way of apology said—"*E necessario per la salute, fratello mio.*" *

We dined yesterday with the Marquis de Sambuca, who, during the whole time of dinner, never opened his lips, either to eat or speak, and looked quite planet-struck. I thought he was seized with some mad fit, or hypochondria, but it came out afterwards that his dismayed appearance was caused by Carlino, the intendant of the king's bakehouse, who had been put in prison for cheating, having made his escape from thence, and was just retaken as he was endeavouring to get to the king to make a discovery of everything;

for *bas la Fischer*, and, being overwhelmed at such a greeting, fell into hysterics.

* It is recorded of the Count d'Artois, that, upon returning to the pavilion Marsan one night from the opera, and entering his own apartments, he gave his hat to his gentleman in waiting, and at the same time committed a similar solecism in good breeding, saying the while, as he coolly looked at his attendant, "*Ah! quel bonheur d'être seul.*" The Persians look upon their slaves as "nobody;" the Count d'Artois appears to have considered his "gentleman" in the same light.

—which it is believed would have strongly implicated Sambuca.

I have visited Dottore Cyrillo's house near Capo di Monte, to see his drawings of Calabria. In his library is the skeleton of a celebrated courtezan who was attempted to be converted by a famous Jesuit. His endeavours proving fruitless, he threatened her that unless she changed her way of life, and listened to his admonitions, she should die on such a day and at such an hour. Accordingly she expired at the precise time, and the Jesuit pretended to have heard her ghost confess she was punished for having slighted his prediction. As this adventure was long the public talk, an eminent anatomist had her body exhumed and dissected.

It is strange that now, the middle of April, Mount Vesuvius should be covered with snow, as well as the Sorrento mountains.

The Prince de Janni has a villa at Resina, where we dined. His gardens are extensive, and have outlet to the sea. We afterwards saw the gardens of the Duke of Montelione, which are very fine; there is a prodigious quantity of pineapples, but poor things. Here the gardeners put the sets of the plants into a hot-house, if it may be so called, where there is no fire, and common mould instead of tan. In a month they produce fruit, which I have not yet tasted in perfection. At Chiaramonte are a great many botanical plants.

Sannazar's tomb is in the church of Mergellina. That of Virgil is nothing at all; it is strangely situated in a nook of the rock. Over the right hand of the entrance into the grotto of Posilipo, opposite to it, is the following inscription:—

> "Qui cineras? tumuli his vestigia!
> Conditus olim ille est qui cecinit pascia rura, duces."

May 23.

I went with Mr. Thomas Pelham a pleasant trip to Capri in five hours. We had charming weather and a smooth sea. The landing-place is one of the most enchanting spots imaginable, embellished by a variety of timber, evergreens, and country-houses, with the town rising above them all.

All fruits thrive there, and no inch of the soil is lost. The points of view are delightful, and vary every moment. The eastern is divided from the western part of the island by immense perpendicular rocks, and the only communication is by a staircase of above four hundred steps. We mounted the eastern heights to the point which hangs over the sea. Here was Tiberius' summer villa, of which the vaults and reservoirs are still pretty perfect. Above his palace now stands an hermitage, from which the view of the Pestan coast, and of all the Gulf of Naples and coast of Romagna, is quite matchless: on a neighbouring point is a ruin which they call La Lanterna.

Having rested to cool ourselves, we descended to the Carthusian convent, which is beautifully situated. There is a long range of arches, called by our guide " the shops of the ancients." Caper bushes, now in flower, grow plentifully upon them. There are the remains also of another magnificent palace of Tiberius Cæsar, and there seems to have been a theatre near it. We dined in a village, then rowed off to Massa, coasting round the cape, and in raptures at every new landscape which opened at each turn of the promontories. No painter can imagine a richer prospect than that of the woody sloping shore of Massa, with its convents peeping up through the woods, with such a variety of verdure as render the tints superlatively mellow and pleasing to the eye. We passed by Sorrento, Castelamare, and returned by moonlight, enjoying a delicious evening, and still sea, with the animating prospect of the lights of Naples.

June 10.

The weather is grown extremely hot, but the country is in high beauty, refreshed by a heavy rain. The walnut trees are good shelter, and the pomegranate flowers very ornamental to the road; the sirocco wind is oppressive. We dined at Portici, at the Maggiordomo's, and afterwards saw the king draw up a detachment of the cadets, Lipariotes and chasseurs, and hold a council of war, like a child playing *à la madame*.

At six, his majesty marched into the Boschetto, where we followed him. The advanced guards, his new Cacciatore, attacked and drove away the enemy's light troops; and after several skirmishes between the different corps, the defendants were obliged to retire into the castle; the besiegers then attacked and took by escalade a house in the woods.

At eight o'clock the company came down to the Pallone, where a large vestibule or card-room was erected for the occasion, at one end of which was a very grand theatre, at the other an immense ball-room. Though run up in such a hurry, and slightly built, they are exceedingly elegant and well proportioned. We had a French play, after which we all adjourned to the card-room to take refreshments, and from thence to the ball. About twelve the king and queen retired, and soon after the assembly broke up, walking to their coaches by the light of a charming illumination, through the wood and large gardens, where the fountains formed a pleasing decoration. The presence of the sovereigns in these parties, instead of causing any formality, seems to make everything more jovial and merry.

Next evening the ball was repeated, and many more English were invited. Mr. Spence and Miss Snow,* by their furious dancing, entertained the king prodigiously; he was in roars of laughter, bravoed, clapped his hands, and encouraged them to skip and jump about. Each of them was conscious how much the other was laughed at, and took care to tell it to all the company, without suspecting that their own figure and performance could be the object of merriment. There was an Italian play, great stuff.

The king continues to divert himself with his

* This lady was so fat that she was called "Double Stout."

camp, pushing on trenches, besieging, &c., till the cadets and Lipariotes have quarrelled in good earnest, and begun doing mischief to each other. One of the latter was very dangerously wounded by being fired at too near. Whilst the villeggiatura was acting, a bomb was thrown into the castle, among the company.

The queen is exceedingly prodigal; at the birth of her son the king gave her 100,000 ducats, which she had squandered away in a twelvemonth, besides her allowance, which is 40,000. It is universally the custom at Naples for the husband to give his wife, on her lying-in, one hundred ounces, and the godfather is at all the expense of the christening. In Russia, whoever visits a lady in the straw must slip a piece of gold under her pillow.

The common people here are not very gallant; one never sees any flirtations going on among them. The fair is a gingerbread representation in the Largo Castello, within a narrow semicircle; a great deal of board-work painted with evergreens, and lanterns hung about, which give a dim light. At noon all the tents are let down, and all the world is asleep. In the evening, till eleven or twelve, the populace crowd hither to saunter, and then retiring to rest, leave the scene clear for people of quality, who take posession of it till one. The fashionable drive on Sundays in summer is along the Chiaia to Posilipo; there are generally fireworks at the Carmes.

Mr. Spence has quite made a conquest of the king by his ridiculous dancing, which I suppose the king takes for buffoonery. He has him to play at tennis with him, and they are as great as inkleweavers.

Count Pennicolto, a Polish general, has come to beg I will be security for him for three hundred ounces! A modest request from an almost perfect stranger. He says he is sent here as agent from the king of Poland, to recover principal and interest from the crown of Naples for a large sum lent upon Naples to Philip II. in 1588, by Queen Bona Sfortia, queen of Poland. The elector palatine has received one half, and the house of Condé pretends to the other, but Poland puts in a juster claim:—*ça m'est bien egal.*

There is a Mrs. Hart here, who was a nun at Milan; she is of the Pietra family, and eloped with an Englishman: she threw herself at Queen Caroline's feet, to get the Pope's pardon for her, and a release from her vows.

The Duc d'Ayen and the Tessés are just arrived in a French frigate.

July 20.

I embarked some days ago for Ischia, with Pelham and Spence, to dine with Prince Francavilla, who has a villa there. Just above it are the stufas or vapour baths, the smell of which is very powerful, even to those who walk in the road below. Myrtles in full blossom are abundant, and numberless flowers perfumed the air; a small honeysuckle in particular, sweeter than anything I ever smelt.

The air is now so hot, that going out of a room at Prince Francavilla's to the window, it struck one all of a sudden like stepping into the steam of an oven; but I cannot say that I have felt, or seen any one feel, any bad effects of lassitude or faintness from the heat.

We came away at seven, and arrived at Naples about twelve, by the mildest moonshiny night imaginable, with just a breeze to keep us going, whilst we and most of the crew lay down to rest. It was altogether a most pleasant evening, with a refreshing breeze to allay the fury of the lion,* which now rages. In addition to our party at the prince's, we there met and made acquaintance with the Abbé Galiani, one of the *beaux esprits* of Madame du Deffand's and Madame Geoffrin's

* The Lion, or Sol Leone—the name given to the dog-days.

society—an extremely clever and witty man, and an author.*

There have been horse races at Portici, and grand fireworks at the palace, in honour of St. Anthony; then a ball.

Figs and melons are in abundance here; filberts are supposed to be aborigines of this country. They have no nuts like our long-skinned filberts, but all of the Spanish kind. Turkey wheat is forbidden to be sold in the streets of Naples, but the police is so inefficient that it is sold in every corner.

From the experience I have acquired from the quarrels and adventures of our servants and neighbours, I conclude there is not such another race of rogues as the common people of Naples.†

A mariner died the other day in a house opposite my windows, and the gesticulations of the widow were truly ludicrous. She tore her hair by handfuls, and yelled horribly; but when her step-son came to seize upon her late husband's effects, she flew at him like a fury, and began fighting. She opposed the body's being removed

* The Abbé Galiani was one of the clique of French philosophers of Voltaire's and d'Alembert's school.

† This, although in contradiction of Mr. Swinburne's previous praises of the Neapolitans, is more near the truth.

to be buried, and afterwards threw herself fainting upon the window, with her daughters all tearing their hair, scratching their cheeks, &c. This is the custom of the country, and is done without the necessity of feeling any real grief.

In Calabria widows are forced to scream and roar, and tear their hair for grief, but the rich people hire women to perform these grimaces for them.

I have observed that the people of Naples never pay any court to the women in public, and never seem to sit making love to them, or appear fonder of one girl than another.

In the *Guardia del Corpo* (body guards,) none but young men nobly born are admitted without very great probation, and those of great houses are soon advanced from the rank of cadet to that of officers in their own troop. Those of inferior birth are slow in getting forward; and as in each regiment there is a company, a lieutenant, and a pair of colours, allotted to the Guardia del Corpo, they are placed out as the vacancies happen. Among them is a very handsome young man, the son of a *valet de chambre*, (which kind of servitude is the greatest bar that can be thrown in a man's way who wishes to enter the service); yet by interest, and particularly that of the Abbé Galiani, who is his real father, he was admitted and kept his ground. He is now the cecisbeo of the Marchioness de la Sambuca, and they say patronised by the queen herself.

The king's *Volontari della Marina*, or Lipariotes, are a most complete and handsome regiment, commanded by all the young men of the highest rank at court. The uniform is green, lined and cuffed with scarlét, and yellow buttons. The soldiers perform their evolutions wonderfully well. The king has been their major, and takes infinite pains with them. He always wears their regimentals. All summer they row his galliots, and in the winter follow him out shooting. I am sorry to add, that this brilliant set of soldiers is composed of the most abandoned wretches under the sun. Scarce one but has several murders upon his head, and I do not suppose all these rascals together would stand the charge of one company of resolute, cool grenadiers.

The queen is very superstitious, and is always going to some church or saint, and now has chosen for the godfather of the child she is in expectation of, the poorest *pezzente* or almsman of San Gennaro, one of those who have their feet washed on Maundy Thursday, and carry the dead poor to their graves: and this is out of devotion! It is a custom in use with many of the ladies here. They often have no godmothers for their children.

August 20.

I have been walking to the end of Posilipo, and enjoying something of a cool day. The king of Spain intended carrying on that magnificent road, taken from the sea, and built with immense blocks of lava, brought from near Puzzuoli. It would have crossed the hill in a zigzag line, and been a most noble work, saving the disagreeable necessity of going through the grotto. His confessor, a capuchin, was the director and supervisor of this work. But the present king, who in all probability will not leave one monument of his reign behind him, has never thought of going on with it. It was his father who built Caserta, the aqueduct, the great hospital, the palace of Portici, made the roads to Bovino and Evoli, dug out Herculaneum and Pompeii, and constructed the whole Strada Nuova and the Molo at Naples.

Paesiello's music is wretchedly sung at the opera, and the dancers are bad, except Le Picq, who teaches the young princes. We had a brilliant gala at court last week for the queen's birthday.

The quantity of water-melons consumed in Naples is prodigious. The greatest part is sold in the cellars or grottos under the streets. One shop under the Porta di Chiaia sells five hundred a day, and six hundred on holidays.

I went with Prince Butera to see the plans of Brindini at Pigonati's, which are making out for the king. It appears that a statue of his majesty is to be erected on a point of land, which is to be changed into an island by a new cut, (to be converted into an oyster-bed,) and called Isola di San Ferdinando;—a most ridiculous idea. The works of Brindini have already cost 26,000 ducats.

The other night, at a ball at Posilipo, the queen was taken ill and retired, and not long after, the roar of the cannon announced the birth of a prince. He has since been christened by the innumerable names of Francis, Louis, Januarius, Jean Baptiste, Pasquale, Balthazar, Melchior, Gaspar, &c. &c. The queen had a new doctor, Mr. Pears, called in, in preference to Viventor, the established one, which has caused a great sensation. Viventor is the son of a practitioner of Nola, himself an ignorant pretender to physic, and only constituted doctor to the queen's household from having married her favourite maid, as everything is done by favour here. By making himself a jack of all trades, and playing with the king, he obtained an almost uncontrolled power in all departments, directed the marine department, modelled the army, and, like a second Struensee, disposed of everything with the greatest annoyance and brutality. He had a scheme for improving the naval affairs, and subduing the Algerines; but the loss of the ships he expected success from, has lessened his consequence; and now the queen, having thrown off her slavery to his will, has done his business, to the great joy of all Naples.

When a person here is in a brown study, or *révant à la Suisse*, they say he is fishing for "Carmelachi;" which are "*manches de couteau*," or razor fish, taken in a very sedate manner; viz. a man walks upright into the sea, and seems quite lost in thought, till he feels something pricking about his feet; then he darts down, and catches hold of the fish.

There are four families here that came from Arragon, and settled in the kingdom of Naples, viz. —Carolina, Count d'Acerra; Gucoaro, Duke of Novino; Cavallanes, Marquis of Santo Mario, and Count d'Avilos. They walk together in the procession of the octave of Corpus Christi, to visit the great altar.

The dissipation of the Neapolitans is really

disgusting. All ranks seem to live only for tawdry show and idleness. Every day there are fireworks and music, with some devotional procession or another; these are so common, that nobody minds them. In one firework, let off before some Madonna, was a paper statue of a doctor giving a *lavement* of squibs to Pulchinello.*

Expense and prodigality are at their height here. The rich are oppressed with debts; the working people always spend the produce of their labour before they have received it; and from the king to the lazzaroni there is not such a nation of idle, irregular fellows in the world.

The queen had three young ladies praying for her safe delivery, who are now to be portioned off as wives or nuns. When one of her children was ill of a swelled face, she sent it regularly to kiss an image of St. Jago, in one of the churches.

The women here seem to give avarice and

* In the ancient part of the city of Antwerp, said to have been built by the Romans, there for a long time existed a small image of the god Priapus. It was suggested by one of the town council that this pagan emblem ought to be effaced, and the niche, in which it stood, purified by some christian image. The proposition was carried, and a small statue of the Virgin, at this hour, occupies the place of the Roman effigy.

vanity the first rank among their passions. Forty years ago there were not ten women at Naples who knew what a cap was; but luxury has much increased since that time, and now the ladies are all *à la Française.*

The politics of this court are very strange, and, in compliance with the bigotry of his most Catholic Majesty, Tanucci's projects of undermining the power of the church are quite knocked on the head. The Hackney has just been presented to the Pope, with more than common pomp, though his Holiness was informed last year that this humiliating ceremony would never be performed again.*

Last year the king named to the bishopric of Aquila the professor of common law in the university of Naples, who immediately wrote a letter to the tribunal and magistrates of that city, notifying his nomination, and descanting upon the happiness of Aquila in being under the sole command of the king, free from all interference of the court of Rome. The pope was outrageous at this, and refused to grant the bulls, or to con-

* The establishment of the tribute, of which the presentation of the palfrey was the emblem, dated from the epoch of the Norman kings, who thereby acknowledged the right or sovereignty of the pope to the kingdom of Naples. This custom was abolished at the period of the French invasion, and has not been re-established.

secrate the recipient. At last the latter was forced to recant, went to Rome, and was consecrated. In the bulls, the pope talks of the plenitude of his power, of his bishops in his city of Aquila, in his fief the kingdom of Naples. When Sambuca expostulated with the king on the disgraceful tribute of the "*haquenée*," Ferdinand shrugged up his shoulders, and said he should have no objections to refuse it, "*ma bisogna far acconsentir il Papa.*"

The king spends in his household about six hundred thousand ducats yearly, and the annual sums paid for masses said in this city alone amount to as much more.

I have been to see the drawing of the lottery, in the great hall of the Vicaria. Five numbers were extracted by a little boy, after the boxes had been shaken by some lazzaroni.

There is no place where music seems to be in less esteem than Naples, or where so little is heard; no one ever attends to it, even from the finest singers and performers, and even the common people appear utter strangers to it. There is no national music, and, except a few drawling kind of sequadillas, probably bequeathed to them by the Spaniards, you never hear any such things as vielles, organs, guitars, &c., in the streets.

All the ladies of quality here, let the circumstances of their husbands be what they will, have a hundred ducats per month for pin-money, and no more. At the birth of every child the husband makes her a present of one hundred ounces, and many other things of value, according to her fortune.

The king, it is said, takes a boat at midnight, or later, to go to his rendezvous on the coast of Portici. The Lucciana's husband has been absent for many weeks, at his country-house near Aversa.

Madame Santo Marco, one of the beauties of Naples, laid a scheme, about two years ago, for making a conquest of the king, at Caserta, which succeeded; but the queen, being apprised of it, gave his Majesty such a lecture as frightened him out of his wits, and brought him back to Naples upon his knees. She forgave him, on his promising never to offend again; to which he willingly agreed. The marchesa was exiled, and the Prince de la Rocca, one of the principal actors, was wise enongh to retire for two years to his estate, where he received the red ribband of San Gennaro, which the king promised him when he was his confident in the affair. On his return to court, he waited on their majesties to thank them for it, and was most graciously received by both; but as soon as the king returned to the inner apartments, he giddily or maliciously told the queen that La Rocca, to whom she was so civil, had been the agent in the Santo Marco business. "You have told me too late," said the queen.

The Abbé Galiani had the other day a religious dispute with some Italian gentlemen, in which he attempted to prove to them that the Gospel of St. Mark was an abstract of St. Matthew. After much wrangling and discussion, one of the company proposed to change the subject, and to talk of the pretty women of Naples; among others of Madame Santo Marco. "Eh?" said the Abbé, "*à che serve? non vi ho detto gia venti volte che Santo Marco é l'epitome di San Matteo?*"*

We see the Abbé often, and he enlivens our conversation by his wit. He has explained some passages of Horace with great ingenuity, and means to publish a new edition, with his observations. The Marquis Tanucci was so envious of all men of any kind of knowledge, that he did his utmost to keep them down, and never liked Galiani after he had heard king Charles say, that he had met him in his library, and found him excessively clever and knowing, upon all the subjects he had questioned him upon.

* San Matteo is the portion of the city principally inhabited by women of bad character; hence the Abbé's bitter sarcasm.

September 8.

The Chiaia was crowded by daybreak with a gay populace, in very splendid holiday clothes, and characteristic national finery, moving from Naples to its environs, to pay homage to the *Madonna di pié di Grotta.* The troops in garrison pitched their tents, and repaired to their posts, lining all the Chiaia towards the sea. The picture was incomparable. All the nobility in gala coaches passed along to enjoy the sight, and to be seen themselves. Great dinners were given at all the houses on the line. The Count de Chatenay and Abbé Galiani dined with us. At five the king passed in his state-coach, with twenty-two carriages preceding or following him; the spectacle was brilliant.

The origin of this ceremony is the supposed miracle of the blessed Virgin, to three or four old women and monks, recommending a church to be built to her honour, where her image was stuck up against the wall; and as the Viceroy, Don Pedro di Toledo, was very fond of Puzzuoli, having already a country-house opposite the spot, the cunning Jesuits fixed the scene of this mummery in that quarter; which induced the viceroy to build the church, and to institute the procession, as he was delighted to find his favourite residence likely to become a place of resort.

The small-pox has declared itself on the fool Don Philip, the king's elder brother, and the whole court is in alarm. There seemed to be great debates about what was to be done; at last it was arranged for the royal family (except the sick man) to set out for Santa Lucia,—to the great vexation of all Naples; with, however, the consoling promise of feasts and rejoicings on their return, at the end of forty days. The queen has invited Vincenzo Montalto, brother of the Duke of Tragnito, to go with her to Santa Lucia.

There are many *Monache di casa* in Naples who make vows, but live at home, and have not the best reputations; also the nuns of San Vicenzo, who are a kind of Magdalens. They go about the streets begging, with their faces covered. One of them the other day came in a hurry up to a groom-boy, at the Duke of Valentino's stable-door, and begged he would give her leave to rest herself in the stable for a short time, feeling very ill from the heat. The boy consented, and allowed her to rest within for a quarter of an hour. She then came out, thanked him, and went her way. Some time after the lad, going in to dress his horses, heard a squeaking under the manger, and found the nun had left them a fine chopping boy.

Neither men nor women walk here, either in town or country, except a little at night; they pass most of their time at the Bassette table.

The "*Cavalli di razzi,*" especially of the plains, are all weak, and unable to perform other work than parading upon the pavement. They are always being bled and physicked. Indeed the air here is the greatest generator of blood imaginable. The horses of the mountains are stout and hardy.

The council for managing the affairs of the Jesuits having refused to let the old tenant at Castelmare continue, as he would not pay an increased rent, the fellow put himself in the king's way, and tendered him the quarter's rent. The king was so delighted at receiving what he called the first money of the Jesuits he had ever seen, that he gave the farmer a fresh lease, on condition he always brought him the money in gold.

October 3.

The Infant Don Philip, an idiot, died upon the 17th instant, and four days after his body was carried in a coach, preceded by twenty-four servants with flambeaux, and the judge of the court on horseback, to Santa Chiara, to be exposed on a Catafalqua. The troops lined the road. The Catafalqua had this inscription on it—*Raptus est, mutant ne malitiâ intellectum ejus.*

All is in gala, and there are no signs of a funeral ceremony. The queen has returned, and is giving *conversazione* at the Belvedera. *

We have been on a villeggiatura to Vietri, where Galiani joined our party. He has many amusing stories and anecdotes. Here are a few of them: A Gascon walking one sharp frosty day, clad in a light summer silk, a friend coming up, asked him how he could do with such a coat in such a bitter cold day. "*Cadedis! comment je fais?*" replied the other; "*Eh! je gêle.*"

The Salernitans and Cavaccioli hate each other mortally. Two of the former were quarrelling: and one called the other a filthy Cavacciolo. "No, no," said the second, "I am no Cavacciolo neither—I am a christian."

A Calabrese beggar being ready to die with

* San Vietri was formerly called Marciana, because it was part of the estate given by Trajan to his sister. I am told a bishop of La Cava broke and buried all the statues found there. The friar's convent was a temple called *Votares.*

hunger at Rome, as no one gave him a farthing, applied for advice to a countryman of his, a beggar also, whose stand seemed to produce a comfortable maintenance. His friend told him he must use a little art, and if he did not excite compassion, he must do as he did—put on a kind of Jewish habit, and pretend to be a "*provero Ebreo fatto Cristiano*," and for that reason ejected from the synagogue. Approving of this counsel, the other prepared his dress in such a manner as to have a very Jewish appearance. Thus accoutred, and sure of success, he repaired to the corner of a street; but in going he totally forgot the word "*Ebreo*," and attacked the compassionate passengers with "*Fratelli, la carita per l'amor di Dio—un poco di limosina a un povero Calabrese fatto Cristiano.*" Although this blunder excited the laughter rather than the pity of the gentry, yet they could not help, in the fulness of their merriment, opening their purse-strings to the beggar.

When Charles the V. returned from Tunis, he travelled by land through Calabria and to Naples, and did much good by the road. Seeing Calabria without corn, and being told it was too mountainous and too cold for it to ripen, he ordered rye-seed to be brought from Germany. It succeeds well, and is now universal over these parts, where it is known by the name of "Germano." At La Cava, the town council met to consider what present they should give the emperor. Some were for pine-apples, the kernels of which are of a vast size; but the majority carried it in favour of a kind of fig, which they cover with mats in winter, and in March (the time of the emperor's passing) the fruit is very ripe, and delicious eating. The emperor received the deputies very graciously, and expressing great surprise at the fineness of the fruit at that season of the year, inquired whether they could preserve any quantity of them, and whether they were in abundance. "Oh!" said the wise mayor, "we have such plenty that we give them to our hogs." "What," said Charles, "to your hogs?—then take your figs back again;" and so saying, he flung a ripe one full in the face of the orator. The courtiers following the example of their sovereign, the poor deputies had their faces all besmeared and their eyes bunged out with the fruit. As they were returning from the audience, one of these sapient senators, taking the whole to be part of the ceremonial of a reception by an emperor, observed to his brethren how lucky it was they had carried the point in favour of figs; for, had they presented pine-apples, they would undoubtedly have had their brains knocked out.

About the period of the revival of letters, the Italians were upon the point of returning to paganism. The passion for Virgil grew to such a pitch, that the holy See thought it necessary to interpose. In order, therefore, to take that author out of the hands of young persons, they prevailed upon Vida and Sannazzaro to compose their sacred poems, *Christiados, &c.*, to supply the place of the Latin poet whose work was so much idolized.*

Galiani has a plan of having the whole kingdom of Naples represented in relievo, with cork, by the makers of the Presepio.

He tells me St. Foix discovered, by the papers in the French Secretary of State's office, that the *Masque de fer*, mentioned by Voltaire, was the Duke

* Of Vida little is known; but James Sannazar, who was born at Naples in 1458, has left behind him a distinguished reputation. His most celebrated productions are his "*Arcadia*," his "*De partu Virginis*," (translated into French under the title of "*Couches sacrées de la Vierge*,") and his "*Salices et lamentatio de morte Christi.*" The latter obtained for its author the title of the "Christian Virgil." Sannazar, who was very wealthy, died in 1530, and was buried in a magnificent tomb in the church of *Santa Maria del Parto* at Naples. The following distich was engraved upon his monument:—

"Da sacro cineri flores: hic ille maroni
Syncerus musa proximus, ut tumulo."

Syncerus was the Latin name given to him.

of Monmouth, supposed to have been beheaded on Tower-hill, but in reality brought to the Bastille after the fall of the Stuarts. James had promised his brother Charles, upon his sacrificing Monmouth to him, by refusing to acknowledge his marriage with Lucy Waters, that he would never take away his life.*

The divers of the Gulf are surprising fellows, swimming in the water with a little basket, into which they put their fish. They dive, and remain working and pulling the shell-fish off the rocks, for four or even five minutes, with their feet

* St. Foix, author of *Ess. Hist. sur Paris*, &c., pretended, but did not prove, that the unhappy captive, known as the "Iron Mask," was the Duke of Monmouth. In a work published at Amsterdam, called *Mémoires secrets pour servir à l'histoire de Perse,* attributed to Voltaire, as well as in the *Siècle de* Louis XIV., it is confidently affirmed that this prisoner was the Count de Vernandois, son of Madame de la Vallière and Louis XIV., who was supposed to have died suddenly whilst with the army of Flanders in 1683. Others again assert that the prisoner was an illegitimate son of Anne of Austria, and consequently brother to Louis XIV. Others opine for the Duke de Beaufort. But the probabilities are, that the victim was the celebrated Fouquet, minister of finance to the dissolute monarch who signed the Edict of Nantes. In speaking of the death of the Count de Vernandois, it may not be irrelevant to repeat the words of Madame de la Vallière, when they announced this event to her. She at first burst into tears, but, recovering herself, said, "*C'est trop pleurer la mort d'un fils dont je n'ai pas assez pleuré la naissance.*"

above water, as I have seen myself (my watch in my hand). They gain sometimes eight or ten carlini a day by their work ; but they die young, the violence of the exertion weakening their chests.

The Neapolitan citizens, or middling sort of people, live very poorly as to eating, their little income being curtailed by the calls of show and finery. When they are invited to dinner, it is scarcely credible what quantities they devour. It is the custom to serve every dish, and send it round, and almost an affront to ask anybody if he will have any of this dish. He will answer—"*Volete! ma non sono ammalato!*" When strangers are invited to dine with you, their servants do not wait, but you give them two carlini, wherewith to get themselves a dinner.

Lachryma Christi is, methinks, no longer a very delicious wine; it is strong and sound, with a burnt, acrid taste.*

* A ridiculous mistake was once committed by a good honest country squire of my acquaintance, who had received a present of some of this wine, and neither understood its name, nor whence it came. "What say you to a glass of wine?" said he one day to me at dinner? I bowed, and he continued, "What shall it be?" "Anything." "Come, then, let us try some of L——'s wine, that he bought at *Christie's!*"

November 5.

There is to be no more mourning, the king of Spain having disapproved of it, which is a rare comedy. There was a grand gala at court yesterday, to celebrate the fête of San Carlo Borromeo. The opera was "Catone."

We visited some days ago the Spirito Santo and the Pellegrini. The monks, when dead, are put dressed into their coffins, which are filled with tufo; the flesh is thus consumed in a few months. They are then taken out, and stuck up in niches, attired in the habit of the confraternity, with their names and the time of death over them, and thus exposed to public view. The number of pilgrims fed and lodged at the Pellegrini is very great; sometimes forty a night going upon various pilgrimages, to St. Jago di Loretto, St. Nicola di Bari, &c.

I took a trip to Lake Agnano, which was beautiful beyond expression. There were many people on the banks, trying to get a shot at the wild deer swimming about in the clear water, which had no appearance of fog, or noxious vapour; but the peasant who lives at the temple assured me it was very unhealthy in summer; and his looks were a guarantee for his words.

I saw some very pretty kingfishers skimming across. After admiring all the charming effects of light and shade on the land and water, and taking a minute sketch of the temple, I went back to Baia, and up a narrow path over the hills, and came down to Lake Furaco, where the king was in a boat, shooting wild-fowl.

The other day the king met an old woman near Caserta, of whom he bought a turkey. She, not knowing the blackguard-looking fellow she was with to be the sovereign, accompanied him towards the palace with his purchase. As soon as he appeared there, the drums beat, and the guards turned out; upon which, the old woman, who knew the signal, pulled him back, and told him to get out of the way, for that "LOU PAZZO" was coming, who would run over them; and that "*lou rey pazzo*" made nothing of trampling people under his horses' feet; that he was constantly running about instead of minding his business, and so everything went *al diavolo*. "There is no justice," added she, "no law; and all things are extremely dear." The king then conducted her in, and you may suppose that she was frightened out of her wits when she found out who it was, by his reception at the gate. His majesty, who was extremely diverted at her terror, made her repeat it all to the queen, who gave her some money.*

He never gives anything himself, but gets everything to be given by the queen. One day, however, he gave his eldest daughter an ounce, and the child seemed so delighted, and hugged him so much for it, that the queen could not help taking notice of it, and asking the princess why she showed such extravagant joy for one piece, when she had had so many from her upon fifty occasions. "Oh, mama," said the girl, "but this is the first I ever was able to get out of papa!" The king was quite affected and absolutely cast down for some time, by this reproach.

It is said he sent the Marquis Pignatelli with a thousand ounces to the Duchess of Lucciano, and that Pignatelli kept five hundred for himself, which afterwards came to the king's knowledge, but he never showed any resentment.

Don Ferdinando di Leon, who is a magistrate, fell in love with the Marchesa di Santo Marco, and lent her a sum out of the Pièta, to pay off her husband's debts, notwithstanding which piece of generosity she always disliked him.

Donna Teresina del Sangro is a merry, agreeable woman, but a sad thief. She has played all

* Lou Pazzo (the madcap) was the nickname given to Ferdinand by the Lazzaroni.

sorts of tricks, pawned other people's effects, &c. She is much in favour, so much that the king ensured her a pension for thirty years, that she might be enabled to borrow money upon it.

Our friend, Prince Francavilla, was the *cher ami* of the late Queen Amalia. His rise was very sudden; from being a neglected youth, taken no notice of, nor likely to be connected at court, he became maggiordomo to that queen. He was very handsome.

When any joyful event happens in the royal family, it is customary to grant an *indulto*;—the most unjust thing ever heard of in any country. The king orders all debtors for money due to *particuliers* (individuals) to be set at liberty, but those confined for sums due to the king's account are detained; so that a fellow who is shut up for not paying debts owing to his neighbour is released, whilst he who is in debt to the king, because that man's failure has rendered him unable to discharge the taxes imposed upon him, shall be detained to rot in prison. No creditor can arrest anybody until the expiration of six months.

The curé of La Madonna di Fiorentini is a great rogue. He pretends he has a miraculous Madonna; and lately a tradesman's wife, having two children ill of the small-pox, made an ex voto to this Madonna, of her last gown. The two children died, and in a furious passion she attacked the curé. The affair seeming likely to entail disagreeable consequences, he managed to have the gowns restored, by means of a bucket drawn from a well. The woman was much surprised, and the curé was called in to explain the miracle. He persuaded her she had received the greatest favour by the children being taken out of the world, as otherwise they were both destined to come to the gallows.

Giannone wrote his Storia d'Italia with an eye to the papal and other ecclesiastical vexations, and it has been thought to have contributed to deliver his nation from its slavish veneration and terror for all papal measures. Abbé Galiani has made thereupon the following ingenious comparison, which I translate:—"Did you never see a smoke-jack, with a little man in red working away, and seemingly turning the wheel, and setting the whole machine in motion? Those that are acquainted with the mechanism of the piece know that, on the contrary, he is carried away by the force of the general motion. Just so when you see an author, or a minister, seemingly in a great spluttering, and acting or writing with virulence and energy, be assured it is not he that stimulates his country; it is the general tendency of the humours set in motion, that sets him at work, and gives him the ideas of his subject."

Victor Amadeus was base and mean enough to have Giannone seized and confined for life, as an enemy to the Pope.

Nov. 12th.

This day there is a promotion of the knights of Saint Januarius.* It is plain that Casamanico and Butera are in high favour, from the number of their relations and friends included in the list.

The old families of Naples, great barons from time immemorial, are, Aqua Viva, Dukes of Atri, now Counts of Conversano, San Severino, Lords of Ringone, Rufo, Prince of Siglio, and Canteleno, Toro, Sango, Colonna, and Orsini, from Rome. From the Seggias of Naples come the Caraffas, Capiccis, Caraccioli, Pignatelli, Spinetti, &c. The papal families are Ludovici, Piccolomini, Gaetani; the Genevese, Doria, Spinola, Grimaldi, and Cataneo, Prince of Miandro.

The Seggias were originally places where the nobility assembled to settle their quota of taxes, &c. When the parliaments were abolished, and the Seggias became considerable, the great barons of the kingdom were obliged to get themselves inscribed in their lists.

* *Ordine di San Gennaro.* This order was established, in 1738, by King Charles, upon his marriage with the Princess Amalia, daughter of Augustus III. of Poland.

Yesterday Galiani and Jerningham dined with us, and we then saw a corso of barbs, and another of mares, both won by English horses. After that we went to a ball at Posilipo, where the queen overloaded us with kindness; the talked to us half the time of the ball, and said she had such a sincere regard for Mrs. S. that, if circumstances would allow, she should have looked upon it as the greatest happiness of her life to have made her her constant companion; and ended by assuring us she was fond, very fond of us all. The king also was very good-natured.

The Cavalier Gatti has had, for inoculating the royal family, a diamond ring, with the cipher of the two princesses, the portrait of the prince on a box, and a pension of six hundred ducats for life. He never prepares for inoculation.

Sir William and Lady Hamilton are just arrived at Naples, where he is come as ambassador. They are very civil and agreeable. We met them at dinner at Prince Francavilla's; also Lady Betty and Mr. Mackenzie, and Mr. Dutens.* We had there a young ass served up for dinner and eaten. It is like bad venison.

* Louis Dutens, a French literary man, much in vogue in those days, especially with the English. He is the author of the *Correspondence interceptée*, *L'Histoire abregée de l'Europe*, &c. He accompanied Lord Mountstuart, British envoy to the court of Turin, as private secretary.

Palermo, December 25.

I believe the date of this letter will surprise you, as, from what I have written before, you had reason to think my scheme of visiting Sicily was laid aside. It was a sudden determination brought me hither. My wife's health not permitting her to move to Rome as soon as we had intended, and it being resolved, in a council of very partial counsellors, that it was much better to spend the carnival at Naples, I then, having much time upon my hands, resolved to pay a visit to this celebrated island.

I now sit down to write out of charity for two persons:—first, for you, whom I suppose immersed in Northumberland snow, huddled over your solitary fire, and half asleep over some musty book that you could never hope to get through except in such circumstances; and, secondly, for myself, who am waiting here till the rain ceases a little, that I may set out on my land tour, for which I have been ready some days, and am only detained in the hope of a few dry hours.

This, you know, is not the pleasantest of all possible situations, and therefore a little babbling with one's friends is a relief. However, I have made the most of the bad weather, having been studying very hard many learned folios, relating to the antiquities and natural history of Sicily; so that I am somewhat better stocked with learning than I was when I landed.

I sailed from Naples in a French sloop, and, without meeting with any accident, or seeing anything remarkable during the passage, arrived here in exactly thrice four-and-twenty hours. We had calms, contrary winds, and dirty weather, otherwise the passage is commonly run in six-and-thirty hours, or two days. The appearance of Palermo is very agreeable from the sea, as the capes advance, so as to form a very large and almost perfect half moon. Its present port is artificial, being rendered secure by a mole running out above a mile. The old harbour is only for fishing-boats. The plain extends to the foot of high mountains, which are tolerably green. To say it is a garden of orange groves, full of villas, is the best method I can take to give you an idea of it. Even at this time of the year it is beautiful; but the soil is so rocky that it is disagreeable to go out of town in a carriage.

Palermo is a small town; its form is almost square, divided into four parts by two straight streets that cross each other at right angles, in the centre, being terminated by four gates, where they join in a kind of octagon, square, adorned with statues of the seasons, and of some, Spanish kings. These streets, though not well paved, are yet bearable; whereas the rest are as bad as the pavement of Chastelheraut, which you cannot but remember. The buildings in these two are handsome, and pretty regular; but, except the palazzi and the convents, the rest of the town is horribly built. There are statues of kings and saints without number; indeed, marble is in plenty, but I cannot say good statuaries are so easily come at.

The Domo is a large gothic edifice, different from the style of our English cathedrals, but, though barbarous, not deficient in grandeur and merit. I have found some antiquities of the Saracens, particularly interesting to me after my Spanish studies; and have also had some success in my *chasse aux medailles*, having had a box full of silver and brass ones given me by the archbishop, who is particularly civil to me. I brought a letter to him from Abbé Galiani; also one to Prince Torremuza, a civil, learned man, who took me to the Museum. Prato Amenos' daughter sent, two days after my arrival, to offer me her coach, and the Duke of Castellana called on me. I have seen Butera's sister and brother-in-law.

The viceroy (Prince of Stigliano) is a blockhead, very stingy, and *fait mal les honneurs de sa place.* The people regret their old master Fogliani, whom they drove out; for he used to scatter his money amongst them, and hundreds of idle hands that lived upon his charities have since found the difference between him and his successor.

I went to the *Ricevimento* for the son's marriage, but never saw anything so stupid. The Princess of Stigliano told me I was welcome to come on common nights, when she did not receive all the town. That was the utmost extent of her civility, though she mentioned my being recommended by her husband's friend Losada.

I never beheld such an ugly race as the Palermitan ladies—quite monsters. The only tolerably pretty woman is the young princess of Villafranca.

The country about Palermo is charming, and so full of orange trees that it appears summer whenever the rain allows one to put one's head out of doors. I have got a good snug room where I pass most of my time, except an hour or two at the archbishop's.

I went to a soirée at the Prince of Patagonia's country-house, where was assembled a collection of frightful women, being the principal belles of Palermo. I am sorry I left Brydone's book at Naples by mistake, for it would have amused me on the road, and I should be glad to see how far he deserves the reputation of lying that most travellers have bestowed on his work. However, he is certainly right in what he says of the scarcity of female beauty in this part of the world. I have Baron Reidesel's voyage with me; it is incorrect and credulous. His Puglia journey gave me a disgust, from the continual blunders he makes; but I am afraid his Sicilian one will prove worse.

I have been to the top of Monte Pellegrino, the ancient Ereta, where Hamilcar Barcas, father to Hannibal, remained five years with his army, during the first Punic war, in spite of all the efforts of the Romans to drive him away, as he was master of the seas. Santa Rosalia is placed there now, and there is a fine road cut up the steep rock.

Among the villas in this neighbourhood are some very showy ones, some in a modern taste; one at the Bagaria, belonging to a Monsignore, is a very pretty elegant house, far beyond any of the gingerbread stucco things in Italy. Inlaid work is done here in perfection, but they only work when ordered, so I cannot purchase any. The silks here are not good. I have hired a muleteer, who conveyed Madame de Tessé round the island, and a very civil intelligent fellow for a guard. His accoutrement is very magnificent, *à la houssarde,* with a velvet cap laced with silver. I have also provided myself with a good travelling cap, that covers ears and shoulders.

I propose going to Segesta, (or Ægesta, founded by Æneas,) but I dare not think on the confounded long route I have to go. I am ready, but the weather is not. I have attempted some excursions in the neighbourhood, and have as often been completely soaked through. However, I am in hopes, as it has become very cold, and the mountains behind us are covered with snow, that I shall get away to-morrow or the next day.

To tell you the truth, I wish I were fairly back at Naples. *Qu'ai-je à faire dans cette galère?* But as that kind of fretting after one's *dieux penates* can do nobody any good, and may do me harm, I shall not dwell upon the idea.

Naples, February 22, 1778.

You have, no doubt, long ago received my letter from Palermo, which, I think, was written in the last week of December. Since that, I have accomplished the tour of Sicily, and returned on horseback through the whole length of Calabria, arriving here on the 13th of February; exactly two months from the day I left Naples. The journey might have been made much shorter, had I not been delayed by rivers, and want of resolution in quitting Messina. Not that the charms of that place detained me, but the impossibility to come home by land, and the want of a ship to bring me by sea.

Luckily I overcame my own backwardness, and all the sinister ideas put into my head about roads and robbers, and have had reason to rejoice at my courage, for the journey amply repaid my trouble. I met with no accident of any kind, performed the route in eight days, and had the finest weather through the finest country; besides which, the season has been so boisterous that my things are not yet come by sea from Sicily.

I know you expect an account of my tour, but I cannot undertake to give it *en detail*, and will refer you to future letters and to my journal for minuter information. I can only now afford you a very slight sketch. You must not be in expectation of anything romantic, à la Don

Quixote or Gil Blas; for I am ashamed to say neither accident nor adventure befel me during the whole of my absence; so, if I wish to excite your wonder, I must make up a pack of lies and nonsensical froth, like Brydone.

To the good archbishop's paternal care I owe the comfort of having had excellent beds and accommodation every night I passed in Sicily. My muleteers were attentive and civil, and their beasts good, but they were rather too fond of short days' journey; indeed, often the unlucky position of the towns and villages obliged us to halt many miles short of the distance we might have accomplished, there being very few single houses in most parts of the island.

From Palermo we followed the coast west and south to Alcano, which is some miles from the sea, among the hills. The country is rich, but horrid for travellers such as I was, after rain. Plantations of manna, a kind of flowering ash, may be seen in all shrubberies. It is the most particular object on the coast, and the principal place, for it is Favarotta.

At Alcano there is a great deal of sumach, which is pounded and exported for the purposes of tanning fine hides. I proceeded due south towards the African sea, and visited the temple of Segesta, one of the finest and most entire of the Doric order existing. I will show you the designs of it when we meet.

At Castel Vetrano, a place where I drank some of the strongest and best white wines that I ever tasted in my life, I was glad to get out of the deep clays and bare hilly country which constitute the general run of the inland parts of Sicily. The rocks are composed of a shining substance, from which the plaster or gypsum is extracted, and these micacious quarries continue far along the coast eastward. The vale of Castel Vetrano is a charming spot; all a woody rich garden, of many miles extent, with a narrow border of sandy hillocks along the shore. Here are the ruins of Silenus, a city which stood on the slope of a hill, with a port at the mouth of a trifling river, and is said to have received its name from the quantity of parsley (selinon) that grew there. Little or nothing of it remains. On the hill above are the remnants of three Doric temples, standing on a flat like those of Pæstum.

I rode for several days eastward along the coast, which is uneven and bare, except the valleys near the sides of rivers. At Sciacca the hot sulphureous waters, which gave it the name of Thermæ Selinuntiæ, still retain their force. Not many miles off, on the top of a rocky mountain, are hot sulphureous vapour and other baths, in caverns under a church,—a thing I do not recollect ever meeting with elsewhere, as such phenomena in nature are generally placed low. It demonstrates the vicinity of the focus to every part of Sicily, though apparently Etna is the only volcano in the island.

At Girgenti, (a shocking poor town on the point of a high mountain four miles from the sea,) I was struck with the beauties of ancient Agrigentum; its situation was as happy as that of Girgenti is wretched. Its temples stand in a line on a hill, where the abrupt rocks formed a rampart to the south. The ground is covered with orange, olive, and other charming woods. The Temple of Concord and others are almost entire; that of Jupiter Olympus was the largest in the world, but never finished. The great pond, though dried up, can still be traced. The Recollets have a convent in the centre of the old town, and there is a beautiful view from their terrace.

This is one of the greatest corn ports in the island; and for the purpose of exportation they have made a harbour where nature never meant one. It does not succeed very well, but is a help and advantage to the place and coast. There is no other on the Southern shore, (Cape Trapani belongs to the western,) and the foreign ships lie in the roads to load by means of barges. There are no Sicilian vessels of large tonnage. The liberty of exportation, though partially granted, and often unjustly withheld, has thrown a deluge of wealth of late years into the island, and they have ploughed out vast tracts of land, in consequence of the great price corn bears. The Sicilians assured me their island could neither produce more corn, nor more inhabitants than it does; but to one who was a witness of their slight mode of cultivation, and who has read that Syracuse alone contained as many inhabitants as all Sicily can boast of at present, such assertions can meet with very little credit.*

I went to Alicata, then on the sands to Terra Nova, where one column of a temple remains. Here I first beheld Mount Etna, covered with snow. About Pietra Persia are high mountains which shut out great parts of Sicily from its view.

Here I altered my course, and struck into the heart of the island, to Calatagirone, through a rich and pleasant country, the almond trees all in blossom, and the sun so hot as to be troublesome.

* The circumference of Syracuse, according to Strabo, was twenty-two English miles. During the reign of Dionysius the Elder, it maintained an army of 100,000 infantry, 10,000 cavalry, and 400 ships of war.

You may guess my surprise to find Calatagirone, a place full of gentry and coaches, which no doubt must have dropped from the skies, for they cannot have got up the mountain it stands upon, in the usual way.

The town is large, towering on the pinnacle of a high mountain, over many finely cultivated hills, clad with vineyards and orchards. A large plain stretches for thirty miles to the foot of Etna, which here appears in full glory, a most stupendous cone indeed! The snow covers about one fourth of its height, then comes a dark brown region, lower down a number of white villages, and at the foot stands Catania.

I met at Calatagirone a vast number of well-dressed, elegant young people, had a most agreeable supper served up by a French cook, and a very sprightly *bon ton* conversation, quite upon a different style from the awkward manner of Palermo. I own I was as much astonished as if I had found it in some remote part of Barbary. Yet this place has no commerce of any kind. It certainly is remarkable for the elegance of manners and politeness of its inhabitants, and I am told there are also other inland towns full of better-bred people than those on the coast.

I travelled on an immense plain of thirty-four miles breadth, to Lentini, which affords nothing curious but its lake, full of trout, of the eggs of which is made a caviar, called *butarga*, that is very good.* This place has the worst malaria of all Sicily, being a long chain of marshy ponds to the sea, abounding with water-fowl. As we travelled along them, the report of the fowling-pieces was so frequent, as to resemble the noise of a regiment exercising.

I next steered south, over a stony country, to Syracuse, where I revelled four days in the bishop's palace, tasting such varieties of exquisite wines as I had no idea of before. The weather was heavenly, and my stay there was the most agreeable part of my tour. The climate is so mild, that on the 14th of January I plucked off the tree and ate a handful of fresh tender almonds. Roses, honeysuckles, and carnations, in several gardens, were in bloom. The situation is matchless; I mean that of the whole ancient city, for the present one is very small; but even that is in a pleasing position. The fortifications that defend the land-gate are strong and in good repair; but to the sea the place is weak enough, and the entrance to the port narrow.

I spent a whole day in riding and walking

* The Greeks of the islands make this *butarga*, which is sold in cakes, of the roe of the mullet.

round the walls of the ancient city, which are of some height above the ground. Strabo's account must be just, of their being twenty-two miles round. This immense city commanded the most magnificent view imaginable. Little vestige of buildings remains in this vast enclosure, except part of the theatre. The Latomiæ, or subterraneous prisons, are curious. That called the Ear of Dionysius is a large quarry, wrought in a circular form, and certainly made use of as a dungeon, as the ear is artificially cut, and has many rings in the wall for fastening chains to, for the hands and feet. At the top it is narrowed and twisted in the shape of an S, till it terminates in a groove, which is conveyed to a small closet high up over the entrance, where the listeners sat. From the breaches in it, the hearing there is now very imperfect, as those tell me who have been let down by ropes from the top. The echo in the cave is wonderful; the tearing of a sheet of paper is like the cracking of a whip: the walls are smooth, cut so as to make it impossible to escape, for the top projects very much over the bottom.

In the middle of a part of the rock was the guard-house, and all around the summit of the rocks runs the water of an aqueduct. The Latomiæ, at the capuchin convent, nearer the sea, are very extensive, and divided into several courts, now filled with a wilderness of orange and lemon trees, olives and almonds, which, from luxuriancy of growth, have taken root in the clefts of the rocks.

The catacombs are lower down, and reckoned more wonderful than those of Rome or Naples. In many of the mouths of the skeletons were found medals. The marks of the wheels worn in the rock trace out the streets of the town.

I went seven miles through a low marshy meadow, upon the winding deep water of the Anapus, up to the fountain of Cyane, now called La Pisma. It is a circular pool of clear water in a flat meadow, where the spring rises. I could not see it boil, or in any violent motion, yet it runs down with great velocity, is full of fish, and its banks are covered with the Egyptian papyrus. I believe this is the only place in Europe where it is to be found. It is called *La Perucca*, from the mop form of its head. So much for sweet Syracuse!

The next night I passed at Augusta, a town on an isthmus in a beautiful bay. Then came to Catania, the finest city in Sicily. It buildings are grand and its streets wide, and the disposition of them peculiarly handsome. It is built upon black lava, vomited out of two hills near the foot of Etna in 1669, which is quite different from that of Vesuvius. It is impenetrable, and unproductive of the least dust that might give hopes of a disposition to vegetation. The Prince of Biscari, to whom I brought a letter, has made gardens and walks upon it, but every tree is planted in earth brought from other places. His museum contains many precious articles. His cabinet of cameos and intaglios is a rich one, and his cretas and vases are curious. I spent some days with him very agreeably. There is a very fine convent of Benedictines at Catania.

The snow lay too low on Etna to tempt me to climb to its summit; but I dined in the tree of the Centi Cavalli, which is the most curious, but not the most striking, of the trees thereabouts, for it is not easy at first sight to believe it ever to have been one trunk, though I saw it was so, upon examination. There are some chesnut trees, as yet undivided, of astonishing width; I measured one seventy-eight feet round—about the size of the dining-room at Capheaton. The wonderful size of Etna makes one think with contempt of the Neapolitan Vesuvius.

At Taormina, the situation of the theatre upon a lofty narrow promontory running into the sea, and affording a full view of Etna on one side, and Italy and the harbour of Messina on the other, occupied my attention very agreeably. The ride to Messina is pleasant along the shore, under woody hills, with many pretty towns on the tops of them. The Palazzata, or semicircular range of regular houses, that runs along the port of Messina, is, undoubtedly, the grandest thing of the kind I ever saw ; adding thereto the noble haven, the very fine citadel, and the opposite mountains of Calabria, which do not appear at the distance of a stone's throw.

The town has two fine streets, and a large cathedral remarkable for its ancient columns and the richness of its marbles. The hills behind are handsome, but there are no rides amongst them, nor any other walk at Messina than along the beach. That near the port is a very fine one: many of the buildings are in ruins, others unfinished.

There is the greatest appearance of depopulation everywhere since the plague, and the ruin of the trade. The harbour is so deep, that ships can only lie close along the quay.

Having waited there six days to no purpose, in hopes of prevailing on a Provençal vessel to carry me to Naples, and the wind being quite fallen, I left my baggage, arms, and almost everything behind, and hired a boat with six oars to take me as far towards Naples as it could.

The tide, which sets very strong into the Faro at stated times, obliged us to lie-to all the evening, just without Cape Peloso; and in the night we sailed and rowed about fifty miles, having a fine moon, and the coast at about ten miles from us on our right, and the Lipari Island about sixty on our left.

Next morning we made the south part of the Gulf of St. Eufemia, and were in hopes of reaching the Cape of Cetraro, but the wind obliged us to put into Tropea, a small bishop's see on a rock projecting into the Gulf. I there hired horses to take me and my two servants to Cosenza. We had delightful weather, and a very pleasant ride to Monteleone, a considerable town, charmingly situated, where I lodged at a convent, and sauntered about while supper was preparing. It commands a beautiful view of the sea: the olive woods are thick and full-leaved on the slopes of the hills, and the corn-fields intersected by roads of fine green sward, upon which I saw several carriages out on airing, and priests without number enjoying the evening sun.

Next day I passed by some rich villages with

great beauty of cultivation about them, passed a large river, and came to sleep at the foot of the mountains at Nicastro. The town is in a valley, with fine woods and lofty mountains; a very romantic situation. On the following morning we ascended the mountains, and travelled up and down them, in forests of chesnut and oak, of prodigious bulk and age; there are immense quantities of fine timber.

Cosenza is an ugly poor city, built in a narrow pass where two rivers meet, and in winter is seldom without clouds and rain. In summer the air is noxious. The river Crato runs to the east, through an immense plain into the sea, near the ancient Sibaris.*

I continued my road over the hills to Morano, through a very mountainous country, where the finest views, most noble timber, richest valleys, and pleasantly seated towns, occur in great variety, with beautiful rivers and torrents. I saw from one mountain the seas on either side, and boats upon them. Then to Lago Nero, a large town worse than the wild villages you have passed in the Alps. I rode through the charming plain of Diano: villages line the spurs of the hills on

* This city was at one time so powerful that it sent 300,000 men into the field. The subsequent effeminacy of its inhabitants gave rise to the appellation of a "Sybarite."

both sides, for the malaria prevents the lowlands being inhabited. It is a delightful tract of country. At the end of it we came to our inn at La Polla. The river Negro, which runs down the plain, goes underground for above a mile, and bursts out with vast impetuosity at the head of another vale, where it winds its course to the plains of Eboli, waters the royal gardens at Persano, and falls into the sea a few miles north of Pesto.

The views during this day's ride were enchanting. At "La Duchesse," a royal hunting-box, we came to a good road, and, descending through the king's forest, crossed the bridge of Eboli, and came to the fine road made by the king of Spain. I took a coach and post-horses, and late that night reached Naples, to my great comfort;—most happy to get back *au sein de ma famille*, and to find all well.

Considering that we are in the height of carnival, and that the king and queen are parading the streets in a most superb masquerade, representing the return of the Grand Signor from Mecca, I think you owe me some thanks for having the courage and friendship to retire from all this gaiety, to write you such a voluminous letter.

This cavalcade is the finest exhibition, perhaps,

ever seen : the dresses, trappings, arms, &c., are *de la derniere magnificence*, not excepting a car for the ladies, perfectly in costume. Twenty-four Janissaries go first ; then the king as Aga to twenty-four spahis or horsemen. Then the divan, with four ambassadors from China, Siam, Persia, and Hindostan. The car of Sultanas, of which the queen is one, drawn by eight horses, musicians, vases as presents, perfumes, horses, camels, &c. This is all performed by the noblesse about court, and the king's guards.

As it has been raining sadly during the carnival, the king was very much afraid of this brilliant spectacle being frustrated by the weather ; therefore he had five hundred masses said, for obtaining fine weather for that one day. It did not rain, and he has been going about telling every body how he prevented it. The masked balls here are extremely splendid this year ; I was at one last night with Sir Thomas, who was disguised *en femme de chambre*, to the great diversion of the king, who took him under his arm, and paraded him about the galleries, ready to die with laughing. Adieu ; this letter is already too long.

Naples, March 25, 1778.

By a mistake of the banker's, your letter of the 10th of January was sent to Messina, and delayed so long that it only returned to Naples yesterday. I do not think any more of going to England this year, on account of the great trouble and expense it would put me to, and because the only affair of consequence that might call me home is the division of the common, which I find from your letter can be transacted just as well in my absence.

I sent you an account of my Sicilian trip in a long letter some time ago, which I trust you received. Naples is very gay, the balls at court more numerous and brilliant than last year, and the play deeper.

We have many English here; the prettiest is Lady Smith, daughter of Tom Delaval.* Lady Maynard is also here, and we have had the devil to pay about her. Lord Maynard has left no stone unturned to get her presented, but in vain; and poor Lady Hamilton has had a great deal of trouble about refusing it. The king has put an absolute negative upon the proposal, and all seems quiet again, though I cannot answer for this cabal permitting the Hamiltons to be long at peace.

* Lady Smith was the Miss Parsons before alluded to.

Sir William and Lady Hamilton are very civil to us, and we live on the most intimate terms with them. We have had a ball at Prince Cariati's, on the occasion of his son's (the Duke of Seminera's) marriage with Donna Margarita Brancaforte. A most noble room was built on purpose; the French ambassador made one in a rich quadrille of Spaniards.

Some days ago the king and queen went to Astroni, and we, as well as all the English, were there to see the wild boars hunted. The weather was delightful and the *locale* charming; the royal pair gracious and affable beyond measure; but the sport was sad—a mere butchery of hogs.

The queen and the company were within a palisade, on a rising ground, under some fine oaks.

The king and several of his courtiers were stationed on horseback, in the plain in front, with large spears in their hands. A body of hunters drove all the game from the hanging woods which line the sides of the immense crater, to the spot where the king was placed; and this was the best part of the sport, for it was a cheerful scene to see such crowds beat the thicket, and to hear their continued firing, shouting, and hallooing. The boars ran down into the open grounds, and there large hounds were let loose to stop them, in order that the horsemen might come up and spear them; but as the dogs were too large and too numerous for these tame animals, the poor beasts generally tumbled about sprawling, for the royal hero to drive his spear into them at his leisure.

The queen was very chatty, made the ladies sit on fagots near her, and was very attentive to the company. The king ordered a wild boar to be sent to each of the English ladies present. The queen then walked from Astroni to the lake of Agnano, where she sat until dark, conversing with some foreigners and two or three of her court. Lady Maynard was present at the day's diversion, and with her companions formed a group apart. None but herself could have supported such a disagreeable situation. They say the queen is not unwilling to receive her, but the king will not hear of it. Lord Maynard asked him in the tennis-court, and was refused plump.

The queen is now thicker than ever with Madame Santo Marco, who patronises Lady Maynard. I saw the latter at a splendid ball given by Lord Tilney, where she and her gang assisted, seceding from the rest of the company to one corner of the room.

We have a beautiful new ballet just now at

St. Carlo, the "Syrosa Persiana;" and Le Picq, who is a great favourite with her majesty, dances like an angel. The queen has projected a grand dance, of a Chinese construction, in which she and the king are to take a part. For that purpose, numberless lessons are given, and rehearsals set on foot; notwithstanding which, I am told this ballet will not take place; indeed, by all accounts it is a very unbecoming one for sovereigns, full of genuflexions and prosternations.

The queen has been very kind to my children, having had them to play with hers, and loaded them with the most expensive toys, silver cages, gilt coaches, &c. We have taken leave of her, having fixed to set out in a day or two for Rome. She was extremely gracious, and pressingly invited us to return; indeed I shall be very, very sorry to leave Naples; *mais il faut faire une fin;* and although I have no mighty reasons to call me more to one place than another, I cannot reconcile to my conscience the staying so long from Rome, where you know I have never yet been. You must direct to me there at Mr. Byre's.

We made our last appearance last night at a grand conversazione, given at Caserta, to celebrate the king's recovery from his inoculation. Gatti was very much *fêté*.

Rome, May.

I am happy if ever man was, *car me voici à Rome, l' unique objet de mon desir*, *(not *ressentiment.*) We arrived in time to behold, besides all its own intrinsic merits, the ceremony of holy week; but in these last I confess I am disappointed; they fall far below my expectations; there is neither decency nor magnificence. Such a noise! such crowding and difficulties! I have seen finer and more imposing solemnities in a French cathedral than here in Rome, except indeed the pope's high mass in St. Peter's on Easter-day, which is a very noble exhibition. His blessing the people from the windows of St. Peter's is one of the most striking sights in the world, and I think the grandest.

Pius VI. does it admirably, and exhibits one of the most majestic figures possible, as he rises up, lifts his arms above his head, and blesses the three points of the compass. The

* Quotation from Corneille's Les Horaces.

Miserere is performed in his chapel by fine voices, without instruments.

On Thursday night, an illumined cross, let down from the cupola of St. Peter's, had a very grand effect. Many painters came to study and take views from it, as well as of the inside of the church by that light. Some I have seen are singularly beautiful, from the strong contrast of light and shade.

Sir Thomas and myself were presented to the pope soon after our arrival. He received us at the door of the apartment, as he was going out to walk. Abbé Grant, who conducted us, talked so much, that the pope could not get in a word. His Holiness is a very handsome tall man, with fair hair, half white, and a ruddy face, with a turned-up nose. He speaks French, but did not to us—indeed he addressed himself entirely to Abbé Grant.

A few days after, Mrs. Swinburne was presented to him, and took the children, as he came up from his devotions in the chapel of the sacrament at St. Peter's. She made the children kiss his foot. He then held it out for her to kiss, and next day he sent her some very beautiful beads and stones of oriental agate. He performs all his ceremonies with much grace, and appears to have practised and studied his actions before he comes out of his room. He is very proud of his legs and feet, and wears his gown short to show them. He sits up very late, and rises early, but sleeps in the afternoon, and takes a mile walk to Ponte Molle about sunset.

Abbé Grant, who generally performs the part of cicerone or introducteur to the English, is a Scotchman, and was brought up to London as a rebel in the year 1745—6, in the same ship with Lords Balmerino, Kilmarnock, &c. Whilst on the voyage, a Scotch servant said to him, "You will be saved;" Grant shook his head, and replied, "I fear not, friend." "You will," said the other; "but you will be the only one."

Not putting any faith in the second sight of his countryman, he had no hopes, both from the inveteracy of the court party, and from his having no friends to intercede for him. By the merest chance no proofs or witnesses appeared against him, and therefore, to his great surprise, he was acquitted. He then immediately set out for Rome, where he has resided ever since. He told me that the cruelty and violence of the Duke of Cumberland's army were incredible, and that a Jacobite house being set on fire, (the inhabitants having been permitted to come out beforehand,) one little girl, crying, said she had forgotten her doll, and ran back up the stairs for it, upon which a brutal soldier dashed her from the window of the house after her family, and she died on the spot.

The approach to St. Peter's does not quite please me; the houses facing the church are so shabby. The vestibule is charming, and the inside divine; yet in some things I prefer St. Paul's. The great door there has a more solemn general effect; yet the cupola roof of St. Peter's, and the unity of all the parts, are quite sublime. The two fountains are delightful; they discharge such a quantity of water in so agreeable a manner, as to realise all my ideas taken from drawings.

Upon Easter Monday we began our tour of all the antiquities, churches, &c., under the direction of Mr. Byres the antiquary, and commenced by the Campo Vaccino, which was originally a marsh, where the Romans and the Sabines fought. In this marsh Curtius, the Sabine, was drowned, which probably gave rise to the fable of his devoting himself. In the north-west corner of the forum stood the temple of Mars, now the church of San Martino. There lay the statute of Marforio, so called from its position. It is now removed to the court of the Capitol. Its rival Pasquin took its name from a barber, a great newsmonger and encourager of seditious wit, near whose door Marforio lay. It was at that time almost the only ancient statue known of above ground. The shop still retained the name of Pasquin after his death, and is, to this day, a school for a similar epigrammatic literature. When Alexander VII. (Ottoboni by name) succeeded Innocent X., Pasquin said to Marforio, "*Allegrezza! per un Papa cattivo abbiamo otto buoni.*" *

The arch of Septimius Severus, in the Forum, is covered with rubbish twenty feet higher than the old foundation, although it was the ascent to the Capitol. Next to it is a part of the rampart, on which stands the portico of the Temple of Concord, where Cicero convened the senate in Catiline's conspiracy. It was burnt by the soldiers of Vitellius, and very ill restored, for the Ionic columns do not match; they are of Egyptian granite, and, like most others brought to Rome, were probably ready cut for other edifices. Next was the arch of Tiberius, of which

* Another of Pasquin's satires on Popes Pio VI. and VII. is worth recording. It was written at the time when the latter went to France and crowned Napoleon.

> "Romani vi diro un bel quadro—
> D'un santo padre chi fu coronar un ladro.
> Un Pio, per conservar la fede, lascia la sede;
> Un altro, per conservar la sede, lascia la fede!"

no vestige remains. All triumphal arches were built over great thoroughfares.

But I find myself getting into a description of Rome, which you will not thank me for; so I will tell you of an excursion we made some days ago, to dine at Frescati, with Lady Betty and Mr. Mackenzie, Mr. Dutens, and Abbé Grant. The hills thereabout are beautiful. Cardinal York was officiating in the church when we went in, and immediately sent to tell the ladies they must pull off their hats, or else go out. This peremptory order of the ex-prince could not very easily be complied with, according to the present mode of ladies' hats being fastened on the cushion by long pins, &c., unless his royal highness had provided a perruquier to extricate them. They therefore refused to obey. Many messages passed and repassed. Mrs. S. sent him word that she had not heard mass, and left the omission on his conscience. He is an ugly, foolish-looking, long-visaged fellow, very like his grandfather, full of pride, and just such another obstinate bigot.

We then walked to the Aldobrandini Villa, and saw the water-works; one is very pretty, as it is seen tumbling down the hill through a grove of trees. Thence we went to Villa Conti, where are a noble wood, shady walks, and lofty jets d'eau.

After dinner we went through Villa Bracciano, a wood and drive very like Gibride. The views from these villas are extensive, but the Campagna is a horrid object.

Abbé Grant told us a comical story of Cardinal York and Cardinal de Bernis. They were sitting together one day, when the floor of the room gave way, and partly fell in. Frightened to death, and thinking themselves on the verge of eternity, they both called out with a loud voice, the one, "*Eccellenza! assoluzione in articulo mortis!*" the other, "*Altezza réale! assoluzione in articulo mortis!*" However, their fears were groundless—I do not mean to pun—for the floor did not fall a great way, and they met with no hurt.

Two days after, we went to Tivoli with the same party. The Campagna is bare, but cultivated *tant bien que mal.* The situation of Tivoli is bold and commanding, the cascade grand, and the temple of the sibyl beautifully placed on the point of a rock; but it would be more conspicuous, were it not for the filthy houses of the town. Its environs are wonderful; below is the grotto of Neptune, where the Teverone rushes through the rocks from precipice to precipice, and then glides through a bridge, perhaps of its own forming. From the walk on the hill-side you see at once the valley, the winding river, the towns of Tivoli, Cavea-tella, the arches of Mæcenas's villa, and the Cam-pagna of Rome; the sea, St. Peter's cupola and the Alban hill. There is not a richer view, nor one more difficult to paint; yet I have at-tempted it; I have also taken a view of Villa Millina.

The ride is delicious through the gardens of Villa Madama, one much neglected, and up a bank of wood of arbor Judas, flowering ash, and other pretty trees. Villa Millina stands on the point of a hill backed by rows of cypresses, and has by far the finest prospect of Rome.

There are many musicians here. Nardini, who is the first violin-player in the world, comes to us in the evening, and Ruffina Battoni, daugh-ter of the famous portrait painter, a beautiful girl, has a divine voice, and delights us with her singing.

Her father has painted one of the rooms in the palace of Monte Cavallo, which is an enor-mous building in a charming situation. The coffee-house where Benedict XIV. received the King of Naples, is a vestibule with a room at each end, and a balcony commanding half of Rome. It contains some fine pictures.

The Coliseo is a stupendous edifice. The *sta-tions* and clean walks which have been made in the inside are very picturesque additions in my eyes, though I would not acknowledge it to an antiquarian ; it was built by Vespasian.

Villa Albani is airy, rich, and elegant; two noble alabaster vases, one at each end of the hall, are valued at 2,000*l*. each ; and amidst a profusion of statues and antiques one must notice the basso-relievo of Antinous, which was found in Adrian's villa—perhaps the finest in the world. The owner refused 40,000 crowns for it, offered by the late pope. It is over a chimney, and is an exquisite performance. The room it occupies is the richest I ever saw with mosaics and grotesques; the ceiling, representing Apollo and the Muses, is by Mengs, the first Muse being done to represent Madame de Prié.*

The family Albani were originally in the service of the Dukes of Urbino, and the last duke, having been persuaded to resign his duchy during his life to the holy see, chose Albani to go to Rome, to make a formal abdication for him. Albani was aware of the duke's fickle temper, and made no doubt that he would change his mind; which he accordingly did ; but, being won by the pope, he bribed the messenger (that was sent to bring him back) to return and pretend

* Mistress to the Duke de Bourbon, regent after the death of the Duke of Orleans.

he was already in Rome before he reached him, and thus the abdication took place. But the ambassador durst not go back to Urbino; and the pope, whose interests he had served, made him senator of Rome, and his son was afterwards Pope Clement XI. The present pope's functions are mostly performed by Cardinal Albani.

Villa Pamphili is the finest of all the villas for rural beauty; there is one charming meadow in it, surrounded with stone pines.

Rome, July 1778.

On the 28th of last month, the constable of Naples, Colonna, presented the white horses, as a tribute from the king of Naples to the pope. The procession of his coaches was grand, but the ceremony in the church was performed in a very hurried manner, it being so crowded that the pope and constable had scarce room for their business.

At sunset, the cupola of St. Peter's was illuminated with paper lamps and large pots of fire, which continued to blaze most part of the night; it was the finest sight of the kind I ever beheld. We saw the fireworks of Castel St. Angelo, which were very fine, from the apartments of

Marquis Rossi. The next day being St. Peter's, the church was richly bedecked; St. Peter's statue was robed in cloth of gold; fine gold chandeliers were placed on the steps of the altar. There was a brilliant illumination there that night, as well as at the castle and at the constable's. The appearance was very grand.

We have had the Piazza Navona overflowed in part, and coaches drove about it all night: few go thither now, but it was formerly much resorted to. The pope ordered the water to be let off at nightfall, which has spoiled all the sport. The custom began under Innocent X., when Donna Olympia, his sister-in-law, who received company every Sunday, had the Piazza filled with water, to refresh the air in August.

Many English are at Rome; among others, the famous Duchess of Kingston, *alias* Countess of Bristol, *alias* Miss Chudleigh; also Mr. Howard, an excellent philanthropist, who makes it the business of his life to travel for the sake of inspecting prisons, and spends his fortune and time in the service of the unfortunate; Lady Catherine and the Miss Beauclercs, Lord and Lady Lucan, and the two Misses Bingham, the Bishop of Derry, Mr. and Mrs. King, the Herveys, Pitts, Moleswortlis, &c.

The Duke and Duchess of Lucciano are arrived, being on their travels by order of the Neapolitan court. It is said the reason of their exile is the queen having found a *billet* from the duchess in the king's pocket, in which she upbraided him for being led by the nose by the queen.

We were yesterday at a grand dinner given by the Maltese ambassador, in consequence of the ceremony of the pope's blessing the stucco, or helmet of the grand master of Malta.

I was present during divine service a few days ago, at the Greek church. They say mass behind a screen with three doors in it. Mr. Sennett, an Irish abbé, who went with me, remarked afterwards to Mrs. Swinburne that it was all said in Greek, except the *Kyrie Eleison*, which was in Latin! He is a capital one for Irishisms. He told us some English lady (I forget who) was come to Rome on purpose to sit to Battoni for her son's picture; and assured me solemnly that my new servant was very likely to *shoot me*. You may imagine how I was startled, but I suppose you are aware that he meant *suit*. He is very unhappy just now, with remorse for having refused alms to a famous beggar on the steps of St. Peter's, who is just dead, and turns out to be a saint, and is to be canonised.

Apropos of Irishmen, I find there has been a

cardinal of every nation except an Irish one; perhaps lest he should encroach upon the authority of the pope in making bulls.

Having obtained permission to inspect the manuscripts in the library of the Vatican, I saw Henry the eighth's letter to his mistress, in French and in English; legible enough, but very nonsensical. The christian museum is curious; also a fine hall of the Papyri for reading in, the ceiling painted by Mengs; a collection of medallions; and some gold ones of Louis XV.

We see much of Lady Lucan and her daughters, who are very accomplished,—sing charmingly and paint well, which she herself does likewise. There is a Lady and Miss Knight here, the latter a *bel esprit*, clever and learned. Her mother is quite the contrary; she is always making mistakes which are very amusing;—she addressed the bust of Numa, (whom, from the termination of the name, and from the veil it wears, she took for a female,) with "your most obedient, Mrs. Numa." She talks of the romantic groves where Tasso composed his *Ariosto*, and of the extraordinary circumstance of a church having been erected in honour of St. John's *latter end*.*

* Lady Knight's mistake was not more comical than that of the French tourist who called it *St. Jean des Latrines*.

I have taken a view of Rome from Monte Testuccio, which hill is one of the greatest curiosities I know. If all the pottery ware of the town were brought hither and broken, it would not make such another heap. It must be a production of the lower ages, for there have been found in it at a great depth two sarcophagi, of the time of Adrian It was probably formed by some pope or christian emperor ordering all the pagan urns to be broken and thrown near it. The prospect from it is beautiful.

I have seen some men play at the ancient discus, a large flat round wooden thing, with a groove all round the edge; in this they put a cord, and set it off underhand by a jerk ; they seem to play for length at long bowls.

We dined yesterday at the Capitol with the Senator Prince Rezzonico, nephew to Clement XIII., in company with Cardinal Rezzonico, Baronessa Gavotta, ambassadress of Bologna, Marchesa Lepri, Monsignor Pignatelli, Comte de Chatelet, and some prelates and *abbates*, which latter are in abundance here. Where the senator's house is, was the *posterna publica*, of which the solids of the pillars remain; close by are three columns of Jupiter Tonnans, of most exquisite architecture, a work finished to a surprising degree of nicety. Augustus erected this temple after his Spanish expedition, because, when travelling in the night, his litter and torch-bearer were struck with lightning, and himself remained unhurt.

Below, on the west of Severus's arch, are the dungeons of the Pallian prisons, now converted into chapels; as it is supposed St. Peter was chained there, and that the well in the bottom one sprang up miraculously, to assist him in baptizing his guards. The Gemonian stairs were adjoining.* The two twin deities holding the horses at the top of the steps represented Caius and Lucius Cæsar, Augustus's grandchildren.

Having carried my little girl to Tivoli for change of air, I took the opportunity of riding towards the site of Horace's villa, described by Abbé Chaupy. We passed over low hills, seemingly Volcanelli, like Montenuovo, heaps of lava, peperino, cinders, and some ruins of the Via Valeria. Casteldama is situated upon a high hill, crowned with olive, oak, or chesnut, a handsome object over the Teverone. Turning into hollow valleys and a narrow course of the river, we came to a view of Vico Varo, the Varia, where Horace's five peasants went to attend the meeting of the magistrates. The situation of the town, which

* It was from the top of these stairs that the bodies of malefactors were cast down to be devoured by dogs.

belongs to the Bolognesi, is delightful. About eight miles from Tivoli the vale of Licenza takes up the course of a small brook or river to Licenza, formerly called Digentia.

At the confluence of the Teverone is San Cosimato, a romantic convent on a hill. In the angle where these valleys meet, stand Cantalupo and Bardillo, the ancient *rugosus Pagus Mandela*. Then following up this riotous little torrent, I came to the Castello of Rocca's Giovane, perched upon a rock. The vale then widens into a kind of plain, planted with poplars, vines, and fruit trees, and in front is the village of Licenza, on a peaked rock, half hid by a chesnut wood, which forms the extremity of a ridge of fine cultivated grounds, joining Monte Gennaro, (Lucretilis,) near which was Horace's bathing pavilion.

The Temple of Vacuna stood on the side of an opposite hill, where its ruins are still to be seen. Fine small meadows, with noble walnut and oak scattered over them, render this a beautiful place to spend a summer's day in ; the Ratini, or Horace's fountain, rises in the middle, which the Orsini proprietors have collected in a basin and brought into a cascade. The fountain springs out high up the mountain, and is always abundant, sometimes committing great disorders, and tinging everything of a whitish clay colour.

On a line with the cascade, on the brow of the hill, is a platform, near the little casino of Orsini. Here stood the main body of Horace's house, and from the plan one may imagine that his baths were at the extremity of his garden, on the flat top of the long ridge. I saw two bits of column and of a capital or cornice: there are many pieces of blue and red stucco in the ruins of the pavilion. Abbé Chaupy's description is very accurate. It must have been a charming summer's retreat, literally a *latebra;* for, till you have advanced a mile or two up the valley, you can see nothing even of Licenza, nor suspect, when looking from the Via Valeria, that any such beautiful spot exists. On my return to Rome, I found it many degrees hotter than Tivoli.

The churches called Basilica are those which were originally palaces. In all these there was a hall of judgment, as every patrician had one in his house for the use of his clients; all the ancient kings were lawgivers and interpreters, therefore the courts of justice were held in their palaces.

The Palatine hill was, till lately, occupied by the Orti Farnesiani and the Villa Magnani, both of which have been destroyed to dig for the antiquities and bricks of the golden house of Nero. The latter is now the property of the present French king's valet de chambre, Laborde, or rather of Madame du Barré, for whom it was bought. The view from the hill is fine, as it commands almost every considerable object. Under some clumps of evergreen oaks, they have collected many pieces of cornices, &c., formerly ornaments of the imperial halls: they are finely wrought and very curiously finished. One may easily trace the origin of the Ionic capital from this sample. Suppose the first builder to have erected a cork tree to support his roof, and finding it not stand even, put a piece of the bark at top to make it level: dryness made the bark curl downwards, which thus gave the curves of the capital; the angular volute was probably taken from a ram's head, and acanthus grows in plenty in their gardens.

There were two hippodromes; one is still entire, with a music-room in the middle of its length. One of these opened into magnificent baths, now far underground: the ceiling is gilded and painted, and is still very fresh. There are many remains of underground apartments.

Between the Palatine and Aventine hills was the Circus Maximus: the emperor could enjoy the spectacle from his palace, and the seats were disposed against the terrace and slopes of the hills. Julius Cæsar was the first who had permanent seats made; before him each person erected booths and scaffolds, which his family occupied or let.

At the foot of the hill were the temple of Neptune and altar of Hercules, where Evander was sacrificing when Æneas came, and from whence (the only place it can be done from) he showed him the different hills of Rome.

> "Miratur, facilisque oculos fert omnia circum,
> Æneas, capiturque locis."

Near this is the fountain of Juturna, sister to Turnus, king of the Rutuli, whom Jupiter changed into a fountain for rejecting his addresses. The twin founders were discovered at this place, and near the spot where their temple afterwards stood, Castor and Pollux were seen watering their horses, after assisting the Romans in the battle of Lake Regillus.

Rome, Jan. 8, 1779.

Since the dreadful loss I met with of my angelic child,* I have been thoroughly incapacitated from continuing any correspondence, or troubling myself with any of the occurrences

* A fine boy, who fell a victim to the malaria.

around me. We have since learnt the death of the eldest prince of Naples, which has plunged his mother into the greatest affliction. He was a sweet boy of four years old, courteous and clever in all his little actions, but weakened by too much care. He was the favourite of both his father and his mother.

The letter we have received on the subject from Lady Hamilton contains this remarkable passage. "Never was anything more terrible than the combination of accidents which contributed to make the scene of the death of the hereditary prince of Naples more horrible. The queen did not suspect his danger till the moment the physicians declared there were no hopes, at which news one of the women, going to call the king, dropped down in convulsions; her companion fell into the same state, and they could not be removed out of the queen's hearing. Six men could not hold them, and at that moment one of these was struck with apoplexy. It blew a dreadful hurricane from the mountains, the roof of the house took fire, and to add to the distress and danger, all the corridors had been filled with hay to prevent noise."

Sympathy of feeling has induced my wife to rouse from the lethargy of grief she has been plunged in these last four months, and for the first time since her affliction to take a pen in her hand, to write a letter of condolence to the queen, who just before this death sent some kind messages to her through Lady Hamilton on the illness of our little boy. I enclose you a copy of Her Majesty's answer.

I have been staying a few days in the country with Count Gastaldi, at Monte Rotondo, fifteen miles up the Tyber, which is an agreeable mixture of hill and dale. The views are fine on the river, and extend over the plains towards Monte San Gennaro, Tivoli, and Palestrina. We rode through vineyards and villa gardens to Lamentana, the ancient Nomentum, a small place with a large palace of Prince Borghese, (Salentinæ,) on the brow of a hill. Then to Ponte Lamentana, on the Anio, where the prince has some game preserves in his noble hanging woods.

I have formed an acquaintance with the Cardinal de Bernis, who is a clever man, and has seen much of the world. His exterior is pleasing, and his manners agreeable. When very young, and an abbé, he solicited preferment, and for that purpose begged an audience of the Cardinal de Fleury, the minister and ruler of France. That minister happened to have taken a great dislike to him, and said very crossly—“ *Monsieur l'abbé, vos sollicitations sont inutiles, et soyez sur que vous n'aurez rien durant ma vie.*" "*J'attendrai, Monseigneur,*" was his reply. Nor did he wait in vain, for he was in course of time raised to the post of minister of foreign affairs, but afterwards disgraced in consequence of a quarrel he had with Madame de Pompadour, who had till then been his benefactress. He was succeeded by the Duc de Choiseul.

The Duchesse de Noailles has left Rome to return to Paris, having finished her journey, undertaken for the purpose of speaking to the pope on the subject of the Jesuits. Mr. Jenkins tells me he has seen a letter from their principal at Vienna to Ricci, (the general of the Jesuits,) who had great confidence in the justice and piety of Marie Therese, and thought she would prove a buckler to the order in their distress, and resist the attempts of the French cabinet for its destruction. His correspondent answered his hopes thus: "Depend not upon her, for if every drop of blood of the Jesuits were demanded, and necessary for the marriage of her daughters, she would without hesitation spill it!"

The frost now at Rome is prodigious; I walked on a pool of water quite hard, and the fountains on the hill of St. John are full of icicles. The travellers for Naples have been detained at San Marino, by the snows of La Faiola.

Last month and October, which is the villeggiatura season here, there were great fêtes at the casino of villa Borghese ; I did not go to them, but heard from those who did, that it was very splendid and agreeable. The prince gave music and refreshments there, with many sorts of diversions, such as tilting at the ring, and grand balls in the evening. There is an inscription there of Cardinal Scipio's putting up, which gives leave to all comers to do what they please there, as the gardens are more for the public than the master. It is near the bust of an emperor which I take to be Adrian, with a curled head, and his hair turned back and twisted on the crown like that of a woman.

The Borghese palace has a vast collection of pictures, and not a good room in it ; it is built in the shape of a harpsichord.

I was persuaded some nights ago to attend the opera at the Argentina. It was "*Adriano in Siria*," the music bad and the theatre dirty, old, and dark, with a great show of diamonds in the boxes. Monsignor Spinelli had published an edict, prohibiting any clapping or hissing, which kept all as still as a mouse, contrary to the custom of preceding years, when there was nothing but riot and confusion, the men standing up in the pit waving handkerchiefs, and the ladies holding out their cloaks as flags of triumph. The music was so dull, that I thought this universal silence and attention rather *de trop*. The singers, however, were good; Ronca was the *prima*, and David the tenor. He sang so well that he was applauded by the governor, who, having tried the dastardly spirit of the Romans, enjoyed his victory, and gave leave to clap twice. The dancers are horrid jumping things, and the fellows in women's clothes (for females are not here allowed to exhibit on the stage) are too ridiculous.

The Irish Dominicans have made an excavation at Santo Sisto, which I walked to see. They have found a rough column, consisting of a very valuable piece of Giallo Antico. The saw was in it, and had already cut off a large slice; they value it at four thousand crowns; also fine slabs of porphyry and green marble: nothing is at present in hand for St. Peter's, in the shape of mosaics. There are fifteen thousand colours among the pastes in the magazines; one man alone has the secret of making them, and he has only imparted it to his sons.

The origin of the story of St. Luke having been a painter is, that about the time of the taking of Constantinople by Mahomet II., the most famous painter of Madonnas was one Luke, and he being looked upon as a holy man, perhaps a martyr, his pictures came to be held in high estimation, and he was very soon confounded by the barbarous western devotees with his namesake the evangelist.

That wonderful picture, the Transfiguration, is at San Pietro, in Montario. No miniature can be more highly finished, nor can anything be more admirable, or better connected, in spite of all the French criticisms on this last work of Raphael. It was done for France, but stopped by the Medici family, and given to the church. At Raphael's funeral this exquisite work of his was carried in procession. Its preservation is very good, and being on the high altar the light is favourable. Another favourite picture of mine is Guido's Madonna, at the Bolognesi palace: its wonderful expression of devotion and inward pleasure is most admirable.

A story concerning the Duke Mattei is much talked of. In rummaging over his family papers, he found, in the handwriting of one of his ancestors, a note, which gave the following *renseignement*:—"Go to the garden, and so many feet from such a corner you will find a bronze nail driven into the wall; take it out, and behind that place you will see a bronze key, with which open a door that you will find built up so many yards north of the nail; enter this door, and go down the ten steps; you will then come to another door, which the key will open, and this leads to a long gallery. You must then break open the wall at the bottom, and in a nitch behind it you will discover very considerable treasures of my hiding."

The duke went immediately to the garden; to his great joy found the nail, and set to work with great secrecy to discover the rest. By the truth of the second and third circumstances, he judged of the certainty of the rest,—and having associated proper persons, and enjoined caution and secrecy, proceeded in his excavation. Everything answered to the directions, and when they came to the last wall, they broke it down, with the full confidence that their labours would be crowned with success: when behold, in the nitch was an enormous pair of horns, which the jocose ancestor had placed there.

Under the Palazzo Massimi great treasures are supposed to be hid, because in the sack of Rome the principal Romans carried their wealth thither, and walled it up in the cellars underneath; they have attempted to open these vaults, but the level of the water is now so much above that of the floor that they have never been able to proceed.

From the Queen of Naples to Mrs. Swinburne.

MADAME,

La consolation que je ressens du rétablissement de votre cher et aimable fils m'anime à vous écrire. J'ai voulu le faire il y a quelques mois, pour vous assurer du vif interêt que je prenois à tout ce qui vous regarde ; je n'ai jamais eu le courage de rouvrir votre playe par des inutiles consolations, et j'en ai gemi en silence, me contentant de m'informer de votre santé, avec cet interêt et amitié que vos estimables qualités m'ont inspiré pour votre digne personne.

A présent, que par le plus affreux des malheurs, j'ai éprouvé quelle douleur c'est pour une mere de perdre son enfant cheri, celui sur lequel elle fonde toutes ses esperances, consolations et, complaisances. J'ai été d'autant plus sensible à la maladie du charmant Henry, et infiniment consolé de son rétablissement. Que Dieu vous bénisse et votre charmante famille, vous le méritez, étant si digne et bonne mère ; comme telle, je suis sûre que vous aurez eu compassion du coup affreux qui m'a enlevé mon cher, beau, et parfait Charles.

Cet enfant etait d'une santé parfaite, augmenté en beauté et capacité, et parfaitement robuste. En moins de 60 heures je l'ai perdu. Ce sont de ces douleurs qui anéantissent. Vous en comprendrez toute la force, et me plaindrez; mais j'oublie que je n'ai écrite celle-cy, que pour vous assurer de ma satisfaction sur le retour de la santé du cher Henry, et point pour renouveller votre juste douleur en vous parlant de la mienne; mais c'est que ne pensant à autre chose j'y reviens toujours. Saluez de ma part votre aimable époux; j'embrasse la chere Fanny et le beau Henry: soyez sure, Madame, que je suis, avec une véritable estime

Votre très affectionée amie,

CHARLOTTE H. N.

Rome, February 8, 1779.

We have great crowds and regularity on the Corso, but no show. The Maltese ambassador makes use of his privilege, and drives down the middle of the street. The Zagorolo and Ceri families were drest like Turks, in blue and white; the other masks were vulgar. I think little of this famous sight. Prince Pirratino went out of his place, and was fined very smartly; the officer on duty was sent to prison for permitting it—a good sample of Governor Spinelli's spirit.

The masquerade at the Teatro Aliberti was well lighted up, with very few good masks; some figures of Terminus Pan not amiss. The American provinces were represented by thirteen men and women, meant for quakers, dressed in round pink hats, encircled with ribbons, on which were inscribed M. W. M. C. and "*devinez;*" short coats, white and pink, with slashed sleeves. The men wore long beards. They gave away English engravings, of an angel breaking the chains of a negro. There was no fun, no noise, no gaiety, no humorous characters. These entertainments do not begin till midnight, after supper.

We went last evening to the Torredinoni theatre, near the ponte St. Angelo. It was the siege of Jerusalem by the crusaders, intermixed with humours of Punch and Briscotto, who being both in love with Armida's maid, they cut cards for her, then fought, and Punch lopped off his antagonist's arm, leg and head, which she put on again. The whole of this motley exhibition is too stupid for a rational creature to sit out.

We have had an elegant dinner at the senator's, with the repetition of Salieri's new opera in the evening. Sir Thomas has brought us the

Petroni collection of medals from Naples. He says Lord Maynard having attended and cured the prince of Marino with James's powders, has made Lady Maynard quite popular, and she and Santo Marco are great friends. We have had a pleasant dinner at Duke Grimaldi's. The Duchess of Cori and the Misses Bingham sang in the evening.

Two evenings after, the duke gave the Intermezzi of Valli, by Cimarosa, to a very splendid audience of cardinals and ladies and gentlemen in masquerade dresses, in the theatre of his palace, with supper, &c.

The festinos here are crowded and brilliant, but there is no wit or drollery. The last day of the carnival the people walk about singing the dirge for the funeral of the carnival, the houses being all illuminated.

There is a considerable feud among the English.* Lady Susan will not visit Lady Berkeley. The latter gave a ball, and many

* It is singular that at all periods English, when abroad, seem to enjoy no sport so much as that of quarrelling with their fellow countrymen and women. Go where one will, to Rome, Paris, Brussels, or elsewhere, the same detestable system of backbiting, defamation, and illiberality, is to be found. Never did any nation so completely depart from the sensible and charitable proverb of *Vivre et laisser vivre.*

English absented themselves; we did not, for Mrs. S. is the friend of her amiable daughter Lady Louisa, who is very musical, and sings charmingly to the harp.

At the Duke of Ceri's we heard a cantata of Metastasio's, (*La pace tra la vertu è la bellezza,*) music by Boron, the singers (amateurs) excellent.

Lady C. Beauclerk has had a raffle of a bas-relief of Casper and Alcyone by Mr. Bankes, which I won and gave to Sir Thomas. The Lucans have given some pleasant dances.

The pope was walking to-day through the piazza di Spagna, and I was struck by the majesty of his figure. They say he is very rich.

I went with some Russians to see the statues of the Vatican by torch-light. It is surprising what a different effect they have, and how much better the expression and merits are understood by these means, than when seen by the false lights all of them are placed in. The Apollo is really a divinity.

I have been spending my mornings in the Vatican library, collating Horace for Galiani, and met there the cosmopolite and his family. He is the king of the mountebanks. The history of this charlatan is curious. In his youth he served a doctor in Peru, and was heir to his secrets. Afterwards he travelled as a quack over Europe; then into the East, where he was lucky enough to cure the scaldhead of some bashaw or nabob, who made him a present of such a large sum of money as enabled him to draw 12,000 crowns a year from the bank of Genoa, where he placed the capital. He travels now with a superb retinue, merely for his amusement; has three servants on horseback, with rich red liveries, and sits himself in a gilt coach. Some people think he has found the philosopher's stone.

My walk to-day was out of Porto San Sebastiano, where the meadows are pleasant. Under a little hill is the fountain of the nymph Egeria, an arched grotto, picturesque enough. Near this cave is the church of St. Urban, evidently a temple of Bacchus. In the valley not far off, near the rivulet, is a brick temple, said to be erected to the god of Ridicule, to deride Hannibal for approaching thus near to the walls of Rome. Near the gate of St. John is the church of Santa Croce, restored and spoilt by Benedict XIV., by whose order the porphyry columns were closed up in huge pilasters and arcades, being the barbarous taste of Borromini's school.

Rome, March 2.

I can now give you an account of an excursion I made with Sir Thomas to Terni. Our first post was a villa of Livia's. The hills there are naked and unpleasant, and the air pestilential. The Via Flaminia remains entire for many miles, and, *pour le malheur des voyageurs,* serves for a road still. Near Castel Nuovo is a forest-like country of stunted oaks, with an immense view over Sabina and the Campagna. About Castel Regnano the country is fine, full of olives and vines. Thence to Civita Castellana is a beautiful country, Mount Soracte or St. Oreste on the right rising up singly on the plain.

Civita is the ancient Vici, so long the enemy of Rome. The castle was built by Michael Angelo, and seems a large magnificent fortress, like castle St. Angelo at Rome. A handsome bridge joins the insulated rock to the country; from thence to the hill, which hangs over the Tyber at Borghetto, is one of the prettiest landscapes imaginable, with woods and groves of oaks, bounding green fields. The mountain of Viterbo is on the left, where Capriola, a grand palace, is distinctly seen, though ten miles off.

At Borghetto we crossed the river at the Ponte

Felice, and re-ascended to Otricoli, which commands a wonderfully fine view, with all the windings of the Tyber, and a multitude of houses on the heights, hedges of pyracantha in berry, and a great variety of landscape, through a woody vale to Narni, a town of some size built on unlevel ground. The view from it over the immense vale of Terni is magnificent. The Nera winds so very intricately, the numberless convents and cottages are so white and beautifully placed, the plains so richly cultivated and wooded, the tints of the vines, elms, poplars, so various, and the mountains of such different hues and appearances, that I cannot but think it matchless.

Ten miles of low roads among vineyards brought us to Terni, a well-built town in the plain, very thin of inhabitants. The palace of the Spada is its most showy building. The walks about it are pleasant, and the rides delightful.

The next day we hired horses, and rode early, through vineyards and olive woods, to see the famous cascade. On the way we came to a turn where we had a pleasing view of the Nera, as it winds out of the mountains between two very high rocks. A couple of villas at the bottom, with their orange gardens, enlivened the scene. The village of Papilia is on a point to the right; the road cut up on the rock, and a ruin on its summit, are fine additions. By a steep winding road we got to the level of the cascade, or the vale of Ricti. The rock at the point was blown up, and the passage widened round it about twenty years ago.

We crossed a kind of canal cut in the petrifaction which is upon the rocks, and were brought by our *cicerone*, a ragged tailor, to a point where we had a near view of the tremendous fall, being on its left side, a few yards lower than the level of the top.

The Velino rushes out of a long canal between two rocks overshaded with wood, and precipitates itself downwards above two hundred feet, with several lesser falls, before it comes to the Nera in the valley. It is wonderfully fine. Unfortunately there was not much water, and one side was dry; but there was enough to make it a noble sight. The steam, or cloud, arising from it, is very considerable, and everything partakes of the petrifaction that is sprinkled by it. Very fine spunges, or petrified mushrooms, are found. I got a piece of a petrified bough.

This cut was made by Curius eighty-five years before Christ, to drain the vale of Ricti. There is a sluice of iron to prevent more than a certain quantity of water from coming over, lest the too sudden discharge, at certain periods of the year, should lay Rome under water. At that time the Velino overflows its banks prodigiously, and does a great deal of damage; but as it vents part of its overplus into the lake of Pié di Luco, the harm is not so great as it might be.

Having seen all we wished at the cascade, we rode up the narrow vale, and, coming in sight of an opening in the mountains, had a pretty peep of the lake through the trees.

Desirous of spending some hours of a most delicious day on the water, we dismounted, and got into a crazy ferry-boat, paddled along by one man with two shovels. He rowed us up the canal which communicated between the lake and the river. The waters of the lake are clear, but not like those of Keswick; they are said to have a petrifying quality. The lake is deep, and surrounded by a great variety of lofty, well-wooded mountains, where we heard the noise of people hunting wild boar,

Pié di Luco stands prettily round the foot of a conical hill, on the top of which is a ruined castle. The fishery is abundant in tench, pike, barbel, and trout of a wonderful size. The fishing in nets is confined to the proprietors, but angling with lines is open to the whole world. People row about in slender flat boats, scarcely sufficiently fastened to be safe.

After enjoying the charms of the prospect, and the different appearances of the land and water, we returned to Papilia, where, leaving our horses, we crossed the bridge, and through the gardens of a ruined villa of Count Castellis, we trudged up the narrow ridge, along the water-side, under thick woods and impending rocks, till we came in full front of the cascade. Glorious indeed! but from the position of the sun we had no rainbow; the steam or cloud was driven about by the wind, but as no rays reached it, the usual phenomenon was not produced.

There is a curious tradition concerning this cascade having been formed by the lava of the neighbouring mountain of St. Arcangelo, which throws back the Velino, so as to form the lake of Pié di Luco. What great antiquity would not that evince, as it was in the time of the Roman republic that the cut was made, to give vent to the Velino!

Our horses were sent down to meet us, and we made the best of our way to Terni. We slept at Narni, and saw the bridge built by

Augustus over the Nar. One arch is entire, of large stones without mortar; the present bridge looks like a dwarf near it.

TO MRS. S.

Rome, May 5.

The heat was insufferable all the way to Capua, nor did I once look out on the country, as I usually do, or make any remarks; for my thoughts were full of Naples, and the dear objects it contained.

We supped and slept at St. Agatha, where we met two ladies who looked like actresses. They had been ordered out of the kingdom, and were on their road, escorted by two ministri.*

Sleeping was out of the question, for my slumbers were disturbed by the nightingales, which made a dreadfully loud concert all night under my window. You will compare me as a Vandal to old Walton, who complained of the horrid smell of fresh violets in the fields disturbing the scent for the hounds.

Next morning we crossed the ferry of the Garigliano, the tower of which passage stands near the ruins of Minturnæ. From Mola da Gaeta

* Officers of the police.

we took a boat and crossed over to Gaeta, from whence the view is noble all round, especially the orange groves of Mola and Castiglione. I was better able to enjoy my journey than the day before, and took notes as I went, which I believe was a great bore to my companion, *qui ne se soucie pas de la belle Nature.* We dined, on our arrival here, at Mr. Monson's vineyard, and met several people we knew. All Rome is in distress at the death of the Marquise de Puymontbrun, niece to Cardinal Bernis. She fell a victim to the small-pox.

Florence, May 15.

On leaving Rome we passed through the valley of Terni, than which nothing can be more refreshing and agreeable. It is a very close and winding dale, with thick young woods of oak and common pine, and old olive trees. Spoleto may well have served as a barrier to Rome against Hannibal. It stands on the slope of a very high round rock. A river, which at present has no water in it, almost makes it an island. Its castle, where the governor lodges, is on the top, and water is conveyed into the city from the opposite mountains by an aqueduct. The plain begins at the low town, and extends beyond Foligno.

The hills behind Spoleto are beautifully wooded and cultivated, and studded with convents and casinos. The city is neatly built, and well enough paved. In the middle of every street is a row of bricks, which make it pleasant walking.

As soon as I had dined I took a ragged cicerone, and walked up the hill to see the curiosities of the place, amongst which is Porta Fuga, which stretches across a street, with an inscription, denoting Hannibal to have been driven from this gate; but I believe it is a piece of building posterior to the Roman empire. There is an arch dedicated to Tiberius.

The cathedral was shut, and the sacristan asleep ; so I saw nothing of it. We turned off below the aqueduct, which at present conveys very little water. It is on many narrow arches of a most stupendous height. Upon the woody mountain, which is connected with the town by the aqueduct, are a convent and about a dozen hermitages, called Monte Luco, full of devotees. Those in the hermitages beg; but the persons in the convent are in easy circumstances, and do not make vows. The situation is beautiful. Charles Vernet has put the aqueduct and castle into one of his views of the Apennines.

Hence to Foligno, the mountain on our right hand is full of villages, convents, and country houses, the largest of which belongs to a Spoletan marquis. At a place called Campetti, a few yards beyond the post-house at Le Vene, so called from the sources of the Clitumnus, a small ancient chapel on the rock is supposed to have been dedicated to the god of the river. In the early days of Christianity, paganism being ousted, it was consecrated to Giesu Salvatore. Its architecture is almost Gothic. Indeed the Christians have added ornaments in the solid of the pediment—a cross and grapes in flourishes. These ornaments, and much work in all the architecture, bespeak a decline in the art. Upon the whole, there is nothing very elegant in this temple. That of the Sibyl at Tivoli had quite another effect upon me.

Just above is Perignano, then a village called Juri. Foligno in the plain is a relief to the eye, after the ups and downs of Spoleto. Raphael's famous picture at the Comtesse is painted on wood. It is much chipped, as if burnt by the sun. The colours are lively. The Virgin in the clouds is very beautiful ; the cherubims behind her look like a cloudy sky. Directly under her is a pretty angel holding a scroll ; behind, a landscape with figures, and a village which gives a crooked look to the whole. On the Virgin's right is St. John the Baptist ; before him kneels

St. Francis, marked with his stigmates; on the other side is a bishop, with his hand on the head of a man kneeling. The latter, who wears a scarlet robe, and tunic lined with ermine, is supposed to be St. Jerome; but that is impossible, as he has no beard, and no lion near him. It is probably some cardinal saint, or the man who bespoke the picture.

The cathedral is plain, but sufficiently distinguished. There is a pretty semicircular walk on the ramparts, with seats, from which one has a fine view of the country.

The better sort of women here wear blue veils; the peasants wear large square Tovaglie on their heads, with a double white veil falling very low behind.

We went on to Spillo, the ancient Flaminia, and to La Madonna degli Angeli, a large convent of Franciscans, who have a vast chapel and cupola. In the middle is the house of their founder.

I walked two miles up to Assisi, a large town on the side of a steep mountain, with a great patriarchal convent about the middle of the ascent. It has a noble refectory, with a large Last Supper by Salernino. There are eighty friars. In the upper part of the town is the front of a temple of Minerva, now a church. This antiquity consists of six fluted Corinthian columns, on separate bases, or steps between each. It is a precious monument, a pleasing piece of architecture. I wonder at its being so little known or copied, for I have never seen a print or drawing of it.

A hilly road brought us to Perugia, which stands in the form of a star, on the crown of a very high eminence. The streets are large, the buildings showy; the *santo anello*, or wedding ring, of the Blessed Virgin, their grand relic, being exposed for rain, made the domo a place of general resort that morning, and most of the pictures were covered with damask hangings. The beautiful Descent from the Cross, by Barbiero, was luckily not among the number of clothed ones, and a wonderful picture it is. Abbé Tonelli, the cicerone, joined us, and took us to the Cambio, a kind of exchange, low and dark, all painted by Pietro Perrugino, with many admirable figures and fine colours. There are also at St. Agostino's many chefs d'œuvres by the same hand; and a billet of his writing is kept in the sacristy, very ill written and ill spelt. At the Nuns of Monteleone is an Assumption, supposed to be by Raphael—his last work.

I crossed the Tyber, which is here a pretty clear river, with fine poplar groves and vineyards along its banks. I observed that the men I generally met all over this country had roses stuck behind their ears, which brought to my mind Falstaff's witticisms, and shows that the same customs were once common in England. The women of Perugia wear black gauze coifs over their hair. The men are very smart.

After passing through very bad roads, we traversed a high hill, finely wooded, to the Torricella, or the Trasimene lake, which is the most beautiful piece of water I ever saw. It has not the wild and grand sublimity of Keswick, nor the monstrous mountains of the Leman; but softness of contour and pretty turns mark it strongly with a character of Greek beauty. A woody range of hills advances into its waters, with a tower on a rock at the extremity of each promontory. Two or three islands, one of which has a picturesque steeple on it, mark the different lines of distance: a high, conical mountain appears far off. The shore is flat, and full of reeds. A boat or two gave life to the surface of the water.

For many miles we had a dreadful road, over the ground where Hannibal vanquished Flaminius. As soon as we got on the Tuscan territories, which are not designated by any guards, barriers, or boundary monuments, I found the roads much better.

We slept at Carnotria, and I was pleased to see all the country girls with little smart round straw hats, coquettishly tied. The faces of the people were quite altered. Here we saw round, chubby cheeks, and small features in proportion to the face; whereas further south the very reverse is remarkable. I no longer perceived the grand large nose and expanded eye.

We walked to Cortona, a very steep mile, and had a fine view every way, especially towards the lake. Cortona is a melancholy town. The day was extremely hot, and no horses being at the post, I took refuge from a broiling sun in the church porch, where I found several grave citizens seated in the shade. They were discoursing concerning a girl that positively refused to own who was the father of her child. They guessed everybody they could think of, but decided on none. At last one wiser than the rest exclaimed, "Do not trouble yourselves with guessing; you will soon learn who the man is, for the Grand Duke is to be here in a few days, and he is sure to find out, for you know he pries into every thing, and knows all that passes."

This royal inquisitor seems, however, to be

very popular among the common people, and takes great pains in making improvements. He is now busy in opening a canal from the lake, to render the navigation of the Chiena more constant, as well as useful.

We next came through Arezza, a large well-built town, and along the rich vale of Arno, to Florence. I lodge at Mrs. Hatchfield's, and dined, on my arrival, at Sir Horace Mann's, where I met Harvey Aston, Smith Barry, Falkenor, Vernon, and Crosbie.

We went to the opera, where, for the first time, I beheld the poor unhappy representative of the Stuart race in the Comte d'Albanie. He goes regularly to the theatre, and always falls asleep in a corner of his box, at the end of the first act, being generally intoxicated. His face is red, and his eyes are fiery, otherwise he is not an ill-looking man. The countess is not handsome, being black and sallow, with a pug nose. She always wears a hat. Alfieri, the Piémontese, is a constant attendant in her box, with her *dame de compagnie*, Madame Malgan.

Le Carcine is a delightful place, along the Arno, with woods and meadows exactly like an English plantation, and a fine ally of stone pines, that grow like fans.

You shall have an account of the gallery, &c., in my next.

Florence, June 10.

We saw the collection of gems, and the cabinet of medals, which are thrown about in a strange confusion; all metals and all sizes, according to chronology—a most uncertain and puzzling mode of arrangement.

Lord Tilney gave us a dinner, where we met a great number of Neapolitans. We dined also with Lady Orford at her villa at Fiesole, in a glorious situation for views, and a very convenient, elegant house, perhaps the best furnished in Italy for neatness and propriety, but too high, too much confined, and on a rock which reflects a burning heat in summer.

The society here seems on a pleasant footing. There appear to be no feuds, no opposition sets, which, among the English, is too often the case. Sir Horace Mann's keeping open house is probably a preventive, being a sort of centre, or *point de reunion.* We see a good deal of Lord and Lady Cowper, whose house is very pleasant. Mrs. S. went with her to Castello, to deliver her letter to the grand duchess, and we were at the opera with them last night. On coming out, we passed close to the Pretender, who was *carried away*, at the end of the performance, being half asleep, and completely intoxicated, which is his invariable custom every night. Such is the force of habit.* I drew my wife's attention to this undeserving object of all her Jacobitical adoration.

Cavalier Mozzi is here, and the Chevalier Lorenzi, a man of great wit and naïveté. He lived much at Paris among the unbelievers and philosophers of both sexes, Madame du Deffand, Madame de Boufflers, &c. When he returned to Florence he heard a church bell ringing, upon which he exclaimed, "What is that for?"—"For illness," was the reply. "*Et quoi,*" cried

* Habit or custom is sometimes exemplified in a manner less filthy than that cited of the Pretender. Segur mentions two instances, both equally pleasant. The Duke de —— had been in love during twenty years with Madame de ——, and had been in the habit of passing almost every evening of his life at her house. At length her husband died, they were married, and of course she removed to the duke's mansion. After dinner, upon the first day, the duchess, seeing her husband absorbed in meditation, said to him, "*Qu'avez-vous, mon ami? A quoi revez-vous?*" "*Ma foi, mon amie,*" replied he, "*je songois à une chose assez embarrassante. Où irai-je à l'avenir passêr mes soirées?*" The second example is that of the learned Marsais, the grammarian. Finding his death approaching, he called to a brother academician who stood by his bedside, and said, "Go tell, tell the academy *que je m'en vais, ou que je m'en vas, car l'un et l'autre peuvent se dire.*"

Lorenzi, "*on dit encore la messe dans ce pays-ci?*"

A quack doctor was called to attend a friend of Lorenzi's who was dangerously ill, and ordered him to take forty of his pills. "*Il est mort au quatrième,*" said Lorenzi, in a rage, as he told the story; "*jugez s'il les eut toutes prises!*"

We intend leaving this place in a day or two for Vienna through Bologna, and I have agreed with a Mantuan vetturino to take us with thirteen horses to Bologna, and nine to Vienna, including all expenses for eating, lodging, &c., for us, our children, and five servants;—the price two hundred sequins,—about twenty too much.

Turin, June 14.

Your letter, which I found here on my arrival, was an agreeable surprise. We came from Florence to Pisa, which is a fine city, and has something grand and noble even in its present deserted condition, that in a melancholy manner reminds one of its former splendour. It is large, well built, and well paved, but so desolate that grass grows in the streets. As a formidable republic, it formerly poured out its citizens to the conquest of distant countries; though now it wears the livery of despotism, misery, and depopulation. The benefits of Leopold's improvements have not yet extended thither.

The Arno, which at this spot is a tolerably large river, divides the city in two almost equal parts. The best bridge is all marble, and it is there that the two divisions of the town meet every third year, to assert, with clubs and coats of mail, the honour of St. Anthony's hog and St. Mary's kitten.

The cathedral is a fine gothic pile of marble, supported on twenty-six antique granite pillars; the roof grand and richly gilt, and the gate of carved bronze. At one end of the church is the famous leaning tower, of white marble. It really bends one way fifteen feet from the perpendicular. Whether built so on purpose, or sunk by accident, is doubtful, and I am inclined to be of the first opinion, as the pillars on the undermost side are longer than the others, and the little turret at top is much more upright than the rest of the steeple.*

At the other extremity of the square, about

* A similar curiosity may be seen at Bridgnorth, where there is an ancient tower, whose summit extends to some distance over the base. This has given rise to the provincial expression of "all on one side, like Bridgnorth tower."

the dome, is the battistero of marble; an octagonal, gothic temple, ornamented all round with columns of divers sorts and figures. The inside is supported on pillars that leave a passage round, and give a light easy air to the edifice. The echo of this building is very strong.

But the most curious place at Pisa is the Campo Santo, near the battistero; a long, square gothic cloister of white marble. In the middle is a cæmiterium of earth brought from the Holy Land, as ballast to the Pisan galleys, in the days of the republic. In the vaults of the cloister repose the bones of the old citizens of Pisa. Around on the wall are fresco paintings done by the first restorers of the art in Italy—which, although they fall infinitely short of the perfection that Raphael long afterwards arrived at, have great merit in the airs of the heads, and also in the whimsical ideas they have introduced into their pieces, some of which would make you laugh. I was myself diverted by the sight of the professors of the university, stalking up and down the town with huge spectacles on their noses.

From Pisa I entered a more interesting though much less famous republic, I mean the existing one of Lucca, the prettiest little toy of a commonwealth imaginable. The city, situated in the midst of a small but rich and beautiful plain, hemmed in on every side by woody hills, is quite round, well fortified, and solidly but not showily built. The ramparts are planted with trees, and afford the most agreeable walk. I have scarce ever felt greater satisfaction than that I enjoyed at the air of plenty, riches, and content, this little tract of land wears; it is the emblem of real liberty. The government is aristocratic, and has a gonfaloniere and nine anziani at its head, that are changed every two months. It really looks upon its subjects as children, for everybody seems to thrive, and double crops are reaped here for one that is produced in other states.

When there was a scarcity of bread some years since throughout Italy, the Lucchese set sentries to prevent exportation of corn, and then distributed it out of the public granaries to the villages, &c., on the easy condition of being reimbursed in the space of nine years.

The nobility are very rich; the men the best made in Italy; extremely polite and affable to strangers. I had an opportunity of knowing some of the Lucchese ladies and gentlemen during the few days I stayed there, having brought a letter from Sir Horace Mann, and was much pleased with their civility and manners.

I could almost have kissed their state's motto,

Libertas, at the proofs I had of its salutary effects, and should have preferred if, instead of a black, foolish daub, (done, as they say, by Nicodemus,) which they call *Il porto santo*, and which is stamped on their coins, they had done honour to the cap and staff of liberty.

The sumptuary laws, which forbid the wearing anything but black, is the only thing I should wish altered in this little paradise, as it gives a rather dismal cast to a naturally gay scene.*

From thence, along the coast, through woods of corks and evergreen oaks, we came to a most picturesque country; the hills woody, and crowned with ruined castles; the river Magra rolling through vast plains, planted with mulberry trees; the valleys enclosed, full of cornfields thick set with trees, on which the vines hang from branch to branch along the road.

We passed through the mountains which

* Although Lucca is no longer a republic, it enjoys as much liberty, and infinitely more tranquillity and happiness, than perhaps was the case in the days of its independence. His Royal Highness the reigning Duke is universally beloved, and has no other object in view, at least as regards the Duchy of Lucca, than the welfare of his subjects. People may wear what colours they please, and say and do what they please. This is real liberty, and is felt to be so, for Lucca is at present a place of refuge to many who can find no shelter elsewhere.

contain quarries of the famous Carrara marble; embarked in a felucca at Lerici, and passed to the Gulf of Spezzia, a place replete with every beauty which land and water, united in a populous country, can procure.

Imagine a large basin of seven miles diameter every way, with three large cultivated islands in the mouth, and Porto Venere and another tower to defend the passage. There are many large fortresses on the shore, along which stand several considerable towns and villages, and round the gulf is a range of beautiful hills rising one above another, entirely covered with olive and fig trees.

We passed this charming bay too quickly, for soon after we had nothing before us but bare brown mountains and rugged rocks. Night luckily relieved us from this ugly view, and next morning, on doubling the cape, about twenty miles from Genoa, we coasted for many miles under the beautiful mountains which form the Riviera di Levante, covered with buildings, allotted to the velvet manufactories; and as we approached Genoa the fairy landscape increased in beauty.

At a few miles distance I enjoyed the grandest and most agreeable view imaginable. The amphitheatre formed by the hills round the city, the palaces and churches, the moles, the light-house, and fine populous coast, are fine beyond description. The port is most beautifully formed by nature, in an exact half-moon.

I took a sketch of the famous light-house, as well as I could by stealth, for nobody is allowed to make draughts of any part of Genoa. In point of beauty of situation that city may vie with any, perhaps, in the world. It is built on a small tract of even ground, which seems stolen from the sea, and occupies principally the eastern part of the crescent. The hills that rise immediately above it are covered with villas, which at a distance appear to be part of the town.

Fish is not very plentiful in the harbour, but the Gulf is much better stocked than is generally imagined; but, as every fisherman is forced to give to the state the third part of his capture, besides heavy entrance duties, they prefer carrying their fish anywhere rather than to the capital. I saw them take many loassi, sardines, and other fish. At night the port is full of boats with lights, at which a certain sort of fish leaps up, and then lies on the surface of the water, stupified with the glare, till the boatman lances his harpoon into it.

Towards the land, for a good way, are the palaces of nobles, painted as most of the houses there are, and very lofty, with terraces to the sea. The roofs of the town houses are covered with earth, and serve as gardens to the great mansions beneath them, being railed round with marble banisters, and ornamented with urns and statues.

The custom of painting the outsides of the houses with representations of deities, &c., and the dissensions in the families, gave rise to a sort of proverb in the Genoese patois, which is something to this purport:—

> Walls thick and servants thin,
> The gods without, and the devil within.

The lower class of people inhabit another quarter, near the gate of the old mole, where the burgesses of the city mount guard, in a guard-room situated near the edge of the rock.

I visited the fortification erected by M. de Boufflers in 1748, when he came to defend the Genoese against the Germans, who had been let into the town by capitulation, and whose troops were quartered in the Borgo di San Pietro d'Arena, and in the mountain near the Borgo della Bisogna. Their officers had the key of the gate which leads to Turin, and the inhabitants could neither go in nor out without their permission. The Genoese nobles, being bound by oath to submit, remained quiet; but the populace, with three determined leaders, rose, and at length drove the Austrians out of both walls.

The ringleaders of this rising were Spagnoletto, a shoemaker, Barbarossa, a peasant, and Carborre, a servant. They fixed a gallows in the piazza della Nunziati, and decreed to hang up all those who should refuse to take arms. They seized on the arsenal, notwithstanding the protestation of the doge. One of their chiefs, on being asked what recompense he demanded, contented himself with asking to be made courier, or postman to the republic. The others were made colonels, and received the pay of that rank for their lives. When the Germans returned the French were come, and their fresh attack proved fruitless.

We stayed a very short time at Genoa. Our road to Campo Marone was all along the river. Upon the hills are an amazing number of country seats, churches, and villages, which, being all white, form a lively prospect, joined to the greenness of the gardens, which are very plentiful thereabouts. We had then a long ascent through a very rough road, and had a fine view of the sea from the summit of the hills.

The haystacks there are made in a particular manner, and so contrived as to resist the fury of the winds, that blow violently on those heights.

They have a thatched roof, fastened at each corner to a thick pole, which serves, when squeezed down, to keep it fixed. The houses of some of the villages are thatched, a thing not common in Piedmont.

In the way to Voltagio the mountains are dull and uninteresting—no rocks, no woods, no variety. This part of the Apennines is far inferior to the Alps in diversity of romantic scenes, and the many pleasing prospects amidst rushing waters, huge rocks, and stupendous precipices, which occur in travelling through the latter.

The road was paved, but very rough ; a torrent, scarcely perceptible, rolls along in the hollow beneath. There is a kind of aqueduct in the valley. These defiles are called La Bocchetta.

Beyond Voltagio the road runs along the sides of stupendous precipices, which are very disagreeable sights. On a high rocky mountain in the midst of the Apennine is the fort of Gavio ; the village is at the foot of the hill. The river Leone runs below in the valley : the sand of its bottom is green.

The women in these mountains and the country about Genoa are very ugly ; all black as gipsies. They plait and twist their coal-black hair in a round upon the crown of their head; then fasten it together with a large silver or steel bodkin. The front is cropped and kept back with pomatum. In winter they wear a veil of white linen, checked with red flowers, which they throw over their heads; it falls down to the hips, and some of them hide almost all their faces behind it.

We passed many mulberry trees planted among vines, and came to Novi, the last town in the Genoese dominions. Its houses are painted on the outside with several colours.

The country about Alessandria is very like that near most of the fortified towns in French Flanders,—low, bare, and intersected with innumerable roads.

Alessandria *della paglia* is called so, as some say, from its ancient walls being only dirt and stones, and therefore so nicknamed by the Emperor Frederick Barbarossa. Others pretend that it was out of derision for the abuse of the great name of Alexandria; or, more likely, the appellation may have come from the great quantity of straw which the capital of so large a corn country might have brought to market. The buildings of this town are poor, the streets narrow. The coaches seem very crazy, for the coachmen stop short at every gutter to go over quietly, for fear of shaking them to pieces. The Alessandrines have a peculiar jargon of their own.

We dined late at Asti. The fortifications of this ancient city (formerly Hasta Pompeia) are now quite demolished. It seems to have had a double wall, and what remains of the outwork is singularly constructed, being all built with small arches, only open towards the town.

We passed San Michaele and Piorino; the latter town cuts a good figure, as it is situated on the brow of a hill, which terminates a low watery valley. From thence to Turin we travelled in the dark, but we could just see the snowy top of Monte Viso, rising above the rest of the Alps in a conical form.

Turin, June 6, 1779.

We have taken up our abode at "*l'Auberge Royale.*" Soon after our arrival we had a visit from Mr. Poyntz, the chargé d'affaires, who obtained leave for us to attend the king's ball at La Venerie, his country palace, about three miles from Turin. There was a brilliant assemblage there, of men in showy uniforms, being the élite of the Sardinian army. They are dressed in blue; the infantry wear white waistcoats and breeches; the cavalry buff: a shoulder-knot distinguishes the latter. The officers wear broad laced button-holes, but no epaulettes. Rows of lace distinguish ranks. The uniforms are very neat.

I was introduced to one or two of the principal Sardinian officers, who spoke to me in Italian. I noticed the peculiarity of their using the B instead of V in their dialect, which illustrates the Sardinian proverb.

"Felices quibus vivere est bibere."

The other sense of it is, I understand, equally correct. There being no minuets, the ball was not so formal as those things usually are, but the room was a perfect Calcutta.

The king was on the point of speaking to us, but his bashfulness could not be surmounted, and he sheered off. The Prince of Piedmont spoke to us, and said he recollected Sir Thomas and Mr. Dillon. He is thin and sickly, like a worn-out man. His wife, Madame Clotilde of France, is as fat as butter, very merry and good-natured. She has no children. The Duke de Chablais seems to be a mere driveller—the rest of the princes are absolute Corsican fairies.* The substance and strength of the stock seems quite exhausted in them. They are the smallest, under-

* Alluding to a famous dwarf so styled.

formed things I ever saw, the Corsican fairy excepted. The queen looks like an old woman of ninety, totally withered and worn out. She has had twenty-one children. The Duchess of Chablais is pretty, like Madame d'Artois. The youngest princess is very pretty, light and elegant, but very short. The Prince and Princess of Carignan were absent on account of mourning.

Many of the ladies who danced were particularly handsome, and more especially Madame d'Arza. The Spanish ambassador, Villa Hermosa, is a most easy, polite, good sort of man, just like an Englishman in his manner. We returned to Turin at ten o'clock, by moonlight.

I have since been to their palace in the morning. The first apartment is a large square hall, the ceiling of which is painted in pannels, but spoilt by the fire the French set to it, when they plundered the palace, during the war in the beginning of the century. There are ten large pictures of ladies hunting, and below ten hunting pieces of Daniel Mieli, which are full of figures, dressed in the habits of his time. The great gallery is superior to that of Versailles for length, height, and breadth, but not so handsomely ornamented. The stables are very extensive, and the orangery well worth seeing. The church is very fine; it has a dome in the form of a

Greek cross; its proportions are admirable, and the architecture noble and elegant. There is plenty of game and deer in the park, and a theatre made by plantations of trees; a labyrinth of hornbeam hedges, a menagerie, several fine broad alleys, and a long mall; but water is prodigiously wanted.

We dined at Mr. Poyntz's with Mr. Head, Mr. Maxwell, and Count Castel Alfieri, a young Piedmontese of the academy. There are few English here, except some youths with their tutors. We drove post to the Valentin, a noble avenue, where we saw several beautiful women; then to the Italian comedy, where the Arlechino was execrable; and after that we paid a visit to Madame de St. Gilles, a very agreeable person.

Turin is supposed to have existed long before Rome, and to have been the capital of the Taurini. There are but few remains of antiquity to support its pretensions. When the old walls of the town were destroyed, to make the square near the porta palazzo, many ancient altars and stones were dug out of the foundations, with inscriptions on them. These are fixed on the walls of the university. The emblem of a bull is supposed to be derived from the ancient Taurini.

The fortifications are strong, and all the walls

are planted with fine old oaks, which afford a very pleasant shade. The citadel is very strong, and underwent a close siege in 1706, till Prince Eugene drove off the French by the victory he gained in the plains on each side of the Dora. It was there, at the Porte de Secours, that Victor Amedius came to get admittance after his abdication, and was refused by the Baron de Remy. The French made several violent attacks upon this place, but were always repulsed.

A soldier in the corps of miners, one Pietro Molo, blew himself up, with several companies of French grenadiers, in order to save the fort, which the enemy was on the point of taking. His children enjoy a pension from the king. His noble intention was confided to his companions, whom he desired to get away, and recommend his family to the duke, having resolved to sacrifice himself for his country.

Turin is divided into two parts, the old and the new. The new is well built, and chiefly inhabited by the nobility, whose palaces are elegant, and contribute to the embellishment of the town. The interior of them is generally well furnished, with extensive collections of paintings, particularly those of the Marquesses de Fana and d'Ormea.

We went to the little opera house of Farignan, which is the only one open at this time of the year. No one seems to attend to the music or representation. The ladies receive visits in their boxes, *e fanno conversazione.* This theatre is but ill lighted. It does to dance in during the carnival, when the opera is held at the grand theatre adjoining the palace, which is very large, and one of the most magnificent in Italy. Its form is exactly that of the section of an egg; the stage is very extensive, and they often have twenty or thirty horses upon it.

The Jews here have a quarter of their own, called Gheto, with a synagogue and burial-place. Every Jew is obliged to wear a yellow ribbon, sewed on the breast of his coat.

The street which leads to the gate of the Po is the grandest in the city, and probably the finest in Europe. The palace of the Prince of Piedmont is very handsome. I have not sufficient time at present to give you an exact idea of this small but beautiful city.

Lyons, June.

From Novalesa we set out *en porteurs*, at three o'clock. The heat was excessive, at which our carriers seemed enchanted! We were seated on a little stool with a back to it, fixed on poles, which two men bore like chairmen; and a rope was placed so as to swing our legs upon. In this equipage we were carried up for three hours, through roads where no horsemen could attempt to ride.

On one side of us, from a cavern in the top of a high rock, gushed forth the river Cencola, which, after falling in several cascades, takes its course along the valley, and discharges itself into the Dora. No words can describe the badness of the roads, which turn incessantly from left to right, from right to left, over rocks and loose stones. A ravine, through which some furious torrent has dashed headlong, and torn up everything before it, is a turnpike compared to this.

We saw no uncommon insects or beasts in our journey. As we ascended, I beheld in succession hawthorn, oak, juniper, larch, laurestinus, beech, barberry, hazel, gooseberry, brier, ash, cherry and sloe, before we reached La Ferrière; afterwards larch, and crimson polyanthuses.

A covered way is constructed here, in order to prevent accidents from avalanches. The pastures in the plains are enamelled with red, white, yellow, and purple pansies, a small flower of bright blue, and plenty of flox adonis. The high peaks on the left are called *la corne rouge*, and *la glacière de Bar.* In front is one of the prettiest cascades in the Alps. After La Ferrière the larch woods cease. There are, however, many hardy pines.

From thence to La Grande Croix is a plain, full of white clover, large blue flowers, and a small yellow cistus. The pastures are covered with white ranunculi, and white heart's-ease.

I thought the lake small and ugly. The larches near it were blighted. The rocks are of a friable marble, like salt.

After descending a short distance, we came to the large woods, which are very fine. Soon after begin the spruce firs intermingled with larches and pines, forming a noble forest.

We arrived at eight at Lans le Bourg, but the baggage did not get down until ten that night, and the carriage not till six the next morning.

The women on this side of Mont Cenis wear an odd head-dress ; it consists of a piece of blue cloth drawn together, which binds up their hair behind; and in the middle of their forehead is a square bit of red or green velvet, with some tinsel sewed round it.

Our road from Modane to St. Michel, a miserable inn, lay over rocks and precipices, the mountains above us being covered with firs and birch trees. From thence the rocks above the highway are quite perpendicular. They consist of a kind of coarse marble, of a bluish gray colour. About St. Jean de Maurienne, goîtres are numerous. Indeed, most of the inhabitants of these countries are affected with them, as well as many of the Turin nobility. This protuberance is attributed to the melted snow, which is drank here in spring.

We travelled along the road above the banks of the Arco, that flows amidst rocks and woods in continual cascades, and crossed it on a bridge of stone and another of wood. The industry of the Savoyards is great; they improve every little spot of land they find among the rocks.

We stopped at Aiguebelle, a small town at the bottom of a hill, hemmed in on every side by the mountains. The setting sun afforded us a sight only to be seen in such a country; its rays, gilding the snowy summits of the mountains, made them appear of a bright fiery colour, and above them the thick white clouds were streaked with three or four reflections of a beautiful rainbow.

We travelled all the way to Chambery between ridges of mountains which kept the sun off us; — their tops were almost always hid amongst the clouds, and their flanks girded with woods.

Montmeilian, noted for its good red wine, stands on the declivity of a hill. High on the top is the fort which was besieged by the French, and taken after a short resistance, in the last wars of Italy. The town is half in ruins, having never been rebuilt since that destructive period. Sudden storms of violent rain prevented our seeing the convent of the Grande Chartreuse, which is much cried up by travellers. Every stranger is treated with a supper, bed, and breakfast. We travelled beneath the shade of the mountains which encompass it, and slept at Chambery, where there is little to be seen.

As we proceeded from thence, we enjoyed the sight of a noble waterfall. It issues out of a cleft on the very summit of a lofty mountain, rushes down its side upon a precipice, over which it sprouts with great violence upon the rocks below, and forms a most agreeable cascade. The height from its source, as our guide assured us, is more than two hundred toises. After the melting of the snow in spring, it falls down with such force that it comes close to the road, which is at a considerable distance.

We next reached a spot where the road is cut through a very large rocky mountain, called La Grotta. Charles Emmanuel, second Duke of Savoy, had it blown up, and a pavement made.

The road is broad but steep, between vast rocks that hang over it, and at the entrance is an inscription in Latin, denoting that, in the year 1663, the passage had been cut by the Duke, for the relief and convenience of travellers.

From the top of the cliff, through a cavity, rushes down a stream so strongly impregnated with iron as to stain the rock red ; and further on there is a large grotto, out of which a considerable brook rolls forth, and forms a cascade. There is also a spacious cavern without water.

We dined at Les Echelles, a small place, near which, on two eminences, are the ruins of two old castles. At a little distance from thence, a guide led us up the hills, to the place where a separation has been made of the Savoy from the French territories. A mountain was blown up with gunpowder, and a passage through the middle of t made for the Guyer, which ran before through several holes in the rock.

We passed along the side of a high smooth rock, polished by the hand of man. The narrow road is rendered safe by a wall of stone cut out of a great crag, which hangs over the precipice. At the end of this passage is a little door, hewn through the stone, by which we came to a narrow wooden bridge, in the centre of which is a pillar with the fleurs de lys on one face, and the white cross on the other. It joins the two roads together. The water beneath rolls over huge stones and precipices, upon which one can hardly look without dread. The prospect terminates in a vast rocky mountain, from behind which the river pours forth its angry waters. The crags on each side are immensely high, and quite impracticable. Their summits bend over the valley, almost near enough to touch each other.

Many ruined castles exist in this part of Savoy, and among them the Chateau de Roquefort, where Mandrin, a famous French smuggler, was taken. The road winds about incessantly, until at length we found ourselves at a surprising height, amidst rocks and precipices, through which rushes the river that separates France from Savoy. The way is hewn out along the side of a large rocky mountain, whose head is covered with clouds. Parapets keep the traveller from tumbling over, which might otherwise happen, as the passage is narrow and slippery. Thickets and rocks hide the precipices; box bushes are common thereabouts.

Pont de Beauvoisin is the frontier town of France and Savoy. The little river Guyer divides the town, and the two kingdoms; the latter join in the middle of the bridge, which is of stone.

On entering France, chesnut and walnut trees are planted in plenty along the road side, and stone pillars are set up at the distance of every half league.

I looked back to take leave of the scenery of Savoy, just after a heavy shower of rain, which had refreshed all the atmosphere, and beheld a ridge of mountains tipped with clouds as white as milk; below, mists rising slowly from the valley, hills covered with wood on one side, on the other rocks of enormous size and height; hamlets and enclosures without number spangled the valley, and a complete rainbow overarched the whole.

Lyons is enclosed with a wall of masonry; it has six gates, all of which are shut at night. The houses near the river are very lofty, and built of white stone. There is one belonging to a magistrate, let out to a number of different families, which brings in 20,000 livres a year to the proprietor. The Place Louis le Grand is spacious and well built, with the statue of that monarch in the middle.

Close to the quay is a famous manufactory of silk and brocades; the designs of which are most delightfully imagined, and the prices of the work reasonable.

The "*Charité*" is a building of surprising

extent, capable of containing ten thousand people. Here the old and decrepit poor are employed at some easy work, according to their capacity, and here likewise vagabonds are shut up and forced to work; for not a beggar is suffered in the streets of Lyons. The work of these poor people is so beneficial, that, besides what is sufficient for the nourishment of those within, every week they distribute fifteen hundred loaves of bread to the indigent in the town.

In front of this building are the ramparts, where the inhabitants take the air in their coaches, as far as the confluence of the two rivers, Rhone and Saone. The difference between the waters of each is as easily perceptible as those of the Rhine and Moselle at Coblentz. The Rhone, rough and impetuous, rushes with fury against the opposite rocks, and dashes back the sleepy waters of the silent Saone a considerable way. As the winds that blow through the openings in the mountains are violent, sudden and unsettled here, no windmills succeed; therefore watermills are built on the Saone, which renders its navigation extremely dangerous.

Desirous of seeing the antiquities, I climbed up a steep hill to an open place, where the convents of the Minimes and the Ursulines are built. The gardener of the latter admitted us into the garden, and led us by the light of a candle down a few old steps into a cavern, which was anciently a bath, or more probably a reservoir, of the Romans, for the waters that were conveyed thither over the hill by aqueducts. This subterranean building is a quadrangular vault, divided into two square rooms, with four doors each, and a gallery that runs quite round them. The walls, roof, and floor are laid with cement, several inches thick, and so hard that not a flaw can be perceived in it, except where it has been broken by hammers, out of curiosity. Two holes are in a corner, one of which served to admit the water, the other to let it run off when too full.

In the vineyard of the Minimes are the remains of a Roman amphitheatre, which anciently had a communication with the palace of the Roman governors, that stood on the ground where a convent of Visitandine Nuns has since been erected. The good fathers have built their house of the stones of this theatre, and are daily destroying it more and more.

From their convent I walked further up the mountains, to the church of Saint Irenæus, a bishop who suffered martyrdom in this place. It is the most ancient in Lyons, and built over a subterranean chapel, where the primitive Christians hid themselves, and secretly performed the sacred rites, until they were discovered and dragged out to death. The saint's body and that of his companions lie in this chapel. On its door is an inscription in Latin verse, and half way up the hill, against the front of a cottage, are the following words, engraved on marble:—"*Souvenez vous, passans Chrétiens, que le sang de nos saints martyrs a coulé dans ce chemin-ci, pour la foi de Jesus Christ.*"

On this mountain stood the ancient Lugdunum. Its old walls yet remain. On its summit are the ruins of a once magnificent aqueduct, which conveyed water over the mountains from a place eight leagues off. A portion of it is still remaining, very solid and thick, built with pebbles, cemented together with a bitumen scarcely to be broken with hammers.

Paris, June.

We passed to Chalons through Villefranche. Its steeple and bridge, with a kind of ruinous citadel behind it, have a lively effect. The men wear little round hats, tied on the top of their heads, with crowns too little to fit.

Near Beaune we entered the famous wine country of Burgundy. The vines are low, and are trained to little stakes, or oaken *échalas*. We passed through a hilly country to Dijon. Its environs are bleak, but the gothic steeples and well-grown trees afford an agreeable view of the city from many points. The streets are wide. There is an equestrian statue of Louis XIV., and in the church two white marble monuments; the one of Philip, first Duke of Burgundy,* of the second race, and the other of his son John, and that son's wife, a Bavarian. He is styled son of Philip of Burgundy, and Jane the daughter of the king of *Bacigné*. What this means heaven knows—it may be Boheme; but Philip married Margaret of Flanders.

We passed a pleasant village, where the Bishop of Dijon is building a fine house. There is hereabouts abundance of excellent fruit. Next day we travelled in an ugly open country, near the serpentining river Yonne, down which much wood is floated to Paris.

The approach to Auxerre is picturesque. Its lofty steeples have a handsome appearance, and the walks round the town are pleasant.

* Philip of Burgundy, called the Bold, was married at Ghent, in 1639, to Margaret, daughter of Louis de Mâle, Count of Flanders. She had been previously married to Philip de Rouvre, Duke of Burgundy, in 1534, he being seven, and she only four years old. He died ere he attained manhood.

Joigny stands well on the river. Sens is an ugly, ill-built city. Its cathedral is large and gothic. In the choir is the mausoleum of the late dauphin and dauphiness, by Corton; a piece of true French confusion, allegory, and want of taste. The country improves near Maret.

We rested at Fontainbleau, where I visited the palace. The king enters it by the gate which opens upon the Bourbonnois road, and leads into a large court. The apartments which are built round this court are of brick, and are allotted for the reception of officers of state and foreign ministers. The Mathurins, who perform in the chapel, live at one end of it.

Two flights of steps carry you up to the palace. The gallery of stags is one of the most curious things to be seen there. It is long and well lighted. Between every two windows are placed, on pillars, stags' heads of plaster, with real horns stuck in them. Every pair differs in something from the rest. Some are of an odd form by accident, some by nature, but all are equally surprising, whether by the redundancy or the scarcity of the antlers, and the positions they grew in. Underneath each, is an inscription, denoting the date of the death of the stag they belonged to. The first are of Henry the Fourth's killing. It was in this gallery that Christina queen of Sweden caused her favourite Monaldeschi to be murdered.*

There is another gallery made by Francis I., crowded with pictures, each supported by two large figures in stone, and each pannel filled with the cipher and emblem of the founder, viz. a salamander. This gallery was one of the first architectural essays after the restoration of the arts in France.

The chapel is very long; full of ancient gildings and ornaments. On the ceiling is painted the history of the creation of the world. The pavement is of blue and white marble. The apartments of the royal family are not very extraordinary. In one of the queen's rooms is a ceiling and floor, which my guide assured me had been there since the days of St. Louis.

I saw a great deal of fine tapestry, among the rest Le Brun's battles of Alexander, copied at

* An Italian by birth, who had long been master of the horse, confident and favourite to Christine. Becoming tired of him at length, she determined to have him murdered, and she put her resolve into execution with so much *sang froid*, that she sent a confessor to him, and bade him prepare for death. Neither the supplications of the victim, nor the remonstrances of her own confessor, could turn her from her purpose. The unfortunate wretch was assassinated by one of her own servants, in the gallery des Cerfs, at Fontainbleau, in 1657.

the Gobelins. There is a good picture of Louis XIII. in the king's bedchamber; the wainscot panels of which are as fine as gold and allegorical paintings can make them. The bed is blue, embroidered with silver.

Next to these is a council-room, where the preliminaries of peace were signed in 1763 by the Dukes of Bedford and Praslin.* In one of the courts is a large piece of water, stocked with carp of a most amazing magnitude.

Fontainbleau is situated in the midst of an extensive sandy valley, encompassed on every side by barren craggy hills or woods. An infinity of straight paths are cut through the forest on every side, for the convenience of stag-hunting. We travelled through a delightful wilderness of young trees and brushwood, and saw at a distance eminences of stone, covered with heath and small birch trees. They convey an idea of the old tumuli raised to the honour of deceased heroes, in the northern parts of Europe.

We proceeded through thick woods of tall old

* John, Fourth Duke of Bedford, who was appointed ambassador to the Court of Versailles in 1762, and on the 10th of February 1763 signed the peace between England, France, Spain, and Portugal, called the peace of Fontainbleau. M. de Praslin, cousin to the Duke de Choiseul, was minister of Marine.

oaks, that intertwined their branches across the road, and arrived about two at the Royal Hotel in Paris. I lost no time in sending the Queen of Naples's letter to her ambassador, Casafacioli, to deliver to her sister the Queen of France.

London, July.

I stopped at Chantilly in my way from Paris. It is low and ugly. The most ridiculous serpentine walks are made round a square pond, without shrubs or variety; and on one side a channel following it, as broad as a basin. We slept at Clermont. Fitzjames is extensive, but dull. The cathedral makes a good figure at Amiens.

We met at Calais the Duchess of Devonshire, with Lord and Lady Spencer, and Lady Anne Spencer, on their way to Spa;—and I had the first sight of my Spanish travels in print, which were lent me by the charming duchess, in the most flattering manner. She has an exquisite figure, and a sweet countenance, though I have seen many more striking as to beauty; but she seems the picture of candour and innocence.

Hamsterley, Sept. 4th, 1779.

I have spent three weeks agreeably at my brother's new lodge at Mounces, on the Moors, where we had fine weather and excellent sport; also some pleasant parties at Lord Percy's castle at Keelder, with Lord and Lady Percy, Lord Aylesford, Mr. Charlton, and Mr. Hall. We had the border toast, viz. "The sheep of the border, that claes our back and crams our weam, and may the shank bane of every sheep mak a whittle haft to cut the throats of our enemies wi'."

At Keelder is a large stone or tomb, called Brand's Well, a famous, but now unknown hero of these hills.

I rode to the head of the Tyne, which is at a sulphureous cold well, where people come to bathe; it is in a wide vale, with bare hills on both sides, from north to south. The place where the water rises is the highest point of the valley, and swells up so as to be able to let the water out either way; the bathers lodge in a kind of village close by. However, I am inclined to think the source of the Tyne is really at the head of Deadwater, a current which comes out east from the northern hills, but is not called *Tyne* till it joins Keelder at the lodge, where stood Bell's chapel, of which nothing remains but part of a cross, and some large grave-stones.

I dined at Beaufront with Mr. Errington, who is as cracked as ever man was. I wonder he is still allowed to be at large, and to see company. He has the mania of fancying he has been created Duke of Hexham. He has erected a pillar in his grounds, with the ducal arms, supporters and coronet, on Stagshaw bank; a most public station, as it is the rendezvous of an annual fair. A foreign title is his idea, for a foreign crown is over his door.

I joined my brother at Capheaton, who is not a little glad to get home, after having been taken prisoner.* We had a large party on the occasion. Lord Adam Gordon and many officers, Sir M. Ridley, Mr. Riddell of Swinburne, &c. Mem. Sir M. Ridley's father was the miller of Blagdon mill. Mr. Riddell's father lived at Fenham, and was called "the auld fox of Fenham", as old Sir John Swinburne was styled "the auld carl of Capheaton."

I send you my adieus to Mounces.

Je quitte donc demain ce montagneux asile,
Où le ciel, à mes vœux rendu moins difficile,

* He was taken prisoner on board a ship coming from the Continent.

A permi pour un tems l'oubli de mes malheurs.
Ah! puis-je le quitter sans repandre des pleurs?
Loin de tous les objets où mon ame ulcerée,
Revoit sous maintes formes une image adorée.*
Loin des ennuis mortels, qu'entraine un peu de bien,
J'avais pu m'etourdir en ne pensant à rien.
Demain donc finira ce train de vie aimable,
Mes soucis renaitront—mon bonheur est au diable.
Que le sommeil est doux! le reveil prompt et frais!
Quand les premiers rayons éclairent nos volets,
De la cime obscurcie écartant les nuages,
Le soleil nous annonce un jour libre d'orages.
Ardens et pleins d'espoir, nos chasseurs empressés,
Grimpent sur ces monts noirs, l'un sur l'autre entassés.
Où l'industrie humaine inconnue
Laisse voir la Nature originelle et nue—
Adam les reverroit avec affection,
Porter en corps l'habit de leur création.
Le chien hardi, nerveux, sur un terrain immense,
Passe comme un éclair, vers le gibier s'avance,
Le suit, s'arrête et reste immobile—attentif—
Le chasseur suit de près d'un pas ferme et hatif—
Un cri s'elève—on part—c'est le coq de bruyere!
Mais il tombe à l'instant sous l'arme meurtrière.
Près du faîte ondoyant de ces Alpes du Nord,
Une eau fraiche et limpide échappe sans effort;
En vain veut elle fuir—la mousse, la fougère,
Par un mur spongieux arrêtent sa carrière.
Ici sur le midi, content de nos succès,
Nous portons au diner grand faim, peu d'apprêts;
Puis sur l'herbe étendus, (sofa doux quoique agreste)
Nous digérons en paix, et dormons la sieste.

* His daughter.

Le zephir parfumé, l'air pur, delicieux,
Assoupissent nos sens—ainsi dormoient les dieux.

Plymouth, Oct. 2.

From Newby, (Lord Grantham's,) a finely furnished house with capital antiques, Sir Thomas and I set out for the camp of cavalry at Exeter. The country is hilly about there, with much moor, and very bad roads, and horrible bridges.

I visited Mr. Parker at Saltram, where we met Lord Grantham, Mr. and Miss Robinson, the Duke and Duchess of Rutland, Colonel Hervey, and Admiral Shuldham. Saltram is in a noble situation, commanding a view of Catwater, Plymouth citadel and Mount Edgcumbe, and has a fine hanging wood and walk of two miles about the water. The house is grand.

Our first expedition from thence was up the Plym, a charming ride for miles, through vales and hanging oak woods of vast extent. Salmon abounds in this little river. From the Barn, four miles south of Saltram, is a glorious view of all the Sound, Plymouth, its forts and islands, the Hamoaze, docks, shipping, Mount Edgcumbe, and the camps.

Our next course took us across the Lavy at

low water, and we rode through Plymouth, which is ill paved and ugly; thence two miles further on to Dock, on as bad a road as any in England; took boat at Malton Cove, crossed the Narrows, and landed near the low gate of Mount Edgcumbe. Avenues lead up to the house; a good approach, low gardens, charming views of the sea, shipping, fort, islands, &c.

The vegetation is surprising—such handsome evergreens, cypresses, magnolias, myrtles, all blooming in the open air. The house is gothic and ill constructed, with an ugly hall of Devonshire marble; but there is no describing the grandeur of the prospects.

There is a new road cut along the side of the hill towards the sea, through a wilderness of pines, arbutus, and other evergreens. Close to the park is Maker Church, from the steeple of which are made the signals; and near it is an encampment.

The dock-yard is a grand piece of work. All the buildings are constructed of the materials dug out to form the docks—a marble excellent for lime.

We went with a large party to meet the Duke of Rutland's regiment, commanded by Colonel St. Leger, coming into barracks; then went on board the Ocean, Capt. Ourry, and sailed into the Sound, saluting the Lord Admiral, &c.

Next day we left Saltram for Bath.

London, Jan. 5, 1780.

I am just returned from a visit at Belvoir Castle, in company with Sir Thomas G——. It is the worst disposed and coldest house in England, and I doubt whether anything can ever be made of it, on account of its exposed bleak situation, and the inconvenient plan it is constructed upon.* The oldest parts are Rose's and Stanton's tower; the latter so called, because the holder of Stanton estate is obliged to come, on summons, with a hundred men, to defend that tower. The cellar under it is curious for its roof. The chapel seems ancient; the rest is modernized and very ugly. Long reaches of even wall render the general appearance of Belvoir, from below and from the other hills, like a Patagonian sheep-fold. The gallery is low, but very long, and the picture-room is good. The bed-chambers are bad; all too low in the ceilings.

The Duke and Duchess were very polite and hospitable. It is impossible to do the honours better than she does, or to be more pleasing; indeed, to look at her is of itself a gratification,

* This opinion has not been confirmed; for the skill of the architect, and the good taste of the present Duke, have rendered Belvoir Castle one of the most comfortable, as it is one of the noblest, habitations in Great Britain.

for she is extraordinarily beautiful.* They have three little children.

The party in the castle, besides ourselves and the family, consisted of Lord Chatham, the Thorotons, Messrs. Pulteney,† Taylor, and Crofts, Sir Joshua Reynolds, and Mr. Chamberlayn, a blind man who rides extremely hard fox-hunting, and tells wonderful stories.‡ The hours were very irregular.

* Few women in Europe surpassed either of the two last Duchesses of Rutland, in grace, beauty, and every good quality that can exalt or adorn the sex. Mr. Swinburne of course alluded to the Duchess Isabella, daughter of Charles, fourth Duke of Beaufort.

† Afterwards Sir James, who was secretary at war and married Lady Bath.

‡ One of the stories attributed to him, though it has been given to another equally celebrated dealer in fiction, runs thus: He was talking of his travels in Switzerland, where, par parenthèse, he had never been; so some one asked him if he recollected Mont Blanc. "I shall not easily forget it," replied he, "for I never had such sport in all my life—Nimrod the hunter, who did things in good form, never bagged such game." "Sport on Mont Blanc!" exclaimed the other. "Yes." "What! chamois!" "No, sir, cherubim—ah, you may well stare! But cherubim, I repeat, as sure as they and seraphim continually do cry." Being pressed to explain, he continued,—"Egad, I had scarcely reached the summit before Bang, my pet spaniel, bolted forward, and in a few seconds ran back wagging his tail, and —may I be set down as a goose if he did not drop a cherubim at my feet. Poor little thing — it had evidently staid out rather late, lost its way among the clouds, and had

There is an extensive, but interesting view from the brow of the hill. The castle looks well from some points of the woods. The library is well stored with old books of history, antiquity, and jurisprudence.

I accompanied Sir Thomas and Sir Joshua to Burleigh, where we saw the pictures. It is far from being a capital collection. The Raphael is undoubtedly a copy, and the Carlo Dolci a very ignoble character. Some heads and sketches are excellent. Two monkeys in fine habits, by Teniers, are very good.

I have, since my return, been to see Sir Joshua's picture of the Nativity, for the new college at Oxford, where it is to be executed on glass. *Non mi piace!* It is a sad, monstrous, bad-coloured thing.

We were at a pleasant dinner yesterday at Mr. John Pitts, where were Lord and Lady Edgcumbe,* with their cub of a son in a high-

been half frozen; so I just wet its lips with a little brandy, placed it in my bosom, and carried it down to Chamouny, where it quickly revived. I then put it into a cage, and had the pleasure to hear it sing. I intended to bring it over as a present to Wilberforce, but my pious intentions were frustrated." "Why! what became of it?" "Confound it, sir, the cursed cat ate it."

* The then Viscount Edgcumbe, who was raised to the earldom of Mount Edgcumbe in 1789. The youth in the highland dress was the present earl's father.

land dress; and Mrs. Greville, a charming woman, whom I sat next to, and whose agreeable way of conversing delighted me. From thence we went to Lady Lucan's rout. Her own drawings and paintings furnish the rooms.

Ostend, Feb. 17.

We were tempted by Mr. Elliot, the British envoy at Brussels, to come hither in his sloop from Margate, after paying a visit to Lord Holland at Kingsgate, so called from the landing of Charles and James in 1683. We embarked at seven in the evening; the sea was extremely rough, and we rolled much all night. Our people appeared to know little of the coast, for when we discovered at daybreak the Flemish downs, they disputed about which was Nieuport, and which Ostend. I convinced them that what we saw was neither one nor t'other, but a place to the north of Ostend; so we had to veer about, and with such unskilful steersmen and so feeble a crew, that it was a work of great difficulty and danger.

By the help of some Tuscan mariners, who were passengers, we accomplished it, and bore away fifteen miles southward along the shore, running with the strength of a high tide over sandbanks and shoals, where few ships ever passed with impunity. About one we came off the harbour of Ostend, but as the tide ebbed, we could not get in. The rain and wind increased; the sea ran mountains high, and the ship tossed about so cruelly, that we boldly ventured into an English boat, and got safe into Ostend, though with great risk and a complete wetting. The ship did not get in till seven hours after.

Mr. Elliot set off for Brussels. We were compelled to remain for want of horses. Many Dutch, English, and Baltic trading ships are in the harbour. Its entrance is dangerous, and many vessels are lost there. The women dress here in coloured camlet hoods and cloaks; the mariners in blue tunics over red waistcoats.

Rheims, Feb. 23.

We left Ostend on the 18th, hired four carriage horses very dear, on account of the tricks of the postmasters, but had no trouble at all at the Douane. We traversed an ugly country to Ypres. They give the horses brown bread in a trough. The price of posting is expensive in the empress queen's dominions.

Passed Menin, a dismantled frontier town. Its remaining gate has the French arms over it. There are a number of harpies in the shape of *commis* on both frontiers, but a few sous set all right and easy.

The road to Lille is almost impassable. The streets are quite infectious, from the cartloads of dirt carried out for manure.

We travelled through avenues of Lombardy poplars to Cambray, in frost and snow. They advertise there the sale of red and black ashes for manure. I bought some ruffles, *fabrique du pays*.

From Cambray we had most abominable roads, over woody hills and deep fields, to Laon; it was hard labour to get there at all. The king's founderies are near La Fere. About Laon we began to get into a wine country. Laon is a small city of an oblong form, situated upon a commanding eminence. The steeples of the cathedral are singular and intricate; the outside is supported by pillars.

We arrived at Rheims after a tedious drive; for the narrow wheels of the carts and wagons cut up the roads, and render them very rough. The country is bare and ugly. My sister, Mrs.

Charlton, who resides here, was much pleased to see me, and persuaded me to remain a couple of days with her.

Rheims is ill built, the houses of wood, and the streets narrow, with a broad kennel in the middle. The great square is handsome. There is a bronze statue of Louis XV., a very middling performance, the hands and arms long and withered, the attitude heavy and ill expressed. It bears an inscription something to this purport—

De l'amour des Français instruisez la terre,
Louis fit ici le serment d'être leur père,
Serment qu'il ne viola jamais, &c.

Two colossal statues support the pedestal, which I took for Peace or Abundance, and Fortitude; but I ought to have suspected French allegory of lying deeper, for in the description of the place I find that one (a woman with a lion and rudder) is moderate government, and the other, (a man sitting leaning on his arm,) the happiness of the people under that government. Œdipus himself would have been puzzled to make out this enigma.

The abbey of St. Nicaise is a beautiful gothic church. It contains an ancient sarcophagus of great size, with basso relievos representing a hero hunting a lion, attended by figures dressed as Dacians; one has a Phrygian cap, and, but for their beards, they might all be Phrygians; but I do not recollect ever to have seen that nation portrayed with beards. The sculpture is not of the best time, but before Constantine.

The *St. Ampoule* is kept at the Benedictine Abbey of St. Remy;* a very ugly old gothic edifice, of the first ages of French devotion, with stumpy, thick pillars clustered together, and clumsy capitals, some of which have binds—an old mode in the gothic style. This architecture, though shorter in its proportions, has a great affinity with that of Durham Abbey.

The cathedral in the centre of Rheims is a stupendous pile, and as much crowded with statues as the Domo of Milan. Though a wonderful piece of gothic magnificence, I confess that York Minster pleases me more. The paint-

* The *St. Ampoule,* or holy phial, which contains the consecrated oil made use of to anoint the French monarchs from Clovis down to Charles X., was, according to tradition, brought down from heaven by a dove, and delivered into the hands of St Remy, who was apprized of its object by a vision. This holy phial was taken from the abbey in 1793, and broken to atoms by one of the sacrilegious deputies of the National Convention; but the clergy now assert, at least they did so prior to the coronation of Charles X., that the phial broken by the terrorists was not the real St. Ampoule, but a fac-simile, the true relic having been secreted and preserved.

ed glass is admirable; the fine red purple among it is peculiarly pleasing to the eye.

To end the evening, my sister took me to an assembly and supper, of very queer-looking folk, but, *en revanche,* we had excellent champagne.

Paris, March 1, 1780.

From Rheims the country improves, and about Fismes grows hilly and agreeable. Soissons has a good appearance, though it is rather a desolate city. We passed extensive forests of beech and other timber of considerable size, cut into rides, belonging to the Duke of Orleans, who has a seat thereabouts. We slept at Villers Cotterets, and next day reached Paris, through avenues pruned up like broomsticks.

I have seen Jerningham, Laville, and my two nephews at the English Monks, where I dined with them, and supped with Madame Martinville, with the Duc de Lauzun and M. de Vismes.

I went last night to see the opera of Atys—the words by Quenault. That horrid screamer, Mlle. des Plaut, was worse than ever. The dances were *moelleuses;* but young Vestris and

Madame Theodore were charming. Edward Dillon has just got the regiment of Guienne infantry.

(*Without date.*)

We left Paris on the second, on our way to Fontainbleau, where the quantity of country seats on the verge of the forest has a fine effect in the landscape. Madame de Montesson's villa is one of the largest, and commands a noble prospect:—the forest, even without leaves, is magnificent. We came in sight of the Loire, near Briare, about noon, and enjoyed the grand and unequalled prospects which that noble river affords—such a fine reach of winding water, with a noble breadth of surface, such luxuriance of culture, and variety of country. As we advanced, all these beauties increased upon us. From the brow above Pouilly is the most enchanting *coup d'œil* imaginable.

Nevers is an ugly town. The motto over its northern gate is a sample of French flattery, viz.—"*Au grand homme modeste, au pere de son peuple, au maître de nos cœurs.*" This was meant for Louis Quinze, *dans les beaux jours de son règne.**

* The name given to Louis XV., *dans les beaux jours de son règne*, was "*le bien aimé*," an honourable epithet that he

Moulins is a pretty city, with walks and fountains. The bridge over the Allier is handsome. There are many mulberry trees, and the environs are gay and pleasant: the female knife-sellers are as tormenting as Italian beggars.

We breakfasted at La Palisse, an ugly seat of the Chabannes family, who reside there half the year. The Loire begins to be navigable about Roanne. Crowds of long slender boats, that ply on it, are loaded with all sorts of merchandise from Lyons, and many with a bad kind of coal. The president de St. Vincent has a large country-house there, with terraces one above the other, and a fine stream below.

At Chateau Morand, a seat of the Mirepoix, one enjoys a most extensive prospect to the north, where the view is only arrested by the dimness of the horizon. From thence are steep

did not long retain; for the love of his subjects was soon converted into hatred and contempt. The following lines were in the mouths of all the people many years before his death:

Le bien aimé de l'Almanac,
N'est pas le bien aimé de la France;
Il fait tout *ab hoc ab hac*,
Le bien aimé de l'Almanac.
Il met tout dans le même sac,
Et la justice et la finance;
Le bien aimé de l'Almanac,
N'est pas le bien aimé de la France!

mountains with snow on their summits, and a most wild landscape. We descended the long Montagne de Tarare, through eminences of very agreeable aspect, and fine woods of oak and silver firs, with country-seats and villages below. The vale of Bresle is very rich and handsome ; but the roads are most abominable.

We met the Baron de Polnitz at Lyons, and went to see "*Les Plaideurs*" of Racine, wretchedly acted. The afterpiece was Midas, with Gretry's music, but so ill sung, that Midas himself, so far from being wrong in his judgment, would have deserved his ass's ears if he had not condemned Apollo. It was a full house, with innumerable ugly women.

We agreed with a vetturino to take us to Turin in seven days, for twenty-four louis, and found it a very comfortable way of travelling, having laid in a good stock of hermitage and tongues. The rivers are delightful on entering Savoy, and we had good roads, which were more enjoyable for being a novelty.

At Turin we dined at Lord Mountstuart's, (the British envoy,) with Lord Herbert, &c. ; next day, at the Comte de Monstresol's. We then continued our route through Alessandria to Fiorenzolo.

I remarked the method of dressing vines in

this part of Lombardy. Among the rows of corn is a row of fallow, in the midst of which grows the vine, supported by small poles stuck in lattice wire. On each side, the twigs are carried out to larger poles, stuck into the ground so as to slope out very much at top; and the arrangement altogether forms a funnel.

On the 22d we arrived at Parma. Went to the Boschettina. I admired the Madonna della Scobella of Correggio, particularly the Infant Jesus—his eyes and graceful attitude; it is Divinity itself. What I found fault with, (if such an expression can be allowable,) was the heaviness of the clouds.

We visited the Benedictine refectory, to see Correggio's Last Supper. I learnt here the manner of the death of the late Infant Don Philip, who fell from his horse, and was devoured by his own hounds.* It was given out that he was taken ill at Alessandria, where he had been to see a favourite lady whom he wished to marry.

His son, now reigning, is a fat fool, doats upon the Dominican friars, gets up at daybreak to go to matins, and plagues the poor priests out of their lives if they do not attend to all their duties. His wife, the Archduchess Maria Amelia, is a

* The Infanta Don Philip of Parma is said by his biographers to have died of small-pox in 1759.

very bad paymistress. She buys a horse one day upon tick, to sell it the next for half price, to raise the wind. The Grand Master of Loretto is just returned hither from Parma, where he has been in vain soliciting payment for his bill of expenses, (400 sequins,) whilst she was at his house. The hereditary prince has a separate household.

There are two pieces of the divine Correggio in a side chapel of the cathedral, which is as dark as pitch.

The palace is pitiful. The plan M. du Tillot had adopted for building it was sumptuous, but as he opposed the duke's marriage with the archduchess, she has taken care it should be laid aside. The old palace was never finished ; in it is the great Farnesian theatre, last made use of when Don Carlos was here. It is in the style of a Roman theatre. The orchestra is on the right hand of the audience, in a recess of the pit. There are no stage-boxes, nor any partitions. The pit can be filled with water, if required, for Naumachias. It holds 14,000 persons, and would require 11,000 francs worth of wax to illuminate it. It is now useless.

There is a bad French bust there of the Infant Don Philip, and one of the empress his daughter, (Elizabeth, first wife of Joseph II.) She was a most accomplished creature;—but to what end were all her talents and charms! In a humble sphere I could furnish a parallel.

I saw many good Parmeggianos, one Schidone, and the beauty of beauties, the Correggio, as fresh as the day it was painted. I could have gazed on it for ever. Such brilliancy, such expression, such truth of colour! The smile of the Virgin is so noble, natural, and complacent, no copy would ever come up to it, and not Raphael himself, divine as he is, can do more for my feelings than Correggio. It is on figtree wood. The picture was painted in 1523, for Donna Cola, wife of Orazio Mergongi, for four hundred livres, equal to one hundred sequins now. She was so pleased with it, that she gave him over and above his bargain a sow, two loads of fagots, and some sacks of corn. This account is taken from a MS. of the Custodes Batistero, and contradicts the story of Correggio having been ill paid, and dying from the fatigue of carrying the picture.

We journeyed to Modena, and saw the hospital built by the late duke, called Pantheon Atestinum. His statue is in coarse white marble, looking like a fool as much as the original could do. The Duomo is gloomy.

We next passed through a country producing little corn, but studded with elms, pollarded to death. At San Arcangelo is a brick and stucco arch, erected to Pope Ganganelli, who was born here. The cultivation is very poor throughout this most charming country.

Near Rimini I came in sight of the Adriatic Sea; the shore is planted with mulberries and vines to the water's edge. The tints in the waves were very singular and strangely marked; the first line dark bluish green, going off into a bright yellow green, terminating near the land in a muddy yellow.

Rimini is large and ugly; the famous bridge of Augustus, though of marble, resembles Tiburtine stone. Its architecture is simple.

At the other end of the town is a triumphal arch, erected in honour of Augustus, repaired with brick. The unfinished Franciscan church was erected in 1450, by Sigismund Pandolfo Malatesta, Lord of Rimini. It is crowded in every part with his cipher and arms. The inside is heaped with statues and embroidered with foliages, of the time of the first revival of arts in Florence.

We passed through Cuma, a large city, prettily situated, the native place of Pius VI., and slept at Pesaro, near which is Gradasa, a seat of the Marchesa Mosca, formerly the villa of the Dukes of Urbino. It is delightfully situated, with a fine land and water prospect, and has a pleasant walk along the river down to the port on the sea. Not a shell is to be found on the sea shore. Tamarisks grow in the hedges, and lambs without end are selling for Easter Sunday.

Pesaro was the winter residence of the sovereigns of Urbino, and at that time the most agreeable place in Italy, and the school of politeness and gallantry. It is a large well-built city, with many palaces, monuments of its ancient grandeur. It is inhabited by a poor nobility, and almost ruined by the change of masters; which is the case of almost all the lesser towns on the coast. The air of Pesaro is not good in summer.

There are very pretty women about Fano, a pleasant town on the beach. Sinigaglia is a more stirring place, and has a canal and quay, with a whole quarter newly built, amongst which the unfinished college of the Jesuits cuts a great figure. The view from thence of Ancona is beautiful; its promontory and buildings advancing into the sea are noble objects; the richest cultivation on all its hills renders its environs delicious. The Lazaretto is a grand pentagon in an island. The ascent and descent to and from the town are very steep, but the roads are good. Trajan's arch is on the pier, several ships are there, French and English.

We journeyed on to Loretto, through a most beautiful country. It stands on the summit of a lofty eminence that commands views over a rich and hilly country on every side, and the sea at four or five miles distance. Its population seems numerous; the buildings are paltry, except the church and great hospital. The outside of the church is not of a pleasing architecture, and the inside is greasy and smoky. I never was in a dirtier place, nor one so crowded with the most filthy nauseous beings in the human form. Villains of all denominations and countries come as pilgrims, through devotion, idleness, or a desire of atoning for their crimes.

We were ordered to leave our canes at the door, and then the soldiers made way for us into the Casa Santa, which is in a blaze of light, from the quantity of lamps reflected by heaps of diamonds, and plates of gold and silver, that cover all the walls. The basso relievos are very fine; the *ex votos* of numberless crowned heads hang in clusters about the inside, and seem neglected, notwithstanding their immense value. The treasury is a large room, with cupboards, containing incredible riches in diamonds, precious stones, pearls, &c. What a pillage may, perhaps, be made here at a future day, by some now unborn Vandal!—enough to buy kingdoms.* There is a fine Madonna by Raphael.

We set off at noon, through a charming country enclosed with olive plantations, vines, and corn, and pulse of all the sorts, except rice. We passed through the gates of Maurata, a large city on the brow of a hill, a picturesque object, with its domes. We got back into the mountains, where the valleys are delicious, but the roads narrow and dangerous; which we experienced by the postilion not locking the wheel, and being obliged to drive full gallop above a mile down the winding roads, with rocks on one hand and a precipice on the other. We slept at Tolentino.

Next day we ascended to a large circular meadow on the highest point of the road, called Col Fiorito. The water is marshy, and here rise the brooks that run different ways—one into the Adriatic, the other into the Tyber. These places must have been craters of volcanos, extinct for many ages, and now are subterranean lakes, or reservoirs, covered with a thin coat of soil. Here very lately was committed a great robbery.

* The Vandals *were* born, for the republican armies quickly disposed of these treasures, and what little escaped the first pillage was afterwards swallowed up by the Imperial legions.

Forty ruffians plundered a number of merchants going to the fair of Sinigaglia.

We came to Palo, a village famous for its paper-mills and grotto, a cavern full of crystallizations, &c. Through a long and superlatively beautiful descent, varied by grand views from Foligno, we arrived at Rome. Fireworks were going on at the Castle St. Angelo. We stayed only to dine with the senator, and left the eternal city for Naples.

Naples, May 25.

We went a day or two ago to Pompeii, and dined in the country house. The city was built on various lavas. The ruins of the temple are of the same order of architecture as those of Pæstum. The paintings of the rooms delighted me as much as ever. The shops, with their stone parapets, are exactly like the modern ones of Naples and Rome.

I have made several excursions with Minasi. We sailed on the gulf, and ran into Meta, at the end of the plain of Sorrento; dined at a fishing-house; then walked up the rich plain, the high cultivation of which exceeds that of the Terra di Lavoro. Another day we went to Vietri, where we lodged at the Dominican convent.

In the mountains above Tropea are large tracts of chestnuts, and the small-leaved ash, the omas, which produces the manna. They do not plant it, but cut down the strong stems, and spring it from the old stocks. In July they make a small gash leaning upwards, the second day another, and form cups with maple leaves, into which the gum exudes.

The tyranny exercised on the poor peasants in this article is very great. The manna is farmed out, and a certain number of countrymen are appointed to gather it, during which time they are not at liberty to absent themselves, or undertake the most necessary labours for themselves. They scarcely derive any benefit from their work, as they are paid five carlini for a rotolo of manna, (thirty-three ounces,) which the farmers sell in Naples for nine carlini a pound (twelve ounces). If they burn or destroy the trees, though wild, their punishment is very severe; and if the smallest quantity is found in their houses, they are sent to prison. Eight hundred poor men, thus oppressed, contributed two carlini a piece for a memorial to the king, but no notice was taken of it.

Vesuvius is now in flames and smoke, and seems to threaten worse.

The queen, on taking leave of us, made a present to Mrs. S. of a pair of diamond bracelets, with her picture and ciphers, and two fine medals.

Rome, June 1.

On leaving Naples we slept the first night at Terracina, and the second at Velletri, at the Palazzo Lancelotto. We travelled twenty miles on the Appian Way, which has been lately repaired; it was a glorious sight. The canal is fine. They have lowered the road, although Trajan had raised it, out of economy; but I fear it will afford the water greater ease in overflowing it again.

There is to be a town built at Mesa. The Forum Appii is a large building of white marble. We dined at Sermonata, and came on next day through new Albano, round by Gensano and the vale of La Riccia, to Rome.

I have had an audience of Pius VI. in the Vatican. He received me very graciously, and conversed familiarly on political subjects for about half an hour, during which time he sat at a table, and I stood by it. We talked Italian.

Florence, June 27.

We left Rome on the 20th, with vetturini; hired horses and mules, and put the heavy baggage in a cart. The appearance of the Campagna di Roma is very desolate; scarcely a house to be seen; a few ruined towers, scattered trees, and a feeble cultivation of arable land left to itself to weed and ripen. If it were well peopled the air would lose its pestilential quality, and this would be a pretty country, though I imagine it would always suffer from want of water.

We dined at l'Osteria di Bacano, a single house in the middle of a large volcanic crater, quite round and free from water, except what is wasted from a fine fountain, or trough, from the houses at Ronciglione, a large town on a high hill, in a pretty vineyard country. A strong sulphureous smell exhaled from a small lake, or pond, with fine poplar groves on its edge.

We went down the chain that forms the crust

or wall of the crater of the Lake of Vico, into one of the most delightful scenes in the world, skirting the edge of a fine large irregular lake, the waters of which are smooth as glass. Moderate eminences, with many pleasing variations of height, covered with woods of aged oaks, beech, and chestnut, encircle the lake. Between them and the water is a stretch of wide meadow land, full of cows and horses grazing. A large cone rises up on one side of the water, and throws it back in a picturesque manner, contributing to a beautiful irregularity of shape on the lake. The woods are noble; they grow thinner as they descend, forming clumps and groves. Near the water's edge are scattered on the green swarth some fine single trees.

We climbed up the opposite mountain, which is woody, steep, and long; it is called La Montagna di Viterbo, and in ancient days was Mons Ciminus. Its passage was the cause of a triumph to Fabius.

Many of the trees on the hills, viz. oak, beech, chestnut, flowering ash, and large sycamores, are decaying from age.

We passed through Viterbo, where nothing is remarkable. It stands on a slope at the foot of the high mountain. There is a tiresome ascent through noble woods and rocks of tufo. After stepped to a door to peep into the church, and almost immediately turned back to the "*buffet;*" but as he returned, he perceived a man passing like lightning from the opposite door. The Pope then came in, and directly took up the cup of chocolate, of which he drank half, but refused the remainder, as he said it had a bad taste. He was not long without being attacked by a mortal disorder, which was of such a virulent and putrid character that his body fell to pieces, nor could his head be kept on his shoulders after death. A nun at Viterbo, who passed for a prophetess, had announced his death, and letters were chalked on the walls of the Vatican, implying that he would not outlive the September of that year.

Pius VI. had a fright like this about two years ago. He was then so burnt up that he could not bear the pressure of his shirt, which was kept from his body by hoops, and his flesh almost burnt the hands of his attendants when they touched it.

We passed through woods of ancient oak to Aquapendente, an ugly ruinous place, on the brink of a precipice, without any appearance of water, but with very beautiful landscapes; and descended a long woody hill, to a river and a good bridge. This vale is full of charming flowers.

We dined at a single house at the foot of the mountain, then ascended the hill of Radicofani, along a steep but good road. We got to the top by the help of oxen.

The master of the posthouse would not receive us, so we proceeded, by starlight, six miles down the northern side, to Ricorsi, a lonely barn; so bad a one that we preferred passing the night in our carriage. We had a little before crossed a rivulet of white sulphurous water, where the incrustations of white travertino are made, of which models are taken off in different moulds. The water falls from on high upon a pavement, where the mould is set sloping to face it, and receives the sprinklings, which in a very short time form a thick crust on the mould, and give a very fine hard basso-relievo of the subject.

Radicofani is a fortress and village on the summit of an extinct volcano. All near it seems to be confusion. On the northern side is a large tract covered with detached rocks of lava. It is seen a vast way off on both sides, and forms the boundary of Tuscany and the papal territories. The country is fine on the Roman side, but the appearance of the natives improves as one enters Tuscany. There are more houses scattered about, more signs of industry, and attempts to improve the cultivation; the people also are better drest. Gentlemen's seats appear on the eminences, and many houses have a general look of comfort and industry.

We dined at Buonconvento, and had excellent wine of Montepulciano, sweet and white, like good mild cider. We then proceeded to Sienna, which stands on the crown of a lofty eminence, and is very conspicuous from all sides.

The Augustines is a handsome modernised church, with large paintings. The most conspicuous are, one of St. Anthony, by Spagnoletti, and a fine Christ bearing the Cross, by Salvator. The church has pleasant cloisters, and a good library. The grates of one of the chapels are of bronze work, representing knotted ropes.

The domo is gothic, of white and black marble; the outside front is loaded with statues, busts, and paintings; the inside is ugly, except the pulpit, which is of white marble, worked elegantly, in the style of the Cinque centi. The stairs are the best thing there; some of the ornaments are charming.

The Chizi chapel is brilliant from the lapis lazuli of the altar, and from the verde antico columns, and rosso antico arms.

Next day we reached Florence, passing Poggibonzi, and through a beautifully hilly country, superior to any other in Italy. We lodge at

Veneni's, where we found many of our acquaintance, and also a general invitation from Sir Horace waiting for us.

Verona, June 21.

We left Florence on the 14th, and slept at Pietra Mala, a horrid inn. Dined next day at Pianora, and thence to Bologna. Saw some fine pictures; Domenichino's martyrdom of St. Agnes—the agony and expression very fine; St. Cecilia, by Raphael; and at the Capuchins, the famous crucifixion, by Guido.

I walked three miles, up to the Madonna della Guardia, under a brick portico, built by subscription and ex votos. There is nothing remarkable about the church but the view, and the image, called a work of St. Luke, now in great vogue during all the earthquakes.

We arrived on the 19th at Modena, and saw the palace, where there are grand apartments allotted to stranger princes. The arsenal is full of arms, and in good order. The great albergo is a noble building and establishment, where old and young, when left unprovided for, are received, nourished, and, if capable, employed.

We went to see a collection of curious medals

belonging to a Jew, some of which are very fine. He assured us that the king of Naples had offered four hundred ounces for leave to select forty pieces. This we would scarcely give credit to, knowing how little his Neapolitan majesty cares about anything beyond macaroni. The Jew supported his fibs by laying his hand upon his heart, and saying "*Je vous jure sur mon ame, que je vous dis la vérité.*" "I suppose he is a Sadducee," said Mrs. S. to me.

Our road from Modena lay through a flat country, the most richly cultivated perhaps in the world. La Mirandola is poorly built, and has a desolate appearance; the grass grows in its streets. The prebendaries wear a crimson ribbon round their necks. The castle is modern, though ruinous.

We took the Verona road, through a wet, enclosed, but luxuriant country, with farmhouses and cottages in plenty, but no villages. With the least rain there would have been no chance of getting on. As it was, we found it far from pleasant.

On reaching Revera, a village on the Po, we crossed in a strong roomy ferry-boat, and slept at Ostiglia, on the north side of the river. The next day we were obliged to have three pair of oxen to travel across the low country, which is intersected in so many directions, that the numbers of steep, narrow brick enclosures can scarcely be counted. Horses could hardly have tugged up the carriages.

We entered the Venetian territory at Ponte Molino, a ruinous looking castle, which we passed through. The doganista (custom-house officers) let us proceed very quietly. There are rice-grounds on the flat. We dined at Isola. Plenty of mulberry trees and Indian corn.

Verona seemed of an immense size as we approached it. We passed through a vast length of town.

Next day I walked out of the east gate, and back down to the river side, where I took a sketch of the bridge,—one of the finest possible, not unlike that upon the Saone at Lyons, but handsomer. The castle and walls are fine objects over the bridge. There is also an exquisite prospect from the castle San Felice.

We went to San Georgio, a convent of nuns built by San Michele, a Veronese architect, about the time of Palladio, whose style his resembles, and he has imitated it in many houses of the town. The church has a lightsome, elegant cupola, but from the shake of an earthquake it has been necessary to support it by cross bars, which have a bad effect.

An antique tomb, serving for a gate near the old castle, has the name of Vitruvius on it;* and as that great architect was of this city, it is supposed to be his, but I think it a modern inscription. In the church of the Franciscans the chapel of the family Pellegrini by Michele, in gray marble, is reckoned by Dutens the *ne plus ultra* of architecture. I think it not to be compared to the Corsini chapel, in St. John Lateran at Rome. Near this chapel is a gate of a gothic order, not opened, and called *porta stoppa.*

The museum of the Philharmonic, adjoining the theatre, is handsome enough. There is an academy for poetry and music, and an association of nobility for exercise, riding, &c. The outer part of the amphitheatre is all destroyed except four arches, but the circus is entire, and has lately been repaired at great expense. This society has great revenues in houses, &c., and a body of gentlemen to direct its funds. The building contains room for thirty-six thousand people sitting, and six thousand in the arena. They are now busy taking away the earth, and reducing it to the ancient level.

* M. Vitruvius Pollio, according to the best authorities, was born at Formiæ. He lived in the time of Augustus.

Clagenfurth, July 1.

We came from Verona along the Adige, through a level plain of vines, trees, corn, &c. Dined at Dolci, and slept at Borghetto, the first place in the Trentin. Our trunks were superficially examined and sealed. We slept next night at Alla. La Chiusa is a very narrow pass between rocks on the river, which is of a bad muddy colour, but rapid and full. Roveredo is an extensive town, with pretty environs. Trent is a large ugly city. The palace is half gothic. We entered the Tyrol near a torrent, two miles from thence. We had payments of barriers without end.

The women wear grey or green caps, like the crown of a hat without brim, or green round hats, which the men have also, or black fly caps fastened behind with a bodkin through the hair. The men wear straps over each shoulder, of green list, like porter's straps, to keep up their lower garments.

We dined at Salerno, where we saw some pleasant rivers and pine woods, resembling those of Tarare, the vale growing narrower and more romantic as we advanced.

Botzen is a large town, at the junction of two valleys; a pretty country surrounds it. We crossed the Adige, which is here a rapid, broad torrent; the mountains then closed in upon us, and there was scarcely room for a road along the water's edge. Noble hanging woods and perpendicular rocks, with patches of cultivation, afford beautiful prospects hereabouts.

We dined at a single house a mile beyond the post of Deutschen, an old mansion belonging to a priest, a most romantic spot; and from thence we had a charming drive to Kollmann, a small village on the hill, commanding such views as can but seldom be matched. A fine castle on the point of a rock, on the other side of the river, is a grand object; and the rivers, fields, hills, and woody mountains are sublime. Behind the town falls a beautiful cascade of sheets of water, from the summit of a mountain. This place reminded me of Bagnères.

We travelled next day through a most beautiful country to Brixen, a large town on the river, in a broad plain, with several valleys ending in it. Here the Inspruck road falls into that of Styria. It was a long evening's drive to Brunecken, through a charming country. Here we found a good inn. The town is moderately sized, with a castle prettily placed on the hill, and has some great works for iron manufacture.

We ascended the course of the Adige, through a delicious valley closed in by laurels and spruce firs. The forests are the most extensive that I ever passed through, with numberless trees, but no large-sized timber. Between Niederdorf and Sillian, we came to the highest lands in the valley. The Adige, which is here only a torrent, descends by a narrow gulley of dark woods from the bare white rocks, which rise loftily behind the woody mountains, which are still full of snow. These are the boundaries of Italy, and are called Staur.

We slept at a single house called Mitterwald, in a dark glen close by the river Drau. We dined at Ober Drauburg, a village belonging to Prince Portia, and thence came to Greiffenberg, a clean village, with good accommodations. We entered Carinthia, near Lienz, and after a few miles of narrow passes came to a very beautiful plain, and dined at Spital, a large seat of Prince Portia, who resides there constantly, being a sort of sovereign prince under the emperor.

The saint of the Tyrol is Saint Florianus, represented by a soldier, with a flag, pouring a bucket of water on a house on fire.

We now passed a charming tract of country. The river flows through the midst of a large plain of flax and meadow land, with many villages; and a ridge of hills running between it and the high mountains is covered with magnificent woods. I saw one spruce fir of thirteen feet in circumference.

At St. Paternion, the next village we came to, we found a variation in the dress of the people, the women wearing black hats with bugle bands, and a brass or studded leathern girdle, from which hangs a knife. Goîtres are almost universal here, and there are many idiots.

We passed the confines of the Venetian states, and dined at Villach, an ill-built town on the Drau, in a beautiful country. Velden, where we slept, is a neat house, on the borders of a fine lake, which seems to be many miles long. Here stands a ruinous pile of buildings, formerly the residence of some great chief. It belongs to Count de Dietrichstein, and serves as a post-house. The women here wear men's shirts, with a red girdle and large flat hats.

We travelled on the side of the lake called the Wertsee, the borders of which are finely wooded, and have many picturesque buildings, especially a church on a rocky peninsula. A canal through a vast plain leads to Clagenfurth, the capital of Carinthia, which is a well-built city, with large though low houses. The streets are straight and wide, but none of them are paved, except the main one. In the great square, Hercules, like a buffoon, is grinning and wielding his club at a colossal dragon, (the arms of the city.) The fortifications are in the modern style.

Vienna, July 10.

From Clagenfurth we journeyed to St. Veit, the poor suburb of a small town in a flat; after which, we passed through rich vales, with woods on each side, and iron mills, in a romantic country; and then entering Styria reached Neumarkt, a small walled town. Thence to Unzmarkt were the finest larches in the world in great quantities, and spruce firs of large size and beauty. I will not reckon among the pleasant objects of the landscape a great many gibbets, with men hanging on them, and heads exposed on wheels, ignobly placed near the road, as a terror to the robbers, which, till lately, infested these parts. Maria Theresa's emissaries have been indefatigable in putting them down.

We saw an innumerable number of Martagon lilies among the corn and flax fields. The Mans, a considerable river, flows through the valley past Unzmarkt to Judenburg, a large ugly town, in a plain surrounded by woody hills. The drive from the pretty hamlet of St. Laurent, along the banks of the Muhr, was beautiful. It wound beneath the hanging fir woods to Leoben.

The roads in Styria are much cut up, and very unpleasant. Leoben is pretty and clean, though built in a barbarous taste. The walls of the houses are decorated with armorial bearings, figures of saints, stories out of sacred history, and various ornaments of architecture. The town stands on the river Muhr, which is the prettiest stream I have seen since I entered the Tyrol.

We dined at Märzhofen, a populous hamlet, and slept at Krieglach. Next day we passed Märzzuschlag, famous for its iron forges, in a fine valley overhung with mountains and pines. We ascended the hills which divide Styria from Austria. It is a noble road, with a grand view towards the plain of Vienna. Schottwien is a most romantic little town, amidst a defile of rocks and woods, beautifully thrown upon each other, with fine streams running down on each side, and a hundred charming points of view. The castle of the seigneur (the Count de Reicheg) is on the summit of one of the highest hills.

We had a fine entrance into the plains of Neustadt, a large walled town, which stands in the plain near a river. A dusty, dreary level took us to Neunkirchen, between which and Neustad is a long village of several houses and a church, lately built on each side of the road, with paled-off gardens, enclosures, vineyards, and walks. This new settlement is called Teresia. The women here wear handkerchiefs about their necks and faces—a frightful costume.

We had a good view of Vienna from the hill; it resembles the situation and country about Paris. The architecture also resembles that of the French capital in the best sort of houses. We passed along a dusty suburb round the town, which is as ugly as anything can be, to the custom-house, where we underwent a severe examination, and paid thirteen florins, duties, for mere trifles; we then established ourselves in tolerable lodgings at the Glanderfirchen Haus in the Ober Bresmer Strass. I called, soon after my arrival, upon Sir Robert Keith, who came directly to see Mrs. S. He had just received accounts from England of the dreadful riots in London.

Vienna, July 24.

The evening after our arrival, we went to the German play, with Sir Robert Keith and the Comtesse de Thun. The theatre is middle sized and well lighted up, but the boxes are extremely small; yet the price of one of them is £100 a year. The greatest part of the pit is taken up for the *parterre noble,* where ladies and gentlemen go as to the boxes.

Sir Robert took us to Prince Kaunitz's, after the theatre, where a numerous party of ladies, ministers, &c., were assembled.* There were cards and billiards.

Next morning we walked in the Lausgarten with Madame de Thun, who is a charming woman, all attention and kindness to us. She has three daughters, all handsome; but Elizabeth, the eldest, is quite a beauty.† We went with her to the widowed Princess Esterhazy, and then to Prince Kaunitz, who has a reunion every night.

The Hoffgarten is a very fine public garden, in an island of the Danube, with charming shady walks, and a great variety of views over the city, suburbs, and hills. The Danube, which flows majestically through the lofty woods and level fields, is traversed by two wooden bridges.

* Prince Kaunitz Rietberg, the celebrated minister of Marie Therese, was born in 1710, and destined for the church; but having come into possession of the family estates by the death of his elder brother, he embraced the diplomatic career, was appointed ambassador to Louis XV., and succeeded in forming the famous league between Austria and France against Prussia. This gained him so much credit, that he was appointed prime minister, and continued to enjoy the favour of the crown until his death, which occurred in 1798.

† The Countess de Thun, daughter to Prince Kaunitz. Her daughter afterwards married Count Razamowski, favourite to the Czarina Elizabeth.

We paid several visits during the next evening, and on the 13th breakfasted with Prince Galitzin, at his casino in the Prater; a pretty box, in a large grove of old trees, with a little garden, like a citizen's world in an acre of ground. We were regaled with a most splendid breakfast, and met a great deal of good company. Most of the ladies came on horseback, riding *à l'Anglaise.* We went afterwards, in Sir Robert Keith's carriage, to dine with Prince Kaunitz at Laxenburg, two leagues distant from Vienna. There are avenues of horse-chesnut and lime-trees all the way, in an open even country. Laxenburg is a small town in the hollow part of the great plain. There is an old chateau, newly patched up, and a strange low palace, the residence of the imperial family. The generality of the nobility have their houses here; but that of Prince Kaunitz is the only grand one, and he has laid out a great deal of money upon it. There is one noble room; the rest are low and small for a person of such consequence.

At dinner we had the Count de Burghausen, the Comtesse de Thun, the Comtesse de Clary, a young widow, the favourite of Kaunitz, and Baron Swieten, son of the famous physician, Mr. Beaky. After dinner the prince treated us with the cleaning of his gums; one of the most nauseous operations I ever witnessed, and it lasted a prodigious long time, accompanied with all manner of noises. He carries a hundred implements in his pocket for this purpose—such as glasses of all sorts for seeing before and behind his teeth, a whetting steel for his knife, pinchers to hold the steel with, knives and scissors without number, and cottons and lawns for wiping his eyes. His whims are innumerable. Nothing allusive to the mortality of human nature must ever be rung in his ears. To mention the small-pox is enough to knock him up for the day. I saw an instance of this; for Burghausen, having been long absent, came out with it, and the prince looked as black as could be all the rest of the day. To derange the train of his ideas puts him sadly out of sorts. The other day, he sent a favourite dish of meat as a present to an aunt of his, four years after her decease, and would not have known it but for a blundering servant, who blabbed it to him.

He is full of childish vanities, and wishes to be thought to excel in everything. He used to have a spiral glass for mixing the oil and vinegar for salads, which he shook every day with great parade and affectation. At last the bottle broke in his hands, and covered him and his two neighbouring ladies with its contents. A gentleman not opening a bottle of champagne to his mind, he called for one to give the company a lesson in uncorking and frothing the liquor: unluckily he missed the calculation of his parabola, and poured out the wine into his uplifted sleeve, as well as into his waistcoat, &c. By-the-bye, he is dressed very oddly; his wig comes down upon his nose, with a couple of small straggling curls on each side, placed in a very ridiculous manner. He is extremely fond of adulation, will swallow anything in its shape, and indeed lays it upon himself with a very liberal hand. One of his peculiarities is a detestation cf musk. He is a sovereign Count of Rietberg, in right of his mother, which brings him in about £3,000 a year. His paternal fortune is £4,000. He has enormous debts, but gets £10,000 a year from the empress, and is never stinted by her. His expenditure in fancies and trifles is incredible. He studied at Leipsic with great reputation, and is an excellent Latin scholar, but no Grecian; he understands English, French, and Italian, very perfectly, and reads a great deal, or rather a great deal is read to him. He has good taste, and has raised the arts from barbarism to great perfection at Vienna. In business he is intelligent, and far above any mean subterfuges or falsehoods. He is always silent when he does not choose to express his real sentiments.* It was he who made the alliance with France, but he has long since been convinced of his error, and would willingly retrieve it; but the times are not proper for a change.

Having never lived much in the world before his present elevation, Prince Kaunitz has neither bosom friends nor bitter enemies; he is cold and insensible;† has made no man's fortune, nor ruined any one.

His wife was a Messalina, and after her death he took to actresses, whose dupe he was, to his cost. He has no affection for his children. The two eldest sons are *bornés*, but gentle, worthy

* "Tongues," said Prince Talleyrand, "are given to men, in order that they may disguise their real sentiments;" a maxim that he pilfered from Euripides, who says that each person has two tongues,—one to tell the truth, and the other to use according as occasion may require. Erasmus employs the same axiom in his "Eulogium on Folly." Prince Kaunitz's system was the most moral, for he preferred silence to telling untruths.

† Helvetius (de L'Esprit, vol. i.) says, "If a minister were deaf to the solicitation of relatives and friends, and only raised men of pre-eminent merit to the first places, this just minister would pass in the world as useless, heartless, and perhaps dishonest. To the shame of the age be it said, (he adds,) men high in office rarely ever owe their reputation of being good friends, relations, benevolent and virtuous, except to acts of nepotism and injustice.

creatures; the third and fourth absolute nonentities; the fifth a sad *roué.*

Kaunitz rides very well, and is fond of showing off. The empress ordered his picture to be taken, and gave the inscription to be placed under it, denoting him to have been for three years her minister, her friend and her confidant. The emperor once entertained a great aversion for him, and a few years ago, Kaunitz, who fancies he can do everything, drew up the plan of a campaign, so supremely ridiculous, that the emperor was convinced he had nothing more than the pretensions and arts of a state quack. Of late, however, *il en est revenu sur son compte,* and is now convinced of his abilities, and is very intimate with him.

After dinner we walked in the gardens and woods, through canopies of fine old oaks and pretty woodland paths,—pleasant enough, were it not for the gnats, which quite devoured me. *La petite Veuve,* Madame de Clary, lives by play, does the honours of the house, and has likewise her affectations. She was married at fifteen to Count Clary, of seventy-five, and soon became a widow. She seems good-natured, and understands English perfectly—which indeed most of the German ladies do.

There is a heronry here, and much hawking.

We heard two French horns in the woods. They almost make that instrument too fine, and unnaturally learned.

The emperor is allowed no power. He wishes exceedingly to go to Flanders, having much at heart a new system for restoring that country to its ancient state of a great mart. But Prince Charles of Lorraine is such a favourite with the empress that he is never to be contradicted, and the emperor does not go for fear of quarrelling with him, which would inevitably be the case, their ideas on the subject not agreeing.

The Prater is a superb park, with a long avenue of horse chesnuts. The banks of the Danube are long and woody. Many hinds and stags graze on both sides, and there is fine scope for riding and driving.

In the Graben is a house so long, and divided into so many apartments, that it lets for thirty-six thousand florins a year. Near it is the stump of an aged tree, leaning against the wall, into which every one, who is made free of the Blacksmith's company, is obliged to drive a nail up to the head. The number of nails already sticking in it renders it difficult *now* to find a spare place. There is no populace in Vienna, everybody belonging to some company or association.

We had a great dinner at Sir Robert Keith's.

The principal persons present were Mr. and Madame Thun, and their daughters, Mr. and Madame de Walthen, the Lucchese and Hanoverian envoys, Starsa and Swieten, with Fludyer, Stratton and Madame de Bassovirtz. I afterwards accompanied Baron de Swieten on a visit to the old Prince of Saxe Hildburghausen, who, at eighty years old, can raise a weight of three hundred pounds. He always retires to his rest at eight o'clock, and as he walks from the salon to his bedchamber, has men posted, who pull off his wig and clothes, so that he is ready for his bed by the time he gets to the door of his bedchamber. Thus scarcely two minutes suffice for his toilette. We have since dined with him at the Belvedere Gardens, and went afterwards to Schönbrun, to wait upon the grande maîtresse of the empress, and of the Archduchesses Elizabeth and Marianne.

Schönbrun palace is of an immense length, and of unequal heights, but with nothing pleasing or really grand in its architecture. It was built at many different periods; that is, whenever the empress had occasion for an increase of apartments. At first it was nothing but a *rendez-vous de chasse* of Charles VI. It was the only place the empress had to live in, when first she came to the throne, being then immersed in a long and dangerous war; and when peace was signed, and all became quiet, she had become too much attached to the place to leave it. Its situation is far from agreeable, being close to the little river Wien, without any pleasant object in sight. The gardens are fine in their way. Opposite the palace is a hill, with a long portico kind of building upon it, as ugly as possible. It is Prince Kaunitz's masterpiece, and what he particularly prides himself upon. Fifty thousand pounds, at least, have been spent in altering and modelling this hill.

The empress has such an internal fever and heat of blood, that she cannot bear to have the window closed at any season of the year. Sometimes the wind is so strong during the night, that it throws down the chairs in her room, blows the curtains against her face, and awakens her. Her son, the emperor, is extremely chilly, notwithstanding all her children were brought up in so hardy a manner, that their attendants were almost starved. The emperor still sleeps upon a a bed of skins.

The empress is generous even to prodigality, and would be miserable if she knew of any one in want that it was not in her power to relieve. The Duke of Saxony, and his wife the Archduchess Christina, drain her prodigiously. The emperor calls him his *dear* brother-in-law.

Kaunitz used always to shut the windows when he came into the empress's apartments, but now he will not come to council any more.

We have innumerable visits and evening parties, and find the society very agreeable. Our presentation to the empress has taken place. The two Archduchesses and the Archduke Maximilian were with her. She received us in her *salle d'audience*, was very gracious, and conversed about our family and that of the queen of Naples. She stood all the time fanning herself, then *nous congedia* with a polite bow.

The Archduchess Marianne is pleasing, and like a woman of the world. The Archduchess Elizabeth was beautiful before she had the small-pox, but is now plain. She complains of never seeing any one, except in her sister's company, who, as the eldest, engrosses the conversation. She is naturally lively, and very volatile, and suffers sadly from ennui. A short time ago an ulcer came in her cheek, which ate it quite through, and confined her many weeks to her room. On Sir Robert Keith coming to condole with her on this accident, she burst out laughing, and told him he was wrong to think it a subject of condolence. "*Croyez-moi*," said she, "*pour une Archiduchesse de quarante ans, qui n'est point mariée, un trou à la joue est un amusement;* for," added she, "no event which breaks through the sameness and tediousness of my life ought to be considered as a misfortune." She told him it was a blot on the reign of Marie Therese to have kept her old daughters under restraint like children, and denied them the pleasure of mixing in society.

Maximilian is a good-natured, neither-here-nor-there kind of youth.

Prince Auersberg is a surprising man of eighty-six, who rides, eats, drinks, and walks, as if he were but thirty. He was in England the year Queen Anne died.

The ramparts are the general place of meeting in the evening. Their circumference is about three miles.

The soil which produces the fine Tokay has so much heat, that Count Collar, the Hungarian vice-chancellor, tells me he went that way last December, through ice and snow, and found none upon that spot. No snow ever lies on the salt-mines either. He also assured me that the Tokay sometimes shoots forth bits of gold, which has been sucked up in the growth of the vine.

The Calvinist reform is tolerated in Hungary, but not the Lutheran. There is no punishment of death in Bohemia. The court wish to make a reform there, by abolishing the *corvée,* viz. the obligation of working for the lords, and giving leases to the peasants; but it has not yet been able to accomplish its desire.

In Poland the nobility contract their marriages in such a manner as always to leave a doubt, and a way of proving their nullity; which gives rise to numberless divorces, and it sometimes happens that a woman sits at a table with three men who had been her husbands, without her character being at all infringed upon in consequence. How the nuncios make out the legality of these dispensations I know not.

August 4.

The other day I accompanied Mrs. S. to Schönbrun, where we walked in the gardens. The temple, or portico, of Doric arches, is a strange concern. There was a sale going on in the middle of it. The empress sent for us to her. She was sitting in a corner of the palace, at a table, *parfilant*. She spoke very pleasingly and good-humouredly, and after some time made a sign to Mrs. S. to sit down, then asked her many questions, and at last told her the Archduchess Marianne wished to see her. Taking this as a congé, we waited upon the archduchess, and were delighted with her. She seems very amiable, showed us great kindness, and appears to have taken a great fancy to Mrs. S.

The empress has a fine face, but is enormously fat and unwieldy. A few days ago her chamberlain, Sinzendorff, waited on her with a petition from some part of her territories, which was very interesting to her. They were alone in the apartment, both standing whilst he read to her the document. Sinzendorff is a thin old man, stiff and erect, and troubled with a rheumatic complaint, which has in some measure paralysed his frame. It happened that the paper fell to the ground. The empress bade him pick it up. "Helas! madame," said he, "*il y a vingt années que je ne me suis courbé!*" She would have stooped for it herself, but was too unwieldy; he was accordingly obliged to ring the bell for the purpose, and the groom of the chambers, on entering, found her imperial majesty in a violent fit of laughter.*

* A similar anecdote is related of George the Fourth (when Regent) and Lady H——d, with this difference, that the latter is said to have dropped her handkerchief when she had a bad cold. Neither being dressed for stooping, and her ladyship's nose requiring assistance, the bell was obliged to be rung, and a fresh kerchief asked for.

Vienna, 13*th*.

On the afternoon of Thursday we went to the empress's drawing-room at Schönbrun, held upon the occasion of the Archduke Maximilian being elected coadjutor and successor to the Elector of Cologne. There was an immense crowd, considering the time of the year, when many of the nobility are absent on their estates. The empress and the ambassadors played at cards, but the former rose often from her seat, to address and coax the French ambassador, (Breteuil,) whom she took extraordinary notice of, indeed rather fulsomely, probably on account of France having suffered the coadjutorship to pass uncontested. She also spoke long and kindly to Mrs. S., who certainly had no hand in the election.

We were there presented to the Duke Albert, and the Archduchess Christina. She is very handsome, and has the most beautiful hand in the world; indeed that is a characteristic of her family. The divine Metastasio was also present. He is a little, old, sheepish-looking, peaked faced *abbate*, with a curled wig, just like those worn fifty years ago. His name was originally Raspi, or rather, I believe, Trapassi.

There was also Marshal Laudohn,* a thin man,

* The celebrated Marshal Laudohn, who commanded the Imperial armies during a portion of the seven years' war. It

with a very withered face; Marshal Haddick, fat and jolly; and Marshal Lacy, thin and amiable looking.

Mrs. S. now frequently spends her evenings with the Archduchess Marianne, and sometimes with the empress. At Kaunitz's we generally adjourn after dinner to his garden, and have fruit and refreshments under the trees.

24th.

I have been presented to Joseph II., who is just returned to Vienna. Some other English were presented at the same time, viz. my nephew Bedingfeld, Messrs. Sheldon, Chaplin, and Stratton. The emperor spoke to me very graciously, and said his mother had mentioned us to him. He is less than I expected, and much better looking. He has harassed himself much, and does not seem strongly built.

The next day the empress herself presented Mrs. S. to the emperor at Schönbrun, where

was to him that Frederic the Great paid the compliment of saying, "*Placez vous à cote de moi; je n'aime pas vous avoir en face.*" Laudohn's name inspired so much terror in Germany, that it was long used to frighten the naughty children. *Nimm dich in acht! Der Laudohn ist da!* was a constant exclamation, just as our nurses talk of "raw-head-and-bloody-bones."

she remained to dine with Madame de Salmour, grande maîtresse to the Archduchess Marianne, the widow of a Piedmontese nobleman, and herself a Pole, being daughter to Lubienski, a Polish grandee. On the partition of Poland taking place, the whole court was assembled in an antechamber, in order to proceed regularly to the chapel, and hear a grand *Te Deum* composed for the occasion. Madame de Salmour was among the company, being in attendance on the archduchess. The empress said to her, "*Madame de Salmour, je vous dispense d'y aller.*" "*Votre majesté a raison,*" she replied; "*j'y serais peut-être tentée d'y faire des vœux contre les oppresseurs de ma patrie!*" Her remark did not offend, for the successful are seldom cross.

All the Poles were presented to Joseph on his return from Russia—that is to say, those whose property was included in his share of Poland. Most of them were dressed in the French fashion, and acquitted themselves respectfully of their homage. A few were in the Polish habit; among the rest an old man, grave, sullen, and backward. Perceiving that he did not approach, the emperor went up to him, addressing him in a courteous manner. The Pole remained sulky and shy. Joseph asked if he amused himself at Vienna. "Very little," was the reply. "I wonder at that," said the emperor, good-humouredly, "for there never were such a vast number of your countrymen here as there are at this moment." "Nay," said the Pole, "I have heard that about a hundred years ago Vienna was filled with Poles!"* The emperor, who tells this story himself, declares he was quite confounded at this speech, and totally unable to say another word; but he was so pleased with the man's boldness and *amor patriæ*, that he felt almost inclined to shake hands with him.

Madame de Salmour told me that when she was Madame de Lubienski, she knew the king of Poland, and that he was so fond of Corregio's Magdalene, one of the forty pictures he bought of the Duke of Modena, that wherever he went, this picture accompanied him in a case, and was hung up in his apartments.

Our friend Madame d'Ulsfield has given us many particulars of the empress's life. The day of her appearing before the Hungarian nobles, they were in a large hall, where a balustrade was put up to keep off the crowd.

* Alluding to the year 1683, when John Sobieski, king of Poland, marched to the relief of Vienna, then besieged by the Turks, whom he attacked and routed, and thus not only liberated that capital, but Hungary, which had been overrun by the Ottomans.

She came in deep mourning, with her infant son in her arms, and began a Latin speech, but as she pronounced the first words of it,—viz. "*Afflicto rerum statu,*" the tears suffocated her, and impeded her utterance. The whole assembly with one movement rose, and, with their fingers upraised, called out, "*Moriemur pro regina Theresa.*"

When Francis died, she was given to understand, from caballing courtiers, which equally exist in all countries, that Joseph would probably seize the reins of empire; and being now emperor (having been elected king of the Romans previous to his father's death), would not consent to be subservient to his mother. She therefore felt uneasy and uncomfortable; but he soon put an end to her fears, for, the first time they met, he threw himself at her feet, saying, "*Je serai toujours votre fidèle Joseph, le plus devoué de vos sujets!*"

The empress is loved by the people, as well as admired. When she lay dangerously ill of the small-pox, Joseph met an old marshal on the stairs, coming from the anteroom of her apartment, where he had been to inquire how she was. He was in a flood of tears, on having learnt that her recovery was despaired of. "Am I then such a tyrant," said the emperor, "that you dread being governed by me?" "No, sir," said the soldier; "but we know what we lose!"

Duke Albert of Saxony is very good looking, and made a conquest, not only of the Archduchess Christina, whom he married, but of her sister Josephine, whose nuptials with the king of Naples were fixed upon by her mother. It was not, however, her fate to be queen of Naples; for, having caught the small-pox, she died the very day that had been fixed on for her departure; and her sister Carolina was soon after sent in her place.

The most earnest wish of their mother was obtained when she succeeded in making her youngest daughter queen of France. The Archduchess Antoinette, was at fourteen extremely pious, and well inclined in every respect; and when the marriage was arranged, Maria Theresa, whose religion did not prevent her giving way to superstitious propensities, visited a nun of a neighbouring convent, who was considered able to see into the future. She expressed her anxiety for the soul of her pious, good child, now about to be separated from her for the rest of her life, and going to so depraved a court as that of Louis Quinze. The answer she received was this: "*Elle aura de grands revers, et puis elle redeviendra pieuse.*" Struck by the thought of her good child ceasing to be pious, which was implied by these words, the empress burst into tears, and was with difficulty restored to calmness. She, however, was not sufficiently credulous, or provident, for the happiness of her young daughter, to put an end on that account to the negotiations for the archduchess's marriage.

The empress is extremely imposed upon by hypocrites of all sorts.* Many an officer has gone to her chapel, and made all the grimaces of a bigot and zealot, which has attracted her notice, and procured him promotion; after which he has never appeared there again. She gives money to all the soldiers that do duty about the palace, and on extraordinary occasions to the officers, and throws about ducats among the poor people when she drives about the streets. She was formerly very rigorous, and as bad as an inquisitor, having ladies and gentlemen carried off for the least irregularity of conduct; which, as

* Mr. Swinburne mentions this as if it were an uncommon occurrence. It would be difficult to name any sovereign who has not been imposed upon by hypocrites and self-interested sycophants. Half the misfortunes that occur to states arise from monarchs being led, instead of leading. The welfare of the people must be that of all crowned heads, for their own welfare depends upon it. The welfare of courtiers, on the contrary, depends upon the downfal of others.

King Croquignolet* says of the fillips, exacted for his nose, "*fatiguoient beaucoup le pauvre peuple.*" However, at present, her fervour has abated considerably. Her affairs are wretchedly managed, without intelligence or ceremony. She gives of late much money to priests to distribute in alms, and of course the poor get little or nothing in comparison of what they had when she herself bestowed her charity, without the medium it now passes through.

Sept. 12.

I rode the other day up the mountain of the Calemberg, towards a house of Count Cobenzel, the view from which place is astonishingly fine. The low mountains of Hungary bound the horizon of an immense plain, through which the Danube flows, divided by large woody islands into a variety of lakes and canals. The bridges may be traced all through, and Vienna lies under the eye. I have also been up to the Camaldolin Convent of Calemberg, backed with large woods of oak and beech. It forms one point of the ridge which advances into the plain; the

* King Croquignolet, the hero of the fairy tale called *Coque d'Œuf.*

Leopoldsberg, or Schlüssel, is the other. This last is a very narrow brow, with a kind of a castle belonging to the crown. The view from it is wonderful, in which the Abbey of Kloster Neuberg is a grand object.

Our dinners and festive parties are innumerable. We breakfasted yesterday with General Pellegrini, at a charming house on the ramparts, delightfully situated, with a fine view of Vienna from its windows. The interior is deliciously fitted up. It contains a salon all painted with cameos well executed. We met the emperor several evenings at Madame de Berghausen's. He was quite easy and chatty; he listens with attention to what is said by others, and talks freely and merrily. One is apt to expect more from an emperor, and to forget that he is one. His accent is rather harsh and nasal. His French is very good, except a few Germanisms. He sometimes puts on his field-marshal's coat, often drives himself in a low phaeton, with a pair of English horses and two servants behind in gray coats, turned up with yellow, and silver-laced waistcoats and hats.

Vienna is divided into towns and suburbs. The former is small, not above three miles round. It is hilly, but not much on a slope to a branch of the Danube, on which side the fortifications are not very considerable. Those on the west, near the Schotten, are extremely lofty, because on that side the ground without is high. The Turks pitched their camp there in the last siege.

There are eight ways out of the city. The gates are never shut. The streets are crooked, narrow, and indifferently paved; with many disagreeable smells, as there are no sewers to carry off the dirt; but the scavengers are often at work. The houses are high, of brick stuccoed over, with heavy leaden ornaments, and iron bars, as at Rome, to the lower windows. It is usual for several families to occupy the same house. St. Stephen's, the cathedral, has a very curious and lofty filagree steeple. The inside, which is gothic, is exceedingly black and smoky.

The squares are not large, except the Hof. The fountains, obelisks, and groups in them are in the style of the Agaglii at Naples. The library is a superb building. The palace is convenient, but not handsome, although the façade of Prince Colloredo's apartments is showy. The hotel of the council of war is a new grand building. The arsenal contains a vast quantity of arms, and many curiosities;—viz. trophies of the Turks, Prince Eugene's armour, which in size is like that of a little boy; also the immense chain which the Turks extended across the river, to prevent succours coming into the town by water; half of it fills the court, round which it is hung on pegs. There is also a monstrous ill-made cannon taken from the Turks.

There was formerly a Scotch college here, but nothing now remains of that nation save the name, which the church and gate still retain. The empress has about eighty capital houses in town, where she lodges her officers of state, &c., besides apartments in particular houses, reserved in their leases. Few of the common people live in the city.

There are two theatres; the French one is the largest, that of the palace the cleanest and prettiest; many houses have doors opening on the ramparts, which is a great *agrément*. The custom-house is a handsome quadrangle. The fish market is in a street parallel to the Danube, and beyond the ancient walls, which still appear.

They say the town is lately much increased, and formerly must have been little more than a castle in size.

Sept. 18.

I dined lately in the suburbs, at the magnificent villa of Prince Schwartzenberg, with Sir R.

Keith, Galippi, auditor of Mexico, and Count and Countess Ohenhausen, from Portugal. She is the grand-daughter of Tavora,* and from a year old was state prisoner with her mother. We also had Countess Daun, and Mr. Harford, son to the unfortunate Lord Baltimore.

We again met the emperor at Madame de Berghausen's, where he was extremely merry and talkative; ridiculed the story of the king of Poland's assassination, and talked of Mrs. Macauley and her hatred of kings. He said he understood she had fainted away whenever they were named, and asked if she put three stars whenever she was obliged to mention one in her history.† He spoke with horror of *lettres de cachet*, and arbitrary unformal condemnations; and I make no doubt, from all he seems to think, and from what others say of him, that his accession to power will be the means of bringing liberty and happiness throughout his dominions, at least if he has moderation and head enough to begin with prudence; but that is still a problem. Of his in-

* The Marquis de Tavora, who was implicated with the Duke d'Aveiro in the famous conspiracy and attempt to murder Joseph I., king of Portugal, in 1758. The conspiracy was discovered, and all the parties and their families suffered death or unlimited imprisonment.

† A History of England.

tentions there is no doubt,—of his success a great deal. He will have much to cope with. The friars and priests detest and abuse him, and there is a strong party of them.* They give out that he has no friendship, constancy, or warmth of heart, and that he is totally incapable of a generous feeling: in short, they know not how to speak ill enough of him. *Mais je n'en crois rien*:—it is something that a despotic potentate should wish for freedom and liberty among his people, and such a hobby-horse can but be beneficial, if only to put it into the heads of others; for as Laville, when he married, told us as an excuse, "*qu'il faut faire une fin*;" I say, *vice*

* The efforts of the Emperor Joseph to extend religious liberty to the whole of his subjects, and to emancipate the Protestants in his Netherland dominions from the exclusive penalties that affected them, were amongst the causes that led to the Brabant revolution in 1789. As a sample of the spirit of the priesthood and of Catholic tolerance, I quote the following reply made to the emperor by the synod of Louvain, when H. T. M. asked their opinion upon his project of according equal rights and privileges to all classes of his subjects, without distinction of faith. "*Tolerance*," said the reverend fathers, "*would be the cause of dissensions, hatreds, and interminable discord; because the Catholic religion regards all heretics, without distinction, as victims devoted to eternal perdition. The Catholic religion impresses this maxim upon her children as an essential dogma and invariable article of her faith.*

versâ, "*qu'il faut à toutes choses un commencement.*"

Sept. 22.

Two days ago the emperor sent for me in the evening to Schönbrun, where I walked with him in the gardens. He was very agreeable, and is certainly very clever. He is on the point of setting out for Bohemia, and yesterday rode in the Prater, showing the empress, who was in her carriage, the improvements that are making. He rides very ill.

I was at a large dinner party of all nations, at Foscarini's, the Venetian ambassador's. D'Ohenhausen mentioned an anecdote of Count Olivaréz:—viz. his artful manner of informing Philip IV. that Portugal was lost. "I congratulate you, sire!" said he; "the estates of the Duke of Braganza are all fallen to your majesty, for he has dared to seat himself on the throne of Portugal.*

We had in the evening a pleasant *réunion chez* Madame de Berghen, where it is the fashion to play at *des jeux d'esprit.* There is no form,—a most agreeable society, with dancing and supper towards

* The renowned Gasper Guzman, Conde Duque d'Olivaréz, prime minister to Philip IV. of Spain during twenty-two years. He died in disgrace at Toro in 1643.

the end of the evening. Such parties often take place here, which, in my opinion, are pleasanter than large and formal assemblies and balls.

I have visited the imperial cabinet of natural history. Baron Baillon, the director, has arranged it systematically, to prove that the polypus system is not here in all its positions, and that great part of those productions are vegetables, and a chain up to life. The petrified woods are curious; the minerals rich, and the precious stones valuable; particularly a large turnip of opal, not to be set a price upon. A Jew offered two hundred thousand florins for it. There is a black diamond, a rainbow diamond, and a nosegay composed of all the precious stones existing. The collection of shells is fine; some are unique.

The medals we brought from Italy are much admired here. We went to see Neuman's medals, and dined with him at the convent of St. Dorothea: he is a learned man, and gave us his book on Nummi Indefiniti—a strange composition. He told us Edenborg, in Hungary, is said to have been called so by Edgar Atheling, who resided there.

Oct. 16.

Kaunitz is the greatest tyrant and bashaw I ever knew; he has always some dishes and cakes (peculiar dainties) reserved for himself, which nobody dares to touch. As he mostly makes me sit near him, Madame de Thun warned me not to transgress, which perhaps put it into my head to do so, for I did not care a halfpenny about him. Accordingly I took an opportunity, and, notwithstanding all the signs and distressed looks of my wife opposite, I succeeded in carrying off some of his favourite gauffres and sweetmeats. He looked very awkward, grew quite reserved, and *me bouda* for several days. I took no notice of his pettishness, which amused me extremely, and in about a week he came round of himself. I was walking from dinner through a long string of rooms, talking to the Nuncio, when I felt an arm thrown over my shoulder, and turning round saw it was Kaunitz, in high good humour. He said he wanted my opinion of a variety of pictures exhibited for his approbation, by Michel, the engraver of Basle, who makes him his dupe, for these pictures are absolute daubs. Amongst others is one of a pope, which the Nuncio and I thought to be one of those exhibited at Rome, at l'Ara de Massimi, price sixteen paoli.

When the Grand Duke Leopold was to be married at Inspruck to the King of Spain's daughter, Prince Kaunitz went thither beforehand to see that everything was in order for the fête. The opera, among the rest, engaged his attention, and he questioned Glück about it. The composer assured him that the performers, singers, and decorations, were perfect. "Well, then," said the prince, "let us have the opera directly." "How!" exclaimed Glück, "without an audience?"—"Monsieur Glück," he replied, "*sachez que la qualité vaut bien la quantité; je suis moi seul une audience.*" He was obeyed, and I heard him tell this with great triumph.

Kaunitz patronized a Diamice.* One day, when he carried his portfeuille to the empress, she began to upbraid him with the scandal of his conduct. "*Madame,*" said he, "*je suis venu ici pour parler des affaires de votre Majesté, non des miennes.*"

On the 10th, Mrs. S. had a long audience of the empress, who said, in conversation, she was sure her son the emperor would not live long, as he imitated the King of Prussia in everything, and had not a constitution for it. She also told her she was certain she herself would soon die, and she only regretted life because she had set her heart upon marrying the Archduke Francis

* A celebrated dancer and courtesan of that period.

to her grand-daughter Maria Theresa of Naples. She has since sent Mrs. S. the cross, patent, and statutes of the order of the *croix étoilée.**

The emperor is returned from Bohemia. I went to court the day after his arrival, and the same evening to the German theatre, in Count Rosenberg's box, to see Madame Sacco as Medea, in a melodrame. She does it almost alone, and a terrible part it is; the music is intended to express the passions, so that the words are few. She acted so well that it was too affecting, and is certainly superior to anything I know of, on any other stage at present. The emperor, who was in the next box,

* This order for noble ladies, called the *Sternkreuz orden*, was instituted by the Empress Eleanor on the 18th of Sept. 1668. Its origin is curious. The house of Austria believed that it possessed a small piece of the true cross. This relic, fixed in a small golden crucifix, was constantly worn by the Emperors Maximilian and Ferdinand III. On the death of the latter, Leopold presented it to the widowed Empress Eleanor, who caused it to be mounted in a small but costly reliquarium, of gold, enamel, and crystal. On the 2nd of February 1666, a fire suddenly broke out in the empress's apartments, and burned with such rapidity and fury, that she had scarcely time to save herself ere the chamber in which the relic was deposited fell in. But, upon examining the ruins some days after, the little case was found almost intact. The empress therefore ordered a procession; the prince bishop of Vienna drew up a *procès verbal* commemorative of the miracle; and, to render the circumstance more striking, a bull was obtained from the pope, sanctioning the foundation of the order.

interpreted it verse by verse to Mrs. S. throughout the play as it went on.

The emperor came one night since his return to Madame Berghen's, and the society was not rendered a bit more formal by his presence. He entered into the amusements, and was very good-natured, but did not stay long. He is always thinking of politics, and one evening at the play looked out of his adjoining box to tell Mrs. S. that the Dutch were taking the part of the French in the most glaring manner; and that if Pitt (Lord Chatham) had been alive, he would have declared against Holland six months ago.

Nov. 29.

The day before we left Vienna, we took leave of the empress and the archduchess Marianne, who has desired Mrs. S. to correspond with her. The empress gave watches to the boys. We spent an evening at Madame Berghen's, where a game was played of subjects given around for verses, On that of Vienna I wrote these lines:

Belle Vienne! délicieuse gîte!
Ville pleine de plaisirs et d'attraits,
Depuis le tems heureux que je t' habite,
Chez toi de jour en jour plus je me plais.

Mais le tems passe, il faut que je te quitte.
Helas ! mon cœur, attristé de regrets,
Au moment du depart encore hesite
A' dire adieu, peut-être pour jamais !

We slept the first night at St. Poellon. The first post after passing Schönbrun is through woody mountains, as handsome as such scenes can be in a tame manner; not the bold savage rocks and waterfalls of the Alps, but the rich flowing hills of Sussex and Surrey. We had some transitory peeps of the Danube; excellent roads; an innumerable quantity of beggars in every place. There are several country-seats in noble situations.

Molck has an Abbey of Benedictines, a most superb edifice; its church has a large cupola and two steeples. The lodging part is endless. Its situation, on the point of a rock, looking both up and down the Danube, is very grand, and the edifice affords a striking object to all the country.

We now drove through a beautiful country with every variety that can be desired in a landscape; noble reaches of the river, and the distant blue mountains of Bohemia and Syria. Many towns and large country-seats give life to the vegetative scenery.

Ens, where we arrived in the evening, is a poor small town, the Lauriacum of the ancients, on the point of a ridge above the river of the same name, which falls into the Danube a quarter of a mile below—a delightful position for prospect. Count Aversberg resides in a large chateau at the end, in the finest situation imaginable. The air is good, but the cold in winter intense.

Mr. Bedingfeld was there to meet us, and we went with a letter from the Nuncio to the Augustinian College at San Florianus, a most magnificent establishment. We were received by the prelate with great politeness. A canon spoke Italian to me, for I am sorry to say I did not learn much German during my residence at the capital, where French is universally spoken. The galleries and apartments for the imperial family are extremely grand. There is the bedchamber of Prince Eugene, hung with military trophies, &c. Two good portraits of him and Charles VI. are reckoned the best likenesses of them existing. There are a fine collection of manuscripts and a cabinet of medals. The church is full of columns of one piece, from the mountains of Saltzberg.

Lintz is a small town, the form of which is square. On the old rampart (for there are no fortifications) is a pleasant walk leading up to the castle—a plain house where Leopold I.

waited the event of the battle of Vienna. It commands an immense view of the Danube, and of the great wooden bridge over it. Boats are constantly passing, laden with cabbages for sauer-crout. It is a beautiful country, with landscapes that might employ a painter for months.

From Lintz is a charming road by the water side. This picturesque country is all a new acquisition of the emperor's. At Scharding, a middle-sized walled town, we crossed the Inn, a broad rapid river, and entered Bavaria, a charming country, like the woody parts of Bedfordshire. The women hereabouts no longer wear the large black hats of the Austrians, but round-eared caps, and their petticoats very short.

Many parts of our journey resembled a park, and that in the most elegant taste. Vilshofen is prettily situated at the confluence of the Danube, with a small stream of very black water. Straubingen is a large ugly town, where we found difficulty in getting horses, as they were reserved for the Archduke Maximilian, in his passage from Magentheim, the residence of the chief of the Teutonic order.

Ratisbon is a poorly built, uneven, and roughly paved town, with a kennel in the middle of each street. Its cathedral is old and gothic, the steeples poor, being covered with tiles, like houses.

There is no monument of any consequence, except a large statue of a cardinal of the Palatine family. At the Abbey of St. Emerand there is an ugly gingerbread monument of Henry prince of Tour and Taxis, and statues of Charlemagne and St. Henri. The diet is held in an old, dark, dismal town-house. The magistracy, with the Chamberlain, are all Lutherans; the bishops, monks, and canons, are Catholics, and as free as the burghers, all their houses being asylums. The territories scarcely extend beyond the walls, which go about two miles out. There does not seem to be a handsome edifice in the town. Every prince, free state, abbot, &c., in Germany, has a minister here. The electors have ambassadors, among whom that of Mayence ranks the first.

The roads from thence to Nuremberg are execrable. This latter is a large ill-situated town; its houses in the antique German style, painted red and other colours on the outside.

On entering the territories of the prince bishop of Wurtzburg, appeared vineyards, the first we had seen since we left Vienna. We passed the Mein at Kitzingen. The appearance of Wurtzburg is grand, as the number of steeples cut a great figure, as well as the episcopal palace, which is built of a darkish stone. It is the grandest and best furnished of any I have seen, indeed too large and magnificent for the petty sovereign lodged in it; he has some fine pictures, by Wouvermans and Brughels. The great hall, painted by Tiepolo, is superb, as well as a cabinet of mirrors painted in grotesques. The bishop has three thousand regular troops, and as many militia, and is allowed forty thousand florins yearly for pocket-money, every other expense being defrayed.

Next day we entered an immense forest, all of reddish sand, and the stones the same colour. We then reached Aschaffenburg, on the Mein, a town belonging to the elector, who has a summer residence there, and has made drives and walks in the forest The palace of red stone is very unsightly, with tall steeples at each angle. He is brother to the prince of Wurtzburg, and is a cross, ill-looking priest.

Hanau, on the banks of the river, is a very pretty regular town; its houses neat and gaily painted. The hereditary prince of Hesse Cassel resides near it, and takes great pains to embellish the place with walks, buildings, roads, &c. At a small distance from the town he has created a water-drinking place, called Wilhelmstadt, where everything is laid out in the Vauxhall style. It allures many people from Frankfort. There is a print of him, dressed as a tapster, inviting people to his rooms. His grenadiers have caps and curls, and enormous pigtails.*

At Frankfort, we put up at a very good inn, l'Empereur. The situation of the town is flat. The fortifications are modern, and in good repair. It is a very dear place. There are a few convents, and a great many Jews. The proverb current here is, that "the Calvinists have the money, the Catholics the churches, and the Lutherans the power." We went to see the golden bull of the emperor Charles IV., which is an old parchment roll.†

* The attachment of the elector of Hesse Cassel to pigtails was exemplified in a laughable manner, upon his return to his dominions in 1813. Upon this occasion he was greeted with the liveliest demonstrations of rejoicings and affection; but nothing seemed to afford him pleasure, or to excite his admiration, until at last an old officer appeared before him with a cue of gigantic proportions. Upon this the elector's countenance expanded, he smiled graciously, and turning round to his principal aide-de-camp, exclaimed: *Gott sey gelobt, der hat ihn noch.*" (God be praised, he has got it still.)

† The famous golden bull of Charles IV., which was regarded as the fundamental law and constitution of the Germanic empire, was first promulgated at Nuremberg in 1354. Its purport is too well known to require comment, especially as its main object has become a dead letter, by the dissolution of the empire. Amongst other ordinances of this bull, was the constitution of the *seven* electors, who were thus nominated in honour of the *seven* candelabras of the Apocalypse.

As we entered Limburg, an ill-looking fellow, all in tatters, followed by a corporal and two sentinels in the same accoutrements, asked us our names, and told us he was the guard of his serene highness the elector of Treves. It is a middling-sized, ugly town.

We crossed the Rhine at Ehrenbreitstein, on a flying bridge, a convenient invention, preferable to our ferry-boats. Coblentz is a pretty town, in the midst of a thousand natural beauties. Bonn is also a pretty town, neatly built, and its streets tolerably well paved, all in black lava. It is situated in a flat near the river. The elector of Cologne's palace faces the south entry. It has no beauty of architecture, and is all plain white, without any pretensions.

We went to court, and were invited to dine with the elector, (Konigsegge.) He is seventy-three years old, a little hale, black man, very merry and affable. His table is none of the best; no dessert wines handed about, nor any foreign wines at all. He is easy and agreeable, having lived all his life in ladies' company, which he is said to have liked better than his breviary. The captains of his guard, and a few other people of the court, formed the company, amongst whom were his two great nieces, Madame de Hatzfeld and Madame de Taxis.

The palace is of an immense size, the ball-room particularly large, but low. The cabinet of natural history is rich, and well provided with birds, minerals, and petrifactions. A large human skull petrified, with all its articulations, is a rare piece. There are also various beautiful corals and funguses, and the efflorescence of lead from the Tyrol.

The elector goes about to all the assemblies, and plays at tric-trac. He asked me to be of his party, but I was not acquainted with their way of playing. There is every evening an assembly or play at court. The elector seems very strong and healthy, and will, I think, hold the archduke a good tug yet.

There are only two English here; one is Mr. Meadows, who is come in search of the Duchess of Kingston, to compromise matters with her; but he has not yet traced her out. She is said to be at Riga with Prince Radzivil.

An avenue of limes, with very little interruption, lines the road to Cologne, than which there cannot be a worse built, uglier, or more dirty city; as black as small coal can make it. The cathedral is a gothic structure, unfinished. The choir alone is complete.

Aix-la-Chapelle, Dec. 1, 1780.

We are now at the town where we were married, and find many old acquaintances still residing here. There is a strange medley of ranks, Russian princesses, English ladies, and German burgomistresses. Madame Klotz has still her whist and faro going on. The Nugents, Lalandes, Lady Cooke, and Count Ricci, are here. There is a kind of club instituted, to meet every evening at Les Rois d'Angleterre.

The Bishop of Osnaburg is arrived here from Spa, and dined with us at the table d'hôte.* He is very young, and rather good-looking. Princess Cazerni asked him to a supper at the Redoute, but he declined it.

I spent a day at Spa, and walked over the hills to enjoy my old dear points of view. Spa seemed still to me the lovely place I always thought it, though the advantage of my honeymoon having been spent there may have enhanced its charms. Some alterations have taken place. A temple has been built on the hill, and a guingette at "Annette et Lubin's" walk. There are a new ball-room and a playhouse. The last season was very numerous, viz. twelve hundred and thirty persons. Gaming is excessive,

* H. R. H. the late Duke of York.

and the profits of the bank enormous: its effects benefit the country, which is very flourishing, and there are great things done in roads, buildings, &c. But the sweet, rural, undressed life and social pleasures of Old Spa are, I fancy, vanished, and there is now as much ceremony, dress, and luxury of all sorts as in a capital.

Brussels, Feb. 10, 1731.

On leaving Aix-la-Chapelle we spent two days at Liege. We went to the apartments at court, where the prince bishop recognised us as old acquaintances, and asked us to dinner the following day.

On our arrival at Brussels, where, *par parenthèse,* we were kept above an hour at the gates, we installed ourselves à l'hôtel d'Angleterre, and were visited by our envoy, Mr. Fitzherbert, the Nuncio Davoust, and many more. The houses here are very neat, and those building at the east end are grand. We have dined with Prince Starhemberg and Lord Trentham.

The Redoute is here a stupid, dirty, ill-lighted ball at the playhouse, with no pretty or well-dressed women, excepting, perhaps, the Duchess d'Arenberg and Countess de Beaufort, née Mé-rode. It was excessively crowded, with a great deal of dancing. We met many English, and supped at Mrs. St. Leger's.

We have Lord and Lady Torrington and their daughters, Mr. Taylor with six children, the Duke of St. Albans, Coombe of the Diaboliad, Lady Juliana and Miss Penn, Lord St. Asaph, &c.

At St. Gudule's the delivery of the keys by Rubens is a fine picture, but the carnations are shaded with blue and other unnatural tints. The drawing is incorrect, and the heads of the sheep not quite exact. At the church, in the Place Royale, monks and nuns were assisting at mass.

Brussels, April 3, 1781.

We had, on the emperor's name-day, a superb gala at Prince Starhemberg's. The emperor is expected here. He never would come during the life of Prince Charles, not to displease his mother, with whom the latter was a great favourite. They say Prince Charles had grown quite foolish latterly; but he still thinks a great deal of his own consequence, and whenever anything occurred which did not please him, his usual remark was, "*Eh bien, n'importe; je n'en serai pas moins le Prince Charles de Lorraine.**"

* This reminds me of one Mr. Thomas ———, only son of Sir James ———, a wealthy Irish baronet, whom Scrope

I have made acquaintance with Mentelli, author of *Cosmographie élémentaire*, rather in a curious way. I happened to buy his *Géographie Comparée*, and finding in it some errors, I made a note of them, and sent them to him, without signing my name. Not long after, the bookseller brought me a letter directed to Mr. ——, and insisted upon its being for me, as the writer had desired he should give it to the person who had bought of him the only set sent to Brussels. This letter was so flattering that I answered it in my own name, and have thus opened a correspondence.

I have made an excursion to Antwerp. Its approach is as pretty as a flat is capable of being made. The fortifications are in poor repair, but the citadel is taken care of. The tower of the cathedral looks beautiful over the town. I climbed to the top of the steeple, which is said to measure four hundred and sixty-six feet. I reckoned five hundred and thirty-five steps, and there is a

Davies and others were wont to rally for his dulness, and to call him "poor Tom." "Never mind," replied the other one day, "you may call me poor Tom as much as you please, but when my father dies I shall be rich Sir James." Scrope Davies asked Tom's valet what he thought of his master. "Why, sir," rejoined the Le Jasmin, "if I may be so bold, I should say that he is one of the *green-hornedest* gentlemen I ever saw."

height above, where it is impossible to ascend. From the steeple I saw Bergen-op-Zoom, the sea, and the winding course of the Scheldt, and an immense tract of country. The churches abound with capital works of Rubens, Vandyck, and other Flemish artists. At St. André is a very beautiful picture of Mary Queen of Scots, over a monumental inscription erected to her honour. At the cathedral I admired the famous Descent from the Cross, by Rubens.

Malines is quite in a flat. Its ramparts are out of all repair, and its ditches, overgrown with bushes and green weeds, are quite offensive. The houses are in the old gable-end form. There are many convents. The cathedral makes a great figure, its tower being of an enormous height, and seen all over the country.

At Vilvorde, the empress has built a stupendous workhouse; but, from an unwillingness in the states to rid the streets of beggars, no use is made of it.*

Since my return, I have been with a party of friends to see Chateau Charles, a country-house built and left unfinished by the late Prince Charles of Lorraine. It stands well, on a hill

* This immense building is now converted into a prison, and is in no lack of inmates. It merits a visit from travellers, as the regulations are admirable.

on the verge of the forest of Soignes. One sees from it Antwerp, Malines, Louvain, and Brussels. There is a want of water to this extensive view. The most remarkable things in the house are a japan dressing-room, which is beautiful, and a chair which goes up to the top of the house by machinery.*

Ghent, June.

We have been remaining here in expectation of seeing the emperor, who, however, went round by Antwerp; therefore, having my family here, I went to meet him at Ostend. He had arrived there the night before, and had been walking all the morning about the port. I went to him at eleven o'clock, and had a *tête-à-tête* with him of nearly an hour, after which he received all petitions till one. General Terzy was with him. He was in the back or ordinary room, which was seen through and through. Terzy stood in the court, and ushered each petitioner in. When I came, I was pushed in directly. A lady in weeds was there with him. He laughed at the interview in public, dismissed her, and began to talk to me of the peace, and made me walk up and

* This chateau, built by the Archduke Charles of Lorraine, is no longer in existence. It was situated to the right of the road near the small town of Terveuren.

down the room, forgetting the people waiting. He showed me the proposals of the people of Antwerp for opening the port, drawn up by a Mr. Hatfield, an Englishman. The citizens offered to defray the whole expense, and well they might, if what I have heard be true, that the vast capital vested in the commercial houses of that city at the period of that commercial ruin still remains unimpaired, and in great part still in specie. The emperor relishes the idea, but he is a man of half measures—a groper in politics, without sufficient steadiness or understanding to adopt and carry through a great and vigorous plan.

He also communicated to me the proposal he and the Empress of Russia had sent over to Belgioioso, offering their mediation for peace. The plan was to appoint a congress in Holland; the British and American ambassadors were to take adjoining hotels, and to open a communication, and the other persons were not to enter upon business till those two were agreed. The plan was sent over to Lord Stormont. The emperor gave me a copy of it, and promised to give me the answer at Ghent.

I returned to Ghent that evening, and three days afterward Joseph II. arrived at the inn of St. Sebastian. Next morning he reviewed a battalion of Clairfait's regiment, and d'Arberg's dragoons, and gave audiences till four. After dinner I waited on him at the town-house, where he had received the magistrates. He there communicated to me Lord Stormont's letter, and refusal of the mediation, at which he felt very indignant. "But," said he, "how can one expect anything reasonable in one's concerns with a man *que j'ai vu pendant deux ans fou!*"

He showed me the official answer, and allowed me to take a copy of it, as well as of his letter. He seemed quite delighted with the reception he had met with at Antwerp and at Ghent, and declared he believed the people would give him their blood if he asked for it. I observed that they naturally rejoiced at the sight of a sovereign, not having seen one since Philip II. He started, and said, "*Au nom de Dieu ne me comparez pas à lui!*"

The crowd was immense all day and all night at the inn where he lodged; so that, in order to pay Mrs. S. a visit, (she being at an inn on the same side of the square,) he and General Terzy were obliged to come by a back way, through little gardens and closes behind the houses, along the river, from one house to the other. When they entered the court where we occupied the ground-floor, our landlord ushered in his majesty with a taper in each hand. He sat with us an hour, then returned the same way. From the silence enforced, and the candles taken about, the people thought it was the sacrament administering to some sick person, and many knelt down.

He gave an amusing account of his entry at Bruges, where petitions were presented to him by a "*drôle de corps, une espèce de fou, qui avoit l'air d'un Marguillier en perruque blanche de travers, qui me parla Italien.*" Never was anything better painted, especially as I had met the person at Bruges.

Next day, by his order, I attended him when the crowd was a little dispersed. He had dined early, and was walking about the room eating strawberries. When he left Ghent he went to Antwerp, making a round by Oudenarde and Alost, without going to Brussels, where the grandees had prepared a brilliant reception.

June 15.

We came by the barge to Bruges, and dined in company with Mr. Burgess, confessor of the Augustine nuns. I could not help laughing when I saw him, for it was he who had presented the petitions to the emperor, and whom he had made such a joke of. My risibility was the more excited, when he boasted of his imperial majesty's great politeness and attention to his speech.

London, July 1.

Having brought a parcel from his brother, General Langlois, I called upon Mr. Benjamin Langlois, under-secretary of state for foreign affairs. The conversation by chance fell upon the question of peace, which he avowed to be the most desirable of blessings, if it could be brought about by any honourable means. I observed, in reply, that it was not likely the present administration should obtain it easily, since they had rejected the mediation of Joseph II., the only friend we had left in the world.

He stared as I repeated, verbatim, all I knew, without discovering my author. Nothing could exceed his apparent dismay; he protested that he was the only person not of the cabinet who had seen the letter. I refused to say more, and the next morning I received a note from Lord Stormont, requesting the favour of me to call on him at his office. I complied, and having no reason for further silence, relieved him from his fears of treachery, by acquainting him from whence I had derived my knowledge. I amused myself, however, a little with his perplexity and uneasiness, before I let him into my secret.

London, April 15, 1785.

Spent a day and night at York with my sister, then came to Parlington, where I was received with great cordiality by the Benedict and Benedictina. She does not appear to me any better looking than she was two years ago, when he thought her so plain; but times and opinions change, one knows not why. I suppose her fondness for dogs has charmed him, though no one is so little of a puppy as himself; the rooms are full of them, big and little.

In my way I went to see Woburn. There is a noble plantation of magnificent timber, fine turf, a large house, but in a hole, and apparently a damp situation. The rooms above stairs are grand, and there is a vast number of valuable portraits, &c. I was much amused by my

* Here there is a considerable hiatus in Mr. S's. correspondence. None of the letters written by him from Paris, upon his visit to that place in 1783, are forthcoming: several others, it must be observed, are also missing. This will account for the want of connexion that is visible now and then.

travels to London on horseback, in the mode of ancient days, when there were neither stage coaches nor good roads. In my opinion it is pleasanter than going in a postchaise; that is to say, when there is no necessity for so doing; for necessity, though it has no law, must, by imposing a restraint, take off all pleasure. However, I conclude they did not mind it formerly, as people would now; it seemed so much a thing of course. It is recorded of our family, that one of our aunts, or great aunts, rode on a pillion, full dressed in hoop, &c., to a masquerade, from Capheaton to Callaby, danced all night, and returned after the ball in the same manner:—about thirty miles distance.

London is full, and dinners numerous. The pleasantest lounge is Ranelagh, where one meets all the world. The routs do not suit me. I was at one last night at old Lady Littleton's, which would have cured me of liking them, if I had been so inclined. I was almost the only man, certainly the youngest. There were plenty of stiff ladies *de l'ancienne cour*, with Lady Mary Duncan at their head, in saques, hoops, and fly-caps at the tops of their toupées. Lady Littleton's cockatoo was the only tolerable piece of life in the apartment.

Perhaps you don't know this anecdote of Lady

Mary Duncan. She was an heiress, and Sir William Duncan was her physician during a severe illness. One day she told him she had made up her mind to marry, and upon his asking the name of the fortunate chosen one, she bid him go home and open the Bible, giving him chapter and verse, and he would find out. He did so, and thus he read—"Nathan said to David, Thou art the man." *

I have met the Prince of Wales at several assemblies. He is a fine looking, fair young man, said to be very like the Pretender in his early youth, when he landed in Scotland. He is pleasing and well mannered.

I have been staying at Cashiobury, where the park is extensive. There is a fine hill and

* A very pretty French widow, Madame Esther de ——, was long the object of the secret affections of a friend of mine, who had not courage to disclose his sentiments. But women's eyes are quick in these matters, and she soon discovered the state of his heart. Being together one day, the subject chanced to fall upon the ancient Testament, upon which she said to him, "Do you know which of the kings of that Testament I, and all discreet women, should prefer for a lover?" "No," replied he. "I will tell you," answered she. "*C'est Assuerus!*" "*Comment!*" exclaimed he. "*Mais!*" rejoined the fair widow, with a very significant smile, "*c'est parceque il savoit aimer Esther (et se taire.)*" My friend took the hint, threw himself at her feet, and was accepted.

hanging wood over a large stream of clear water, full of trout. The house is in the shape of a Greek Π. The left wing is more modern than the right, which is very old. There are fine old trees in the shrubbery, but an air of neglect prevails throughout.

Sewell, publisher of the European Magazine, a work now in vogue, has written to Elmsley to request memoirs of me, and my picture, to publish in September. He thinks it proper to comply with the request, for fear of some ridiculous misrepresentations.

London, Feb. 1785.

In consequence of your request that I should write often and in detail, I will give you some account of our goings on in this gay metropolis, where we have been yet but a short time, but have had plenty to do with many people we know, and dinner invitations pouring in by cartloads. Yet I think you are better off in the country, for the cold weather and the fogs here are very unpleasant.

My business with ministry occasions my being in town, as it is of no avail to trust one's interests in other hands, without attending to them oneself.

However, I am hitherto not much further advanced, for Mr. Rose cannot get Mr. Pitt to give an answer about the purchase.* I have written to him myself, and received a very polite letter in return, apologizing, and promising an answer as soon as possible; but that is already a fortnight since. *Pazienza! en attendant* we amuse ourselves.

Some time ago, at a great dinner at Mr. Wilkes's, we met Barons Weissembourg and Leinkowitz, Barthelemy, Conway, and Mademoiselle d'Eon, who is a very curious personage. M. de Ste. Foix, who has known her from her first appearance, has given me her story. She was always in male attire, and supposed to be a man. She began by being a *commis* in the bureau of M. de Sauvigny, Intendant de Paris, and as a *délassement* she attended the fencing-school, where she attained great skill, which gave her an inclination for the military profession, and she obtained from the intendant the post of "lieutenant de milice de l'Isle de France," but continued to write in his office. When France wished to renew its connexion with Prussia, it was thought proper to send an obscure person, *pour tâter le terrain*, and sound the in-

* Alluding to the purchase of Mr. Swinburne's West Indian property.

clinations of that court. One Douglas, a refugee Scotchman, was chosen for that purpose, and he took d'Eon for his secretary, and employed her in carrying his confidential despatches backwards and forwards; which brought him acquainted with more people in France, and with Ste. Foix at Vienna, where he was chargé d'affaires under Praslin. When the Marquis de l'Hôpital was named ambassador to Russia, d'Eon was thought likely to be useful, and was appointed secretary, with the brevet of captain of dragoons. From that time till 1761 she was employed in the diplomatic line, when she asked the Comte de Broglie to make her one of his aides-de-camp, and in that capacity she made half a campaign. Next year she came with Nivernois to England, to settle the preliminaries of the peace; and, having carried over the ratification, was decorated with the croix de St. Louis, and employed under Count de Guerchies.

The discovery of her sex, and her being forced to put on female attire, arose, I believe, from a duel she was engaged in; but I have not heard this very accurately accounted for, though I am told it was certainly by the orders of the French government. She is very masculine looking and ugly, and looks more like a captain of dragoons than a gentle belle. She still wears the croix de St. Louis.

I thought she appeared quite out of her element, as she accompanied the ladies up-stairs after dinner, and cast a longing look at the wine she was leaving.*

I have met Count Oginsky, chief of the confederates of Poland, a man of spirit and enterprise, but unfortunately almost the only one of that sort in a nation of degenerate, corrupted wretches.† If Poland had six or seven like him, perhaps Poniatowsky would never have been king, nor Poland divided by its ancient enemies.

We had a magnificent concert at Mrs. Conway's, with all the first-rate performers,—Ten-

* Charles Geneviève Louise Auguste d' Eon de Beaumont—such were the names of this celebrated personage, who was born at Tonnère in 1728. The motives that induced the court of France to force d'Eon to disguise himself as a woman, have never been cleared up. The doubts that hung over his sex were entirely removed, however, at his death, which took place in London in 1810. A certificate to that effect was signed by Mr. Copeland, the Pere Elysée, and in which it is distinctly stated that d'Eon was a man.

† The recent struggles in Poland have shown that the people of that unfortunate country do not merit the severe epithets applied to them by Mr. Swinburne. Had he said spirited, but rash and improvident, he would have been more just.

ducci, Cramer, and Cherubini. Therese Decamp, a charming girl of fifteen, played, danced, and acted vastly well. The Prince of Wales was there. Mrs. Fitzherbert wears his picture in full view round her neck; therefore I suppose matters are settled between them.

I dined shortly after at General Paoli's, Townley's, Madame Pinto's, and Mrs. Walsingham's,* where we had agreeable parties. The latter is a very pleasant woman, and very discriminating, for she has bound up my Spanish tour in the most magnificent folio imaginable, with illustrations of her own putting in, of prints, landscapes, and portraits, appertaining to the work. It was lying on the table, and met my eye one day that I dined there; so, if I proclaim her a woman of taste, you will say *je suis payé pour cela.* Her daughter is just come out in the world, and is highly accomplished as well as amiable. Lord Exeter has had a folio illustrated of my travels, in the same sumptuous manner as Mrs. W.

We have morning concerts at Mrs. Hamilton's, (Sir William's sister-in-law,) where her second daughter sings extremely well. I met Mrs. Siddons there; she is handsome, but too

* Mother to the late Baroness De Ros.

stately for common life. I thought her acting in the "Fair Penitent" very fine. I am told she never gets off her tragedy-queen manner; and if she asks at dinner for "the mustard, if you please," or, "I'll thank you for the potatoes," it is in the same dignified style.*

I went to see Mrs. Abingdon act Scrub in the "Beaux Stratagem," for her benefit, which she made an apology for having chosen, in an epilogue which was wonderfully well received. But I confess I was surprised at her making such an extraordinary choice of a part that is totally unsuited to her. She was at Mrs. Walsingham's the other evening playing at cards, when some people came in from the play, in raptures at Miss Farren's performance of Lady Teazle. † She was much piqued at these encomiums: fancying them meant at her, she said, "It would

* This is true. Mrs. Siddons almost always, to use her own expression, spoke in the language of Shakspeare, and accounted for it by her mind being constantly absorbed in meditating upon the works of our immortal bard; so that she identified herself, as it were, with his phraseology. The last time almost I met her, she said, "How fares your good lady?"—"Passing well," answered I. "Bear my kind greetings, and commend me to her favour," replied Mrs. Siddons, waving her hand. Then again one day at dinner, I proposed to help her to something, "I cry you mercy,' said she, "I've feasted sumptuously."

† Miss Farren, who married Lord Derby.

be very strange if she could not play Lady Teazle well, she must have seen me in it so often !"

At Paoli's I met Boswell, whose Tour in the Hebrides with Dr. Johnson I had just been reading. It entertained me exceedingly, and I think has a fund of good stuff in it. They say he has a constant custom, before he retires to rest, of writing down all the interesting parts of the conversations he has had in the course of the day. This practice being known, his brother barristers on the circuit made him sign a paper of penalties, to be recovered if he kept any journal or made notes of private discourse during their journey together. He says, Dr. Johnson thought very meanly of Mrs. Montague, and declared he could never get through her book upon Shakspeare. That is my sentiment exactly.

I have been reading Cagliostro's Memoirs, which are quite a romance.

People seem to be crazy about balloons, which are quite the rage at present, and even supersede politics, notwithstanding that some of the new Icari seem to have shared the fate of their predecessor.* I went to see Arnold's balloon go

* Apropos of balloons. This reminds me of Dr. F——, a learned philosopher, aeronaut, and great admirer of the canine race to boot. He had a poodle, to which his family were much attached. "Being desirous to make an experiment

up. From his son's forcing himself in, the balloon could not raise the parachute, which was dashed against the pales and torn from the car. Arnold, with half the gallery, was pulled down, and his son left to fly up with only a few ropes to hang by. He ascended rapidly, but soon, from the machine's bursting, or his opening the valve, it descended, and was almost reduced to a heap of flat rags, which brought him down unhurt into the Thames, where a boat took him in directly. It was a very affecting scene; poor Arnold fainted away.

March 25.

At a dinner at Mr. Vaughan's, in the city, I met Romilly, Shipley Bishop of St. Asaph, three Americans, &c. The behaviour of the latter at table was truly ridiculous; it is not possible to conceive anything more vulgar, and contrary to the manners of polished countries. A low farmer in England would not do so many awk-

upon the effects of temperature on 'Moustache,' I resolved," said he, "to take him up with me in a balloon; but was compelled to renounce this interesting project." "Why?" demanded I."—"Why," replied he, ingenuously, "it blew so hard that my wife interfered, and said it would be too cruel to expose *the poor dog* to such peril."

ward and improper things, because he would feel more shamefacedness.*

Mr. Peachey has shown me some curious drawings of the pagoda of Mudina, brought over by Captain Paterson, who also penetrated fifteen hundred miles into the continent of Africa, from the Cape of Good Hope. He shot two camel-leopards, one of which the lions ate in the night; the other he has brought home stuffed. It is the first seen in England, and the first in Europe since the Cæsars. He says the natives spoke confidently of unicorns, and that he was within

* Amongst other anecdotes illustrative of American manners, there is one that I heard lately worth recording, for, *si non é vero, é ben trovato.* An English officer, Colonel A——, was travelling in a stage to New York, and was extremely annoyed by a free and enlightened citizen's perpetually spitting, across him, out of the window. He bore this patiently for some time, till at last he ventured to remonstrate, when the other said, "Why, Colonel, I estimate you're a poking fun at me—that I do. Now, I'm not a going to chaw my own bilge-water, not for no man. Besides, you need not look so thundering ugly. Why, I've *practised* all my life, and could squirt through the eye of a needle without touching the steel, let alone such a great saliva box as that there window." Colonel A—— remained tranquil for some time; at last his anger got up, and he spat bang in his companion's face, exclaiming, "I beg you a thousand pardons, squire, but I've not practised as much as you have. No doubt, by the time we reach New York, I shall be as great a dab as you are." The other rubbed his eye, and remained *bouche close.*

a few days' march of the country where they abound.

We had an agreeable dinner at Lady Betty Mackenzie's; a small party—Lady Mary Coke, Dutens, William Townsend, Horace Walpole, and Poyntz. Mr. Mackenzie told me several anecdotes, one of Lady Yarmouth. She was at a large dinner, seated at no great distance from a rich clergyman, and some bishopric having just fallen in, he carelessly expressed a wish that he were so lucky to be named to it. "Do you expect it?" said she to him. "No indeed, I do not," he replied; "I fear I am not so fortunate." —"What say you to a bet?" said she. "I'll bet you five thousand pounds that you will get it." —"Done," said the clergyman; and soon after he had the vacant see.

Lady Betty told us, that after her uncle's death, (her father was the great Mac Cullamore, as he was called amongst his clan,) she and her sisters could not bear to recognise as Duke of Argyll their cousin Jack, (first cousin to her father,) having always been accustomed to dislike and quarrel with him.* He called on them, and sat some time, but nothing could prevail on these girls to give him the title of my Lord Duke. At

* John, fourth Duke of Argyll. Lady Betty Mackenzie and Lady Mary Coke were daughters of John, second Duke.

last he rang the bell for his carriage, and when the servant came he gave no orders, leaving to them to say, "His Grace's carriage;" but Lady Betty was determined not to do so, and pointing to him, she said, "The carriage! the carriage!"

Lady Betty could never have been pretty, but they say Lady Mary was. It must have been in days of yore indeed, for she is now so deadly pale that her face is absolutely cadaverous. They say Mr. Walpole was in love with her, but she was persuaded to marry Lord Coke, who was quite a madman, and shut her up for a long time in a cage.

On Thursday, at Almack's, the Prince of Wales never moved from Mrs. Fitzherbert's side, and supped *en petit comité* with her, Lady Beauchamp, Lady Horatio Waldegrave, and Mrs. Musters, who all paid her the deference they would to a Princess of Wales. About two she yawned, and his Royal Highness, pulling out his watch, showed her the hour. Up she rose, he called her chair, and off she went, he following directly.

We spent a day at Mrs. Garrick's villa at Hampton, which is very pretty, and must be still more so in the summer. We had Mrs. Walsingham, Mrs. Wilmot, Mr. Bowdler, and Miss Hannah More. Mrs. Garrick is a good-natured and rather agreeable woman. She and Garrick were never asunder for twenty-four hours. She was educated and patronised by Lady Burlington, who paid her great attention when she was Mademoiselle Violetta, dancing on the stage. The moment her dance was over, she was summoned to Lady B.'s box, to remain there until it was her turn to perform again.

She has not the least appearance of ever having been pretty; has very small eyes, and a wide mouth. Her good-humour and elegance captivated the heart of Garrick, and it appears that she not only captured, but retained it during life. She has a box at Drury Lane, bestowed on her by the managers, rather in the skies. She lent it us to see the Beggar's Opera, which was ill attended, not as it must have been in those days when it made *Rich* gay and *Gay* rich."

May 19.

We had a turtle dinner at Wilkes's yesterday. I had met him the day before on the parade, and the warmth of the weather and walk had carried off all the powder from his bald pate. He is a great complimenter, and would stand talking to me with his hat in his hand. A drummer and his son passed us, and as I was going their way, I overheard their discourse. " What a queer-looking bald fellow that was," said the boy: " Don't you know him?" replied the other; " 'tis Johnny Wilkes, and that bald head has more brains in it than all our regiments put together, drummers and all." I told this to Wilkes, and it made him chuckle. He was very amusing, and told me several droll things.

In 1783-4, the House of Commons went up every day with an address to the King, praying to remove Pitt and his ministry. The King always received them on his throne, and gave them an answer. One of these days, at the club, George Selwyn had been asking the Prince of Wales some questions, to which he did not choose to reply otherwise than by " Pshaw! nonsense!" Not long after, as they were both leaning on the balcony looking at the speaker going to court, the prince said, " I wonder what will be his majesty's most gracious answer." " I cannot tell," answered George Selwyn, " what may be the gracious answer of his *present* majesty,—but I can tell what will be the answer of our *next* gracious sovereign." " Well, what will it be?" said the prince. " Nonsense!" he replied.

The other day, at a dinner, in company with the Prince of Wales, Wilkes being called upon for a toast, gave "The King, and long life to him!" — "Since when have you become so loyal, Wilkes?" said the prince, laughing. "Ever since I have had the honour of knowing your royal highness," said he, with a respectful bow.

When the prince was a little boy, having been very troublesome in his father's room, and several times turned out of it by him, he returned at last, and thrusting his head into the doorway, screamed out, "Wilkes and Liberty!"

Wilkes told me that Churchill had sold to George Kearsley twelve sermons for five hundred pounds, and that he had only nine to produce. The bookseller would not pay the money unless the number was complete, so Wilkes himself composed the three wanting, which were so much superior, (for Churchill wrote bad prose,) that he was afraid they would be found out not to be by the same author as the other nine.

When Churchill was dying at Boulogne, two capuchins insisted upon seeing and exhorting him, which Wilkes daily refused. At last he persuaded them to depart, by hinting the danger they would run of being perverted by the sick man, who was a divine, and one of the most eloquent of the Church of England.

What a fine sample it is of party spirit, to choose Alderman Skinner for the auctioneer of the Portland Museum,—although he does not know a cameo from an intaglio, nor a cockleshell from a nautilus,—merely because he is a stickler in the city for the coalition, and is chairman of the committee formed against the administration.

END OF VOL. I.

LONDON:
IBOTSON AND PALMER, PRINTERS, SAVOY STREET, STRAND.